ROBERT
LAIRD
BORDEN:
HIS
MEMOIRS

VOLUME I

1854-1915

ROBERT LAIRD BORDEN: HIS MEMOIRS

EDITED AND WITH A PREFACE
BY HENRY BORDEN
ABRIDGED EDITION EDITED AND WITH
AN INTRODUCTION BY
HEATH MACQUARRIE

VOLUME I

1854-1915

The Carleton Library No. 46

McClelland and Stewart Limited
Toronto / Montreal

THE CARLETON LIBRARY

A series of Canadian reprints and new
collections of source material relating
to Canada, issued under the editorial
supervision of the Institute of Canadian
Studies of Carleton University, Ottawa.

Copyright © 1969 by McClelland and Stewart Limited

By permission of Henry Borden, Q.C.

Robert Laird Borden: His Memoirs was first published
in two volumes in 1938 by the Macmillan Company
of Canada Limited, St. Martin's House, Toronto.

The Canadian Publishers
McClelland and Stewart Limited
25 Hollinger Road, Toronto 374

Printed and bound in Canada by
T. H. Best Printing Company Limited

Contents

Introduction to
the Carleton Library Edition

The 1896 election which swept the long-entrenched Liberal-Conservatives out of office brought Robert Laird Borden into the House of Commons. He had become a candidate at the urging of the able, but aged leader of the party, Sir Charles Tupper. His contributions to the Eighth Parliament were not outstanding, but in the election of 1900 he retained his Halifax seat although his party suffered an even more severe setback than that of 1896. Tupper was personally defeated and resigned the leadership. On February 6, 1901, the Conservative members of the House of Commons and Senate, after two days of deliberation, chose Borden as his successor.

The selection stirred little interest among Canadians, although some wondered why the Parliamentary caucus had not chosen someone more widely known or with more political experience. Borden himself was surprised at being asked, and lacking any great fondness for politics, was reluctant to accept the leadership of a party which had just been administered another thumping defeat by the ebullient Liberals.[1]

Borden never did become fond of politics, and it was many years before his party developed a high degree of respect and affection for him. He was unlike the political wizard who had founded the Conservative Party, and quite dissimilar to the reigning Liberal chieftain. Macdonald had been warm-hearted, genial, gregarious, a thoroughly lovable human being who inspired a lasting emotional loyalty among his followers. Laurier was brilliant, eloquent, and blessed with the happy faculty of seeming always to strike just the right note in appealing to groups and individuals. With their dynamic and attractive public personalities these men could stir the hearts of their countrymen and be popular leaders in every sense of the word. By contrast the quiet, reserved, and unemotional Borden appeared an almost insignificant figure and his leadership qualities were not easily or readily detected. Indeed to many he seemed to lack most of the attributes of mass appeal; the charisma, the arts, and appetites of the political animal were foreign to him. His selection as party leader and his eventual

---

[1] In the 1900 election the Conservatives won 79 seats, a drop of 10 from their 1896 standing. The Liberals won 130 seats, a gain of 13.

success in a role for which, superficially, he seemed so unsuited make for a highly interesting chapter in Canadian political history.

Although his public personality may not have seemed particularly appealing to many Conservatives in 1901, Borden did have real qualities which were to prove immensely valuable, both to his party and to the country. He was a prodigious worker. His judgment was generally sound. His sincerity and integrity were unquestioned. He also possessed a consultative disposition, a valuable attribute in any party leader and especially so in the Conservative Party which was then anything but a unified or cohesive group. Although in his *Memoirs* he often records his irritation at lengthy and discursive discussions, he invariably sought the advice and counsel of his colleagues and gave those about him an opportunity to express their views and utilize their abilities.

His close and continuing liaison with provincial leaders was an essential part of the process by which the Conservative Party slowly recovered from the disheartening defeats of 1896 and 1900. While the result of the 1911 election is generally attributed solely to reaction to the reciprocity proposals, it should be noted that the Conservative resurgence in the federal field followed the establishment of strong provincial Tory regimes in Ontario, British Columbia, Manitoba, and New Brunswick. With the premiers of these provinces Borden was always in frank and friendly contact. This political friendship took tangible form when the provincial party machines became totally involved in the 1911 campaign.

Moderation is an essential attribute of the conservative, and surely it is a necessary quality for any politician who would be successful in this heterogeneous and disparate country. Borden was a man singularly bereft of religious or denominational bigotry in an age when, regrettably, it was a far too common characteristic of Canadian social and political life. He stood above the bitterness which was stirred by such divisive debates as those on the Autonomy Bills in 1905. There were those about him who were not averse to inflaming racial and religious prejudice for partisan purposes. On more than one occasion the party suffered from the activities of such extremists.[2] To his moral repugnance at such unworthy manipulations

---

[2] Borden regarded the distribution of the pamphlet "The Duty of the Hour" by Conservative Orangemen as rendering service to the Liberal cause in the 1908 election campaign.

of the democratic process was added his pragmatic judgment of their inefficiency.

Fidelity to party label was a much more important part of the political process in Borden's day than it is in our era of more flexible electorates and changing voting patterns. Then a large majority of the voters considered it the natural and normal thing to adhere to the party affiliation of one's ancestors. To many it would be apostasy to depart from the ancient political moorings. Borden, who in his youth had been a Liberal, was never an intense partisan. In 1911 many of his colleagues warned him of the dire results of his associating with anti-Reciprocity Liberals. But without the support of such people it is not at all sure that his party would have won power. He again stirred misgivings and hostility among some of his hard-line longtime Conservative associates when he included the ex-Liberal W. T. White in his cabinet. White proved to be one of his ablest ministers and became one of Borden's closest friends and advisors.

In 1917, too, he was able to bring to his cause powerful and prestigious Liberals without whose support a coalition government with real electoral appeal could not have been established. Had he not formed a liaison with such people, his own party government might well have failed at the polls. In the Union cabinet he often found himself more in sympathy with the views of his new colleagues than with those of his associates of many years. While we must not push the comparison too far, it would appear that Borden possessed the capacity of political ecumenicism which brought success to the efforts of John A. Macdonald and Mackenzie King.

While he succeeded in broadening the base of his party's support sufficiently to win two elections, Borden, like some Conservative leaders who followed him, encountered frustration and eventual defeat in his efforts to develop a strong and lasting liaison with the French-speaking sector of the electorate. In his efforts to win Quebec's support he faced overwhelming difficulties. The Conservatives had been a declining force in the province, their erstwhile stronghold, ever since the hanging of Louis Riel in 1885. The Liberals on the other hand had gained ground and were led by a son of Quebec whose popularity Borden would be unlikely to challenge even under the most favourable auspices. In no federal election has Quebec failed to support the national party which had a French Canadian as its leader.

Borden was painfully aware of his and his party's problems in reference to Quebec, and he devoted much of his energy to vain efforts to remedy the situation. The alliance with Laurier's ex-Minister of Public Works, Israel Tarte, the champion of protectionism, proved futile. The party won only 11 out of 65 Quebec seats in the 1904 election and contact with Tarte was soon terminated. Apart from the dwindling Castor elements and the tycoons of Montreal, Borden had little upon which to build a power base. The moody and mercurial F. D. Monk, at times the nominal Quebec leader, was a weak reed. Never did there emerge a Conservative of the stature of George Etienne Cartier or Ernest Lapointe who could speak with authority for and to Quebec. The near annihilation of the provincial Conservative Party compounded Borden's difficulties.[3]

Borden's inability to establish rapport with French Canada may well be regarded as the cardinal failure of his career. In his first administration he had immense difficulty in maintaining cabinet representation from Quebec.[4] The Union government had no French-Canadian members, yet it had to conduct the affairs of the country in the face of the deep-seated and occasionally violent hostility of French Canada.[5] Thus while Borden was the leader of a vigorous and efficient government which rendered outstanding service in the difficult years of war, he was heading a political group which had ceased to be a national party. Whether, given the circumstances and inhibitions under which he operated, he could have avoided such a tragic cleavage in the party, and more importantly the country, is a question which must be more fully explored before the final assessment of Borden can be made.

Then, too, Borden faced unique problems and pressures which added to the traditional difficulty of maintaining a measure of balance and harmony between the two founding ethnic groups. The Ontario government, in introducing Regulation 17 respecting the use of the French language in the public

[3] In four provincial elections 1900, 1904, 1908 and 1912, the Liberals won a total of 248 seats to 46 for the Conservatives.

[4] F. D. Monk resigned on October 28, 1912. L. P. Pelletier and W. B. Nantel resigned on October 19, 1914. T. C. Casgrain who succeeded Pelletier died in office December 29, 1916. Coderre served in the cabinet from October 29, 1912 to October 5, 1915. E. L. Patenaude served from October 6, 1915 to June 12, 1917 and did not run in the 1917 election. Albert Sevigny was a Minister from January 8, 1917 to March 4, 1918, P. E. Blondin was in the cabinet from October 20, 1914 to March 21, 1917.

[5] Blondin and Sevigny were included in the Union cabinet, but were defeated in the election.

schools of that province, stirred furious and bitter protests.[6] Even Laurier was not above fanning the flames of hatred and feeding the fires of prejudice. Many of the militant anti-French and anti-Catholic bigots were within the fold of the Conservative Party, and their actions and utterances made it easy for equally bigoted elements in Quebec to direct their followers' resentment against English-speaking Canadians and the British mother country. In the dark days of war many Quebec audiences were regaled with stories of the oppression of their suffering French-speaking compatriots at the hands of Ontario Tory "Prussians."

But along with an exceptionally agitated domestic situation Borden faced problems which had their origin beyond Canadian shores. The French-English cleavage within his party reached acute proportions over the Naval Bill of 1912 and over the imposition of compulsory military service in 1917.

Of all the episodes in Borden's career perhaps the most difficult to understand or to applaud is his rôle in reference to the Naval question. In 1909 he urged that the "best course was to establish a Canadian Naval force," although he stressed the necessity of acting in close consultation with the British Admiralty. He also pointed out that the day might come when the only practical way in which Canada could assist in her own security would be through a financial contribution to the British Navy. But in the end he and all his party voted in favour of the Laurier government's resolution leading to the establishment of a Canadian Naval Service.

In the parliamentary session of 1910 his attitude seemed to have changed significantly. In the debate on the question he appeared to place priority upon a contribution. This change of emphasis was soon reflected in serious strains within the Conservative Party. Before Parliament met Borden had announced a national convention for June 15.[7] In March he had to call it off because Monk and most of his Quebec colleagues, opposed to any naval action, had signified their intention not to participate in the convention. The explosive propensity of the naval issue could not have been made more apparent. With charac-

---

[6] The impact of the provincial measure upon the Dominion scene is shown in the exchange of letters between Borden and his Quebec Ministers reproduced in Chapter 26. The same chapter recounts the long and intense House debate on Ernest Lapointe's motion which would have had Parliament admonish the Ontario legislature on the matter.

[7] The convention was to discuss policy and organization, not leadership. The Liberals had held a similar type of convention in 1893.

xii – BORDEN: HIS MEMOIRS VOLUME I

teristic understatement Borden described the situation as "full of embarrassment."

On his first trip to Britain after assuming power, Borden tried to get Monk to accompany him. Failing this, he took Postmaster General L. P. Pelletier along. But it is hard to believe that with the division of 1910 in mind he did not anticipate the sharp break in caucus solidarity which his own Naval Bill of 1912 would bring. He had included Monk in his cabinet and he had selected the other Quebec ministers only after consultation with Monk. After the break of 1910, and the campaign in Quebec in 1911, could he expect to carry his Quebec supporters with him on a contribution policy which was even more unpopular among French Canadians than the Canadian Navy project?

It would seem that after 1910 Borden was prepared to press strongly for a contribution at the risk of widening the breach with his Quebec wing. It is unlikely that he was led to this course by the advocacy of the Fosters, Roblins, and McBrides who so vigorously denigrated Laurier's "tin-pot" navy. Although he gives few insights in his *Memoirs* it is probable that Borden was primarily influenced by what he saw and heard on his trips to Britain and the Continent in the summer of 1909. From this visit he returned with misgivings about the adequacy, for Canadian and Imperial defence, of the recently established Canadian Navy. His 1912 trip, when as Prime Minister he was privy to the Admiralty's confidential assessment of Britain's defence position and formed a friendship with Winston Churchill, impelled him to the view that world factors transcending considerations of domestic politics demanded a meaningful and immediate measure of aid to the British Navy.

Perhaps more noteworthy than the loss of some of his Quebec supporters was the number who stayed with him.[8] Among these were Conservatives whose nationalist sentiments in 1911 were intense and open. His opponents had denounced the 1911 victory as an "unholy alliance" of Bourassa-ite nationalists and Imperialist Tories. Borden's appointment to his

---

[8] In the *Parliamentary Guide* of 1912 Borden's Quebec supporters listed themselves as Conservatives, not Nationalists. In 1913 on the Naval Bill six members of his caucus voted against the measure but sixteen stood with the government. Even on the Conscription Bill five voted against the party; eight (including C. J. Doherty, H. B. Ames and F. R. Cromwell) supported the government. There were, however, many abstentions. Sevigny, Blondin and others required considerable physical courage to stand as candidates for the Union Government in 1917.

cabinet of L. P. Pelletier, W. B. Nantel, and Monk and the designation of P. E. Blondin as Deputy Speaker were represented as "pay offs" for a nefarious deal. But if Borden was to build a base in Quebec, he had nowhere to turn but to those dynamic non-Liberal elements on the political scene who shared his views on Reciprocity, the issue which he regarded as the overriding one in the campaign. Had the strains and sufferings of a great world war not come upon Canada soon afterwards, it is conceivable that in time a party more Conservative than Nationalist might have developed. But the experiment was not to be carried out and once again events beyond the country's shores profoundly disrupted the political life of Canada.

On the Conscription issue Borden, it would seem, had less freedom of choice than in the pre-war Naval question. The dreadful casualties of 1917 and the terrible toll of Canadian soldiers had deeply moved Borden and had led him to the determination that come what may adequate reinforcements would be sent to the decimated Canadian forces on the Western Front.

It was the thoroughly dedicated war leader, not a calculating politician, who said in 1917:

> *If what are left of the 400,000 . . . men come back to Canada with fierce resentment and even rage in their hearts, conscious that they have been deserted and betrayed, how shall we meet them when they ask the reason. I am not so much concerned for the day when this Bill becomes law, as for the day when these men return if it is rejected. It is easy to sow the wind of clamour against the imposition of equal duty and obligation upon all Canadians for the preservation of their country; but those who make that sowing may reap such a whirlwind as they do not dream of today.*[9]

As his correspondence with Archbishop Bruchesi shows, Borden gave anxious thought to the dangers which might flow from Quebec's animosity towards the imposition of conscription. But he was also aware of "intense and vehement" feelings in the other provinces against a continuance of the no-conscription policy.[10] He believed that a failure to introduce conscription might lead to disorders outside Quebec perhaps graver than those which the Archbishop anticipated within the province if such legislation were enacted. The accuracy of his appraisal of

[9] *Canada, House of Commons Debates*, June 11, 1917, p. 2195.
[10] Public Archives of Canada, *Borden Papers*, Memoir Notes, p. 2119.

the strength of the pro-conscription sentiment was demonstrated by the extent to which the Liberal Party and the Liberal Press outside Quebec parted company with Laurier and came out for conscription and Union Government.

It is unwise, of course, to be dogmatic in a judgment of Borden's handling of the conscription issue. But it is possible that the prime minister of Canada in 1917 could no more withstand the conscriptionist pressure than could Laurier prevent the involvement of this country in the Boer War.

In any event the conscription policy was not of itself difficult to defend. The records of the Canadian Expeditionary Force offer compelling evidence that something had to be done to step up the rate of recruitment. Recent studies have demonstrated that the enactment of the Military Service Bill achieved its purpose in bringing to the Canadian forces the required flow of reinforcements which for many months the voluntary system had failed to provide.[11]

Naturally Borden deplored the further deterioration in relations between English- and French-speaking Canadians which conscription brought. Also, as head of the government he had to assume some measure of responsibility for the insensitivity and ineptitude which marked much of the recruiting effort in Quebec. But the cleavage was not created by the Military Service Bill. The unity of his party and the nation had been shattered long before. It would be naive to believe that it would have been restored by a refusal to impose conscription in 1917.

But while he had arrived at the conviction that conscription was a military necessity he made Herculean efforts to preserve national unity at the same time. No political leader could have gone farther than he did in his efforts to establish a coalition government. He offered Laurier half the cabinet posts and a virtual veto over the selection of the Conservative half as well. Only the most cynical would believe that he made this startling

---

[11] G. W. L. Nicholson in his *Canadian Expeditionary Forces, 1914-1919* (Ottawa, 1962), notes that following the passage of the Conscription Act 129,569 men reported for military service. Considering that the government's goal was the raising of a maximum of 100,000 reinforcements, he concludes that the Act was "neither a failure nor ineffective". (p. 353)

Another scholar who has challenged the long-held view that conscription was an ineffective measure is A. M. Willms. In his article "Conscription, 1917: A Brief for the Defence", *Canadian Historical Review*, xxxvii (December, 1956), he points out that average monthly enlistments in 1917 were less than 6,000, but for the first eight months of 1918, the figure was over 18,000. (p. 350)

offer to Laurier with the expectation that the Liberal leader would refuse. Such a tactic might come naturally to a cunning Mackenzie King, but the blunt, straightforward Borden would not be so devious. Totally involved as a war leader and in any case never much moved by mere partisanship Borden was making a sincere move to strengthen both the military and domestic fronts.

Another notable initiative by Borden was his nine-day pilgrimage to Quebec in the summer of 1919 where he sought to persuade Sir Lomer Gouin, Rodolphe Lemieux, Jacques Bureau, Ernest Lapointe, and other Liberals to join the Union Government and end the isolation of their province. But the anti conscriptionist sentiment and the cohesive strength of the Liberal Party was too much for him. His visit was pleasant but fruitless. No Quebec Liberal, however moderate, would join his government. Most of them would become experts in the use of the conscriptionist bogey as a potent weapon against any Conservative efforts to win elections in Quebec.

Although he may not always have been successful in advancing the objectives and strength of his own party, Borden's record as advocate and champion of his country's interests in the international arena was a triumphant one. With dogged determination and impressive firmness he insisted upon a voice for the Dominion in the highest councils of the British Empire. Under his leadership Canada advanced beyond the stage of adolescent rebellion against the hegemony of the mother country. More than any other statesman he gave leadership in an important transition period which saw the end of the Empire and the beginning of the Commonwealth of autonomous nations.[12] It is no exaggeration to designate Borden as the chief architect of Canadian independence. He had assumed the prime ministership as a colonial politician. When he laid down the reins of office Canada had attained a status of autonomy within the Commonwealth, had been a signatory of the Versailles Peace Treaty, and had become a charter member of the League of Nations.

It is clear from the *Memoirs* and from other records that Borden, in London and Paris, was much more than a parochial

---

[12] An Australian historian, L. F. Fitzhardinge, attributes to Australian Prime Minister W. M. Hughes substantial credit for advancing the status of the dominions. His abrasive aggressiveness influenced Borden to assume a more assertive role than he might otherwise have done. Hughes, Borden, and Dominion Representation at the Paris Peace Conference," *Canadian Historical Review*, XLIX (June, 1968), pp. 160-169.

or peripheral spokesman. His outlook and interests were broad. We find him playing a leading role in a special committee dealing with rival claims of Greece and Turkey, assisting in the drafting of the Covenant, and generally bringing to those momentous days the wisdom and concern of a man who had a realization of the magnitude of the changes which had come over the world.

The reader of the *Memoirs* will regret that Borden did not carry the story through the years after his resignation from the prime ministership. Perhaps no other Canadian politician filled so fully or so gracefully the role of elder statesman. Both Arthur Meighen and R. B. Bennett assigned him major diplomatic responsibilities.[13] He headed the Canadian delegation to the Washington Naval Disarmament conference in 1921-22 and led our delegation to the League of Nations Assembly in 1930. He delivered the Rhodes Memorial Lectures at Oxford and the Marfleet Lecture at Toronto. He served as Chancellor of McGill University and later held the same post at Queen's. He was a well-known friend to many scholars and in 1930 served as President of the Canadian Historical Association.

In his Halifax days Borden had shown an aptitude for the business world and he devoted considerable time and effort to that field in the years after he left the political arena. The Borden papers at the Public Archives in Ottawa are heavy with correspondence of this latter period.

One wishes too that the Borden diaries could be made public. The portions which Sir Robert included in the *Memoirs* whet the appetite for more. Here in his unpretentious, unvarnished style the man as distinct from the statesman emerges. The stalwart aggressive champion of Dominion autonomy was also a deeply sensitive man, moved almost to tears by the suffering of Canadians at the front, delighted by the affectionate response of a child with whom he struck a friendship while enroute to London for important deliberations. His kindness to children was one of his most endearing qualities. Ottawa residents remember seeing the former prime ministers of Canada demonstrating to tots in his neighbourhood the art of making "angels" in the new fallen snow.

The seemingly blunt, pedestrian, and unimaginative man

---

[13] Although he avoided intruding upon his successors he was often consulted by Meighen and Bennett. He once advised the latter to delegate more responsibility to his ministers. Some of his other suggestions bore more fruit. While many Conservatives were shocked by Bennett's 1935 New Deal program, Borden regarded it favourably.

had an appealing streak of the romantic. On his Caribbean cruise with Admiral Jellicoe he arises before dawn to behold the majesty of the morning star. A widely travelled man, he cherishes as the world's most beautiful spot the rolling hills of his Nova Scotian birthplace. Formal and sedate he might seem to many, but the quiet humour which made him known to his friends as a rare raconteur is never far below the surface. He is amusedly sympathetic at Arthur Meighen's tendency toward seasickness. He is clearly in his element as he takes the sanctimonious Sir George Foster out for a night "on the town" in Paris. Not only the achievement of Borden, the decent determined and brilliant internationalist, but also the personality of Borden the man merits further study and appreciation by this generation of Canadians.

The publication of Borden's Memoirs in 1938 was generally welcomed by scholars and statesmen. Reviewers praised its objectivity and fullness. Few major Canadian political figures have set forth the record of their public life and in chronicling the events of his long career so fully and frankly Sir Robert made a significant and valuable contribution to a more intelligent appreciation of a formative period of Canadian political development.

The *Memoirs*, of course, have their weakness. What the autobiographical work gains in intimacy it loses in objectivity, although Borden is one of the least of sinners among those who write their own history. Doubtless his judicial temperament and modest mien kept him from the excesses of self-glorification which often mar autobiographical writings.

The judgments on Borden's contemporaries recorded in the *Memoirs* have been upheld in the main by subsequent and more searching studies. The impartiality and fairness of Borden's appraisal of such men as Sir Wilfrid Laurier, Sir Sam Hughes, the Duke of Connaught, and a host of others have stood the test of time. The student of Canadian politics in the first quarter of this century will find the *Memoirs* a reliable guide.

Of course there are discreet omissions which tantalize the reader. The role of Henry Bourassa in 1910 and 1911 is only lightly touched upon as is the whole question of the financial arrangements between Tory tycoons and Nationalists in the 1911 campaign. (But party financing is still an "unmentionable" thirty years after the publication of the *Memoirs*!)

Was Borden really prepared to hand over the leadership to Premier Richard McBride in 1911 as the telegram of March 25 (reproduced on page 147) seems to indicate? Or was this "call" to the British Columbia premier a master move to smoke-out the pro-McBride faction in the caucus and expose the British Columbian as a less attractive chieftain than the one they already had at Ottawa?

His friends afterwards described the exercise as a skillful gambit on Borden's part to retain the leadership. The *Memoirs* do not answer the question but they may convey a hint. It was but six weeks after the telegraphic appeal to McBride that Borden tendered a dinner to caucus members and provincial leaders. After referring to the fact that J. D. Hazen (New Brunswick leader) and McBride spoke, Borden records: "The impressions derived by the members on this occasion did much to abate the intrigue from which I had suffered. . . ."[14]

In our somewhat more research-conscious age the writing of the *Memoirs* of a man of Borden's status and calibre would be a much more elaborate and proficient exercise. It is clear that Sir Robert in retirement was too active to be freed for long periods for undisturbed and undivided attention to the production of his *Memoirs*. Nor did he have a staff of specialists devoted to the careful execution of the task. In consequence the *Memoirs* sometimes show evidence of insufficient editing and arranging. Some of the chapters are tediously long, others could have profited by more liberal use of extracts from the diaries. There is some avoidable repetition; for instance, the substance of excerpts from the diaries is occasionally repeated in the text.

Book reviewers often appear to delight in the number of factual errors they find in another's writings. While Borden had a capacious memory and an orderly mind he sometimes erred. For instance the ship on which Earl Kitchener was drowned was the *Hampshire* not the *Hampstead*. The conscientious student may find some discrepancies between the original documents and those quoted or referred to in the *Memoirs*. But a wide-ranging review of the House of Commons Debates and state documents of the period is not likely to indicate that Borden misrepresented any event or incident in which he played a major part.

While not a sparkling piece of literature (as is Meighen's brilliant introduction) the *Memoirs* is one of the major examples of personal reminiscence in Canadian political literature. Even after the passage of thirty years it retains its value as a starting place for any student of Canada's eighth prime minister and his times.

[14] *Memoirs*, I, p. 315.

For purposes of the abridgement necessary for publication in paperback form, I have deleted about one third of each volume of the *Memoirs*. Wherever possible all the entries from Sir Robert Borden's diary have been retained. Portions of the text excluded deal with events now generally familiar to most Canadians or cover in detail subject matter of a somewhat specialized or technical nature. In this category fall the chapter on the nickel situation and some of the lengthy accounts of railway development. All such passages are marked by ellipses. Frequently I have added brief connecting passages to bridge gaps in the story's transition. Such additions to the text are marked by the symbol ∼. Quotation marks have been used within these connecting passages to show material taken from the *Memoirs*.

There are three distinct sets of notes in the Carleton Library edition of *Robert Laird Borden: His Memoirs*. The first are the notes supplied by Sir Robert Borden, which are not otherwise identified. The second are references and comments added by Borden's nephew, Henry Borden, Q.C., who prepared the *Memoirs* for their first publication following Borden's death in 1937. These notes are marked by the abbreviation "[Ed.]". The third group of notes, those added by the editor of the present edition, are enclosed within square brackets.

The division between the volumes of the Carleton Library edition comes at the same point as in the original edition: i.e., following chapter 25. An index to both volumes will be found at the end of vol. II of this reprint.

HEATH MACQUARRIE
House of Commons,
Ottawa, 1969

Preface to the Original Edition

Some months after his retirement from active public life in July, 1920, Sir Robert Borden recovered his health in large measure and from then until his death on June 10, 1937, led an exceedingly active life. During this period and particularly between 1929 and 1935 he found time to write what he sometimes referred to as "memoirs" and occasionally merely as "notes." At the time of his death the bulk of the manuscript had been revised by him and it is certain that he regarded such portion as completed. A portion, however, had been merely read over and undoubtedly he would have revised it somewhat and enlarged upon certain incidents of his career had not death intervened. It had been his intention to deal with the years subsequent to 1920 but this was never done.

From time to time before his death my uncle discussed the manuscript with me and in assuming the heavy responsibility of editing it I have endeavoured to bear in mind what I understood to be his intention and his wishes. Nothing has been added to the text but I have taken out references to certain incidents and details which I felt would have been deleted by my uncle before publication. Occasionally a sentence or a phrase has been altered for the purpose of more clearly indicating the meaning which I felt certain was intended to be conveyed. All footnotes added by me are indicated by the abbreviation "[Ed.]".

I wish here to record my gratitude to those who from time to time during the editing of the manuscript have given me their assistance in various ways. I particularly wish to acknowledge the invaluable assistance given me by my uncle's former secretary, Miss Kathleen Kearns of Ottawa.

I acknowledge the kind permission of the University of Toronto Press and of the Oxford University Press, publishers of *Canadian Constitutional Studies* and *Canada in the Commonwealth* respectively, in the use of quotations from these two volumes.

HENRY BORDEN
Toronto, Canada,
October 11, 1938

Introduction to the Original Edition

There has at times been comment on the reluctance, or at any rate on the failure, of Canadian public men to write books. Statesmen of other countries, and particularly of Great Britain, have added much to general information by compiling in the form of autobiography or historical review an account of the times and events in which they themselves played a part. Some, indeed, of the more gifted have in that way made permanent contributions to literature. In Canada, whether from lack of inclination or because of a too limited area of readers and of market, the practice has made little headway.

Sir Robert Borden has in this as in other respects set an example. His *Memoirs* put together during the last years of a long and exceedingly toilsome life are now offered to the public. Few there will be who will not be disposed to welcome with generous hospitality this final evidence of his insatiable industry and devotion to his fellow-countrymen.

The broad features or divisions of Robert Laird Borden's career are well known—the birth and rearing on the Grand Pré farm in Nova Scotia; the urge to learning from an extraordinary mother; the early qualification as teacher; the law studies and law practice; the House of Commons adventure; the War Premiership; the Empire statecraft; and, throughout all, that solid success with which by intense concentration he crowned every stage before the next was reached; these things are familiarly known in this and other lands. What is most worth noting is that there was lying in his path, either as boy or man, no adventitious fortune. Latent in him throughout all the long journey from an humble childhood to the height of his great achievements there was a firm conviction that he and he alone was master of his destiny and that no one could assist him much and no one thwart him long. The reader of these volumes will have no difficulty in determining what was the secret of their author's imposing accomplishment in at least three crowded fields of endeavour. It was his genius for work, his power of intelligently directed toil.

Something which was always well understood by Sir Robert's friends and colleagues becomes known to everybody in these pages—though politics was in overwhelming degree his life work, and though he earned therein an enduring place in our history and in the history of the British Empire, it was by no means the kind of life he wanted, and certainly not the kind of life he loved. To Sir Wilfrid Laurier the House of Commons was an arena designed and appointed to his taste. It was the home of his intellect and he liked it. To Sir Robert Borden the House of Commons was a workshop and little more. He had capacities which made him extremely useful, sometimes incomparably useful, in that Chamber, but he had not the faculties which would enable him to grace all occasions and drink delight therefrom. He was a weighty but not a happy warrior. The futilities of ill-considered discussions irked him. Waste of time in Parliament or in Council was a burden for him to endure. When he came to a conclusion as to what was in the public interest, he wanted that thing done and was impatient of restraints imposed by the clamourings of what the Press calls "public opinion." Many a time in the course of this narrative there will be disclosed irritations and discouragements which distressed him much and which only his stern sense of duty enabled him to surmount. What he really longed for year after year was an honourable release from public responsibilities, an opportunity to return with dignity and credit to a sphere where he would depend less on the loyalties and frailties of others and more upon himself.

It is interesting to examine the qualities which account for the advance to high place and high achievement of one to whom the atmosphere of his life work was uncongenial. The key, of course, was toil—ceaseless, indomitable toil. But toil requires will-power, and as well it must be directed by a mind of native strength, a mind of resource and vision, able to adjust itself to emergencies. Sir Robert entered Parliament at forty-two. Already he had attained a creditable standard of scholarship and had moved steadily and irresistibly to the forefront of the Canadian Bar. A student and a lawyer he remained throughout his life. Never did he cease to gratify his love of literature, not only in his own language, but in German and in French, and to an extraordinary extent in the ancient classics. And in the House of Commons or at the table of the Privy Council those of us who listened over many years to his elaborations of policy and disquisitions on all manner of subjects never failed to recognize in action the thoroughly trained and abundantly stored legal mind. His pre-eminence was reached only when his responsibilities became immense. Then it was that he proved himself not only the consummate lawyer, comprehending clearly the manifold implications of diverse courses opening out before him, but the business man with an organizing brain, meeting new conditions with new methods, selecting his pivotal officers and fearing not to change them, keeping his perspective true and striving toward a long range of objectives in the order of their consequence. His mind was essentially constructive, but he was able to see the reverse as well as the inviting side of any project and to weigh its advantages and disadvantages the one against the other. The soundness of his judgment will, as time goes on, be more and more impressed on the student of that harrowing period when he was at the head of affairs. It is not too much to say that there stands against him on the ledger of Canadian public service no major error, the penalty of which now weighs down upon us. If he made mistakes, they were mistakes more of manner and of method than of business statesmanship.

There will be those who differ from the author of these volumes in views expressed and comments offered on some pages. It is quite understandable that Sir Robert, in setting down his impressions and recollections at the close of a long career, may not have felt himself under the same necessity to exhaust all pains in making certain that his opinions thus recorded were wholly justified, as he had always considered himself to be under when, upon his decisions, depended the welfare of his country. Whatever criticism may be sincerely directed against his public conduct, this at least never can be said: that at any time in the discharge of the terrific responsibilities which crowded upon him through the most critical period of Canada's history, he failed to give to every duty the maximum of thought and care. It may be doubted if any political leader ever exercised such scrupulous supervision of the written record. Evidence to support his conclusions was documented and preserved with admirable system. Caution born of two decades of lawsuits was always with him. At no time did he find himself embarrassed by mis-statements of the past.

A public man is constantly engaged in controversies of every sort, verbal and written. Of the latter art Sir Robert Borden was a master. The reader is referred to one, fortunately reproduced in these *Memoirs*—that in which he engaged with His Royal Highness, the Duke of Connaught. Others with Canadians still prominent in public life do not appear—an omission which the student of effective disputation should never cease to lament. In similar tasks he was equally successful. The preparation of a State paper, such, for example, as that which embodied

Government conclusions on the matter of titles; the formulation of policy on a defined subject, of which the Resolution on Naval Defence in 1909 is an instance—in these things he had no superior.

This Dominion has produced very few, if indeed it has produced any, who would be entitled to a place in the front rank of public speakers. To such distinction the subject of this sketch would not at all lay claim. He was a competent speaker on the hustings, a still more competent Parliamentary debater, and the basis of his competence was at all times discernible. He knew with admirable thoroughness the subject he was undertaking to discuss: he knew just where he was going, never by any chance beyond his depth, and never venturing on a flight above the natural level of his eloquence. The construction of his addresses was almost invariably good. His memory was capacious and dependable, something of a valuable calculation on the floor of Parliament. On the other hand, Sir Robert lacked a certain versatility of expression, a power of illustration, an instantaneous command of phraseology—gifts rare indeed but necessary to the justly pre-eminent. He was by nature and by training under complete self-control— so much so that his hearers caught the same spirit. Knowing their leader was at his best when aroused, his followers would find great joy if only the enemy would bait him, and one can remember being happy when word went round that

the angry spot doth glow on Caesar's brow.

Once he entered the lists he feared no foe; he stood to his part in form worthy of a leader's rôle; but his highest title to the esteem of his countrymen will be his record as a man of action.

During the Great War and for a time thereafter, relations of the British Dominions with the United Kingdom were more intimate than they had been before or have been since. Conferences under various titles were frequent; they were burdensome in length and grievous in agenda. The heads of States, assaulted daily for four long years with news of poignant gravity, confronted in sombre succession with all kinds of unprecedented exigencies, were literally tried as by fire. Among those who were not found wanting was the Prime Minister of Canada. As he grew in the confidence of his associates, special tasks were assigned him, and all were discharged with notable ability. Some, particularly at the Peace Conference, he was compelled to decline. Mr. Asquith, and, more importantly, Mr. Lloyd George came to depend much on his prudence and sagacity. When in 1921 it was decided that statesmen from a dozen leading nations should meet at Washington to re-shape on more enlightened principles the foundations of world security, there was sincere satisfaction expressed at Westminster that Sir Bobert Borden was named to attend on behalf of Canada. His friends will ever be proud to remember that he took a laborious and distinguished part in the most practically useful international gathering of this twentieth century.

There are those whose desire it is to bid farewell to the things of earth in the full flush of their everyday activities, to drop, as it were, beside the forge. Others plan their journey in the hope of a restful eventide when the weary but rewarded traveller can stroll leisurely along the glades, conscious of having wrested something of victory out of life, and looking back in unspoken pride on the storm-torn terrain over which he has fought and toiled. It cannot be said that Sir Robert Borden chose to be of the latter class, but such was the disposition of fate. An overwrought nervous system, which an iron will had held to the post of duty through heavy, torturing years, at last gave definite signals which could not go unheeded. As the summer of 1920 opened, retirement became inevitable. Thereafter, with a slow restoration of health to a point where to live had meaning once again, he was privileged for seventeen years to enjoy a serene and honoured but by no means idle repose and to survey from the vantage ground of an unrivalled experience the puzzling transformations of what he had confidently believed would be a better world. Throughout this whole period he, himself, never ceased to contribute as best he could. In the League of Nations he had the deepest interest. In the formulation of its covenant he had taken a not inconspicuous part. It was the expression and embodiment of that spirit of International Co-operation which, in his view, alone could keep mankind at peace. To the advancement of the League's mission in Canada he gave generously in many ways, but best of all he gave leadership. One is saddened indeed to think that within the space of his own fast fleeting years he should witness the inexorable receding of the horizon of his hopes, and that before his eyes should close, the very soul of the new dispensation should have been surrendered.

To the last his passion for work and aptitude for affairs never left him. The texture of his mind equipped him for a place of commanding usefulness in business, and when such responsibilities were entrusted to him, as they were in three important spheres, he devoted himself to his duties with unstinted energy and as if to the manner born. On at least one occasion he was sought from across the seas for a very difficult mission in Ireland, but for this he did not feel himself in the best position to ensure success. Within his own country though, for which he had laboured long, and which he truly loved, he held himself at all times prepared to assist every good cause and to respond to every worthy appeal. A series of lectures was prepared and delivered in the University of Toronto, and another in the University of Oxford—lectures which have become text-books in their fields. Many—very many—came to seek his counsel, some from the care-laden seats of statecraft, some with other troubles, and, we may be certain, they never failed to get the best that was in him, whether former friends or former foes.

Happy indeed are they who, as the night of life approaches, find that the inner vision does not fade. Happier still are they who, as the shadows lengthen, have full assurance that they bore with head unbowed a strong man's measure of the heat and burden, who are conscious that they enjoy the undimmed confidence of everyone who shared with them their struggles and anxieties, and who have just cause to hope that when all is over there will be heard from their fellowmen the simple but sincere benediction: "He served his country well." Of these was Sir Robert Borden.

ARTHUR MEIGHEN
Toronto, Canada,
October 1, 1938.

1: Early Days *1854-1874*

During the past eight years since I retired from the Premiership of Canada in July, 1920, many friends have urged me to write my memoirs and especially to give an account of my activities in public life. Some preparation has been made from time to time in the arrangement of very voluminous files, but many labours which I have undertaken in the meantime have hitherto prevented me from giving attention to this task. On this fifteenth day of October, 1928, I am making a commencement. . . .

My father's family came originally from Headcorn, a hamlet on the verge of the Weald of Kent, where one Henry Borden made his appearance about 1370. It 1638, Richard Borden, born at Headcorn in the eighth generation from Henry, removed to New England and settled at Portsmouth, Rhode Island. His great-grandson, Samuel Borden, who was born in 1705, visited Nova Scotia and acquired real estate in the County of King's which he devised to his son, Perry Borden, who was my great-grandfather. My grandfather, whom I distinctly remember and who was also named Perry, was born in 1773, and was married to Lavinia Fuller. He died in 1862, in his ninetieth year.

My mother, Eunice Jane Laird (or Leard), was born in 1825, and I was her eldest child. Her grandfather, Robert or Robin Laird, came from Scotland by way of Ireland and, having quarrelled with his father who desired to apprentice him to a dyer, ran away from his home and emigrated to New England. It is a family tradition that while living in New England he heard of Nova Scotia and left to chance the question of migrating to that province. Holding his staff upright he let it fall and as it fell in the direction of Nova Scotia he determined to follow its guidance. Being of frugal Scotch temperament he acquired a competence in Nova Scotia and gave a good education to his son, John Laird, my grandfather. . . .

The County of King's in Nova Scotia lies in the famous Annapolis Valley which extends from Annapolis Royal (where Champlain founded in 1605 the first white colony on the Atlantic Coast, north of Florida) to Windsor in the County of Hants, eighty miles distant, finely situated on the banks of the river Piziquid, as the Indians called it, now known as the Avon. In all my journeyings throughout Canada and elsewhere in the world, I have yet to see any spot more beautiful than that which is still enshrined in my earliest memories. The house in which my father lived at the time of my birth was situate upon a hill overlooking the great meadow known as "The Grand Pré," a portion of which had been reclaimed from the sea by the early Acadian settlers.[1] To the north of the meadow lies the beautiful Basin of Minas (a corruption of the French word *mines*); far in the distance towers the great cape, Blomidon, and beyond are the Cumberland shores. To the south the hills slope down to the picturesque valley of the Gaspereau, beyond which rises a range of hills, then forest covered and locally known as the South Mountain. The village of Gaspereau, nestling in orchards and extending to the low river bank, possesses unusual charm, while further back in the hills the stream rushes headlong over a steep cliff. The waterfall, at that time in its virgin loveliness, is now chained to the prosaic task of supplying electric power to the surrounding country-side. . . .

In 1858, when I was four years of age, my father moved into a house which he built during that year and where members of my family still reside. Across the interval of seventy years there is still fresh and vivid in my memory the outlook, the orchards, the upland fields, the distant meadows, and the quiet village streets with their fine Lombardy poplars and old willows. I can still hear the surf on the shores of Long Island, which lay north of the Grand Pré meadow, and the soughing of the south wind in the evening often lulling me to sleep.[2]

My father, Andrew Borden, was born in 1816 and died in his eighty-fifth year. He had a considerable farm, but for some years occupied himself in business affairs at which he did not succeed. He was a man of good ability and excellent judgment but he lacked energy and had no great aptitude for affairs. In temperament, he was calm, contemplative, and philosophical. In middle life he entered the service of the Windsor-Annapolis Railway Company as station-master at Grand Pré; he remained for many years in that service. . . .

My father was born in the "Old Borden House" (so-called)

[1] The village of Lower Horton, as it was then called, was said, like Rome, to extend over seven hills. I could never identify them.
[2] I have a most distinct recollection of the Saxeby Gales (as they were called) which broke the dykes and flooded the dyke-meadows, not only at Grand Pré but elsewhere in Nova Scotia. The spring tides in the Bay of Fundy and in the Basin of Minas sometimes raise the waters to a height of sixty feet above low-tide level. This is due to the peculiar formation of the Bay of Fundy, through which the western sweep of the tide pours as through a funnel. Thousands of cattle and horses were on the meadows at Grand Pré but very few of them were drowned. At dusk there was a broad sweep of 3,000 acres of meadow; in the morning part of the ocean.

at Grand Pré which I purchased as a community centre for that village. The house seems to have been erected about 1800 by my great-grandfather and illustrated the habit of life in the early days. There was a huge fireplace in a large room which appears to have been both kitchen and living-room. In this fireplace great logs were burned and the embers were carefully covered with ashes at night so that the fire could readily be rekindled next morning. In those days there were no matches and if, unfortunately, the embers expired there was resort to flint and steel. . . .

My mother was a woman of very strong character, remarkable energy, high ambition, and unusual ability, which she probably inherited from her father. She had received a fair education and had a considerable acquaintance with English literature. In her later years she was greatly cheered by her interest in the works of Dickens, Scott, and Thackeray and loved to discuss the events and characters depicted by those authors. Her brightness and vivacity as well as her brilliancy of repartee made her conspicuous in any company. She had very keen likes and dislikes and, although she was of remarkably vigorous physique, had a highly-wrought, nervous temperament. She was passionate, but wholly just and considerate upon reflection. The outstanding feature of her life was her love for her children upon whom she exercised a dominant and most beneficent influence. Having a profound respect for the ability of her father, she hoped and believed that her children would inherit it. She died in 1915, a few days before entering her ninety-first year. . . .

My father belonged to the Anglican Church, while my mother was a Presbyterian. As we often lacked facilities for attending the Anglican Church at Wolfville, three miles distant, I frequently went with my mother to the Presbyterian Church and attended the Presbyterian Sunday-School where I was inducted into the mysteries of the *Shorter Catechism* and the *Confession of Faith*. However, we occasionally attended the Anglican Church of which Rev. John Storrs was rector.[3] He was very bald and my youthful curiosity was so much excited by this interesting phenomenon, which I had never before witnessed, that during one of his pastoral visits I hurriedly ran a chair from the side of the room and mounted upon it immediately behind Mr. Storrs in order to obtain a closer view. I was less than four years of age at the time but I still remember

[3] Rev. John Storrs was the grandfather of Sir Ronald Storrs, the distinguished Imperial administrator. [Ed.]

my mother's stern reproof which caused me to leave my position of vantage with the utmost suddenness. . . .

During the summer vacations and at other times my brother and I worked assiduously upon my father's farm, especially during the season when the hay crop was being cut and garnered. In those days there were no mowing machines and the mowing, raking, and gathering of the hay were done almost wholly by hand. It was a common sight on the great meadow to see half a dozen men moving *en echelon* and swinging their scythes in unison. At that season the weather was usually very warm and the work pretty severe. At an early age I was instructed in the mysteries of building a load of hay but my first venture met with little success as, owing to my inexperience and lack of skill, one corner collapsed, much to the indignation of the men below. The removal of innumerable small stones from land that had been ploughed and harrowed and the stowing away of hay in the great barns are two impressions in my agricultural education to which I look back with no pleasurable recollection.[4] To these may be added the extremely disagreeable task of hoeing potatoes in land infested by a terrible grass called "couch" which was very difficult to exterminate. However, the muscular exercise afforded by these unpleasureable activities as well as by the sawing of cord-wood for the winter supply of fuel was beneficial and healthful, although not so interesting or desirable, from our standpoint, as the schoolboy cricket and other games in which we greatly delighted. Then in winter we had coasting on the hills, skating on the frozen creeks and ponds and ice hockey of a very crude type. . . .

I was eager to devour books as soon as I had learned to read and at a very early age I read *Pilgrim's Progress*, for the sake of the story and without the slightest comprehension of its spiritual significance.

After preliminary training under a schoolmistress I was sent as a day pupil, at the age of nine, to Acacia Villa Seminary, a school which had been founded some ten years before and which from 1860 was in the proprietorship and under the direction of Arthur MacNutt Patterson. . . . The school was principally a boarding-school, but there were a few day-pupils. Patterson was an excellent disciplinarian and he never failed to impress upon his pupils the need and value of truthfulness,

[4] While stowing away hay in our great mow I nearly lost my sight through the impact of a three-pronged pitchfork carelessly thrown up by one of the men. I still bear the scar. In 1869 I had a narrow escape from drowning.

self-control, manliness, and industry. Each morning he read to us a chapter of Proverbs and occasionally he enlarged upon the lesson thus instilled, being especially concerned to make us realize the sharp distinction between knowledge and wisdom....

~ A quarrel between Patterson and the assistant master resulted in the latter's abrupt departure.

Borden, at the age of fourteen years and nine months, was "projected into the duties of assistant master." He stayed in this difficult rôle for three years, his modest salary being a necessary supplement to the family finances. ~

Very early in life, especially during this period, I pondered much upon the mysteries, meaning, and purpose of existence. In fact during the period from twelve to twenty years of age I had perhaps a more serious outlook upon life than during the subsequent years. My mother used sometimes to laugh at my extreme seriousness, although on occasion I thoroughly enjoyed games and outdoor life. A most intense appreciation of the value of time possessed me, and uppermost in my thoughts was the duty to utilize it to the utmost for the development of any intellectual qualities with which I was endowed. Very carefully I divided the hours of the day and prepared time-tables setting forth the amount of time which I should devote to each particular study. My younger brother, who was somewhat of a wit, affixed to one of them a note which he had copied from a railway notice, "All time-tables of a previous date to be destroyed." Outside of my daily labours as assistant master and the hours devoted to study I had but little leisure. In the result I succeeded in reading a good deal of Latin and Greek, the odes and some of the satires of Horace were an especial delight, a little German also, and some French; I delved also into higher mathematics. To English literature I gave inadequate attention through lack of sufficient library, but I read Milton's and Byron's and other poems, with some of Shakespeare's plays, Macaulay's *History of England*, all the works of Scott, Dickens, and Thackeray, and many old numbers of English quarterlies which had been stored in the attic. To read the whole of the Old and New Testaments as well as the Apochrypha was a recognized duty which I did not neglect.

In 1873, when I was nineteen years of age, Hamilton, who had taken charge of Glenwood Institute, a school at Matawan, New Jersey, invited me to proceed thither as assistant master and I accepted the offer; it was my first prolonged absence from home. Hamilton had a weakness for high-sounding titles and upon arriving at Matawan I was astounded and horrified to find that in the school calendar I was announced as "Professor of Classics and Mathematics." The pupils were principally from the village of Matawan which had been settled by a fine type of German, Dutch, and Scottish colonists. There was a flourishing Literary Society of which I became a member. The people of Matawan with whom I was brought into contact were highly educated and cultured. . . .

2: Student at Law and Member of the Bar *1874-1896*

In August of 1874, I became an "articled clerk" in the office of Weatherbe and Graham who were in practice at Halifax as barristers and solicitors. Then, as now, there was no division of the two professions in Nova Scotia. The period of service was four years and although, by the terms of my articles, I was entitled to be instructed in the knowledge and practice of the Law, the members of the firm were far too busy with their professional duties to give any attention whatever to such instruction. Like other law students of the day, I worked laboriously in the office from nine a.m. until six p.m., receiving a trifling remuneration for keeping the account books. In the evenings one occupied oneself in endeavouring to master, as best one could, the mysteries of the Law. There was no law school in Nova Scotia at the time and none was established until 1882, four years after I had been admitted.

During my apprenticeship, I made the best possible use of my time. Besides my work in the office and my reading of Law, I read several books of Homer, a Greek play, *Oedipus Tyrannus*, Victor Hugo's *Les Miserables* and *Maria Stuart* in German by Schiller.

During the last year and a half of my apprenticeship my finances were at pretty low ebb, but eventually I came through without owing a dollar. In 1877 I earned one hundred dollars for some work in connection with the Fishery Commission which sat in that year.

However, in the course of the four years I acquired some knowledge of the principles of Law and a pretty thorough knowledge of the practice. Thus, when I passed my final examination in 1877, one year before I could be admitted, I was fortunate in leading a class of some thirty men, many of whom subsequently attained distinction in the profession and in public life. Among them were the late Sir Charles Hibbert Tupper, the late Arthur R. Dickey—both of whom became Cabinet Ministers; the late Mr. Justice James J. Ritchie of the Supreme Court of Nova Scotia; and the late William B. Ross, for some time leader of the Liberal-Conservatives in the Senate of Canada.

In the winter of 1878 I went through the Military School at Halifax which entitled one to a bonus of fifty dollars. It was a hard grind, especially as leaving one's office at six one had to be on hand at the drill hall at seven o'clock, besides doing a mile to one's lodgings and a mile back to the drill hall. . . .

After my admission to the Bar, I had carried on a practice in Halifax with my friend, the late John T. Ross. In the first case in which I appeared at the Bar, an action in the County Court, I was opposed to John S. D. Thompson, then Attorney-General of Nova Scotia. This was early in 1879, and during the next four years I acquired a good deal of experience in Court.

From the beginning of 1880 to the summer of 1882 I was in partnership at Kentville, the shire town of my native County of King's, as junior partner of John P. Chipman, afterwards a county court judge. . . .

Counsel work was in the first instance a tremendous ordeal to me. However, I was inspired by invincible determination to shrink from no task however responsible and arduous that lay before me. But during a week, sometimes ten days, of continuous counsel work I would be in a condition of such extreme nervous tension that I could hardly eat or sleep. Curiously enough this condition did not in the least manifest itself while I was in court, as I possessed perfect self-control and the intense activity of my mental powers was unaccompanied by the slightest outward sign of what is usually termed nervousness. Whatever success I attained as counsel is to be attributed to the faculty of working at tremendously high pressure but under absolute self-control.

Thus, when I began to practice in Halifax in 1882, as a junior member of the firm of Graham, Tupper, and Borden, I had gained more experience than most men of my age. We had a very large practice, and at once I plunged *in medias res*. When the term of the Supreme Court *in banco* drew near in the autumn of 1882, some fifteen cases for argument before the court *in banco* were assigned to me. I was a rather prodigious worker; then and for many years afterwards I usually worked in my office every evening. Almost immediately I began to take briefs on circuit where I attained all the success I could reasonably have anticipated. . . .

In 1888 Sir John A. Macdonald invited Hibbert Tupper to enter his Government as Minister of Marine and Fisheries. During the same year I received from Sir John Thompson, then Minister of Justice, the offer of appointment as Deputy Minister of that Department. Graham had begun to lean more and more upon me in our practice and, when I discussed my possible acceptance of the offer, I found that he was greatly concerned. In view of his extremely generous treatment and of my warm affection for him, I felt it my duty to decline. The offer was then made to Robert Sedgewick who accepted. Often I have pondered upon the remarkable contrast between the career I then desired and that which with some reluctance I afterwards pursued.

If I had accepted Thompson's offer I should probably have become a judge. The career which afterwards lay before me was by no means of my own choosing, as I shall indicate but, while it was more arduous, it was in many aspects a far wider and on the whole a finer career.

In 1885 Mr. Justice Thompson resigned and became Minister of Justice in the Government of Sir John A. Macdonald. During my student days I had learned to realize his outstanding ability as a lawyer and during the three years of my practice before him in Halifax I began to regard him as one of the ablest men I had ever met. He was a polished speaker, had a wonderful command of English, and possessed a remarkable faculty of vivid expression which he could use with devastating effect in court, on the floor of Parliament, or on the public platform. . . .[1]

In 1885 Canada was startled by the incident of the Riel Rebellion, the massacre of settlers, and the defeat of the Mounted Police. In Halifax, as elsewhere in Eastern Canada, the event produced intense excitement and fierce determination to put down the Rebellion. Up to this time Nova Scotia hardly regarded itself as included in the Canadian Confederation. The Repeal agitation had by no means spent its force but the Rebellion evoked a new spirit. A composite regiment was

---

[1] After appointment to the Bench Thompson found ample leisure for winding up the affairs of Thompson and Graham. He sent out statements to lawyers and business firms who were indebted for professional work. One evening at our office, in reporting his activities to Graham, Thompson mentioned a certain lawyer, well known for indifference to demands for payment of his just debts and made the following observation, "I sent him a statement of his account together with a promissory note which I requested him to sign and return, and he has paid no more attention to that promissory note than he would have done if he had signed it." On another occasion in dismissing an appeal by a solicitor who had put forward an unworthy defence and whose evidence had not been accepted by the trial judge, Thompson, after commenting most severely upon the dishonourable character of the defence, observed, "It was apparently in an endeavour to save the defendant from the disgrace of this defence that the learned judge disbelieved his evidence on oath."

formed in Halifax, recruited from the three local militia units, and young men were invited to enlist. Among those who embraced this opportunity were William J. Tupper, son of Sir Charles Tupper; James A. MacDonald, son of the Chief Justice; and William Young, a nephew of a former Chief Justice, Sir William Young. It was a great occasion in Halifax when the regiment entrained for the West; the city took a holiday and citizens thronged the streets in thousands. During the succeeding months there were rumours from time to time of battle and casualty. The regiment underwent many hardships, took its part in the campaign, but returned without having been actually engaged. Striplings who had gone forth as boys came back bronzed and stalwart. Again the streets were lined with thousands acclaiming the regiment's return. The Riel Rebellion did more to unite Nova Scotia to the rest of Canada than any event that had occurred since Confederation.

In 1887 I made my debut in the Supreme Court of Canada; it was a very strong court at that time and its membership comprised representatives from each of the four original provinces. . . .

On the first day of term the Court made a dignified and impressive entrance in their robes of scarlet and ermine. The session began at eleven o'clock in the morning and lasted until four o'clock in the afternoon without intermission; however, the judges, in turn, absented themselves from the Bench for about ten minutes at a time for the purpose of light refreshment. In the Nova Scotia appeals I usually held many briefs and at the conclusion of a long list I often found myself greatly fatigued.[2] To continue argument day after day in important cases without any opportunity for luncheon was a rather trying experience. The Court House, wholly unsuitable for its purpose, had been in the first instance merely a temporary structure used in connection with the construction of the Parliament Buildings. During my premiership I made preparation for the erection of a suitable building, and a considerable area extending along the shores of the Ottawa River was expropriated for that and other purposes. The outbreak of war prevented us from carrying out our intention. . . .

[2] While I was practising my profession in Halifax an English solicitor visiting that city learned that it was my custom to argue appeals in Ottawa. He was astonished that counsel should make a journey of 1,000 miles for that purpose and expressed the opinion that there must be great disadvantages in such a system. In reply I told him that counsel journeyed 3,000 miles from Vancouver to Ottawa for the like purpose.

When I first visited Ottawa in attendance upon the Supreme Court, it was a city of about twenty-five or thirty thousand people and had hardly emerged from the village state. The streets and sidewalks were those of a village rather than a city. In social life the political element was dominant. All this has entirely changed. Ottawa has become one of the most beautiful cities on the continent. Its business interests have developed immensely and it has a fine social life altogether apart from Parliamentary associations.

In 1888 I visited England and France for the first time. The early history of our family in England was then unknown to me but was subsequently revealed by researches undertaken by the American branch of the family. The visit naturally was of intense interest and I was especially anxious to see the working of the courts. Sailing from Halifax in a small steamer of about four thousand tons we had a delightful passage across the Atlantic. I remained in Liverpool over night and had an opportunity of seeing the opening of the Assizes the next morning. The ceremonial was a revelation. It happened that the judges were lodged at the London and North Western Hotel and I chanced to be outside the door when two trumpeters in Elizabethan garb arrived on the scene and trumpeted for a few minutes; after retiring they came again and repeated the performance. Presently the sheriff arrived with numerous attendants, entered the hotel and returned with the judges and their retinue. A procession was formed which moved in stately measure to St. George's Hall, and after entering divided, one judge going to the criminal side, and the other to the civil side . . .

In 1889 I had become engaged to be married and on September 25, I was married to Laura Bond, daughter of the late Thomas Bond of Halifax, whose devotion and helpfulness during all the succeeding years have been the chief support of my life's labours.

Three days before our wedding my senior partner, Wallace Graham, told me of his appointment to the Bench of the Supreme Court. Our honeymoon was thus cut short as within a few days I was obliged to return and take briefs on circuit that had been assigned to Mr. Graham. Within a few weeks I formed the firm of Borden, Ritchie, Parker, & Chisholm. . . .

From 1889 until my entry into public life in 1896 my firm had probably the largest practice in the Maritime Provinces. I was very fond of outdoor life, but for nearly forty years I almost entirely gave it up and devoted myself with all my strength first to my professional and afterwards to my public duties. . . .

In 1891 I was in attendance at the Supreme Court of Canada when the tolling of all the church bells in the city announced the death of Sir John A. Macdonald. The Supreme Court adjourned until after the funeral and there was practical cessation of business throughout the city. It was my good fortune to be in the House of Commons when Sir Hector Langevin and Sir Wilfrid Laurier paid their tributes to his memory. I had heard Laurier when I was practising at Kentville in 1881; he was then making a political tour of Nova Scotia with his leader, Edward Blake. Blake's speech was cogent, but Laurier's was eloquent and impressive. Thus, in 1891, I heard him for the second time and he rose to the full height of his splendid eloquence. On neither occasion had I even the faintest idea that in future years it should be my fate to enter the political arena against him. In those days it was my ambition to continue in the practice of my profession until some undefined date in the future when I might be selected for a position upon the Bench. . . .

In 1894 I was invited by my friend, Sir Charles Hibbert Tupper, to accompany him on a visit to British Columbia where he intended to address audiences at Victoria, Nanaimo, and other important points. His brother-in-law, Wallace McDonald, was a member of the party which, until we arrived in Winnipeg, included also Honourable N. Clark Wallace and Honourable John F. Wood who were to address political meetings in that city.

During the journey across the prairies I was impressed by the intense loneliness of the early settlers' life. The treeless aspect of the vast level plains was rather depressing to one accustomed to the forests, hills, rivers, and lakes of Eastern Canada. Then came the thrill of the Rockies and finally my first glimpse of the Pacific. . . .

During our journey to Vancouver Tupper had asked McDonald and myself whether we could keep a secret and without waiting for a reply he told us that he thought it extremely improbable that Sir John Thompson would live to return to Canada. We were greatly astonished and dismayed when we learned that the Prime Minister was in so precarious a condition. Tupper had noticed that Thompson's ankles were abnormal in size and had urged him to consult a physician. Thompson came to him afterwards and reported the diagnosis which was extremely unfavourable. "I am under sentence of death," he said. A few years before Thompson had said to me in the course of an intimate conversation, "Seeing that one must die, it does not seem to me that the time is a matter of much moment." As will be remembered he died very suddenly at Windsor Castle. . . .

In 1895, the British Parliament was dissolved while I was crossing the ocean to argue an appeal before the Judicial Committee. Upon my arrival in London, I found that the courts had adjourned and that the hearing could not take place for several weeks, as many of the leading counsel were candidates and were obliged to proceed to their constituencies. My wife and I spent the interval in visiting the beautiful lake country. We spent election day in Keswick. I was impressed by the extensive use of cartoons which were posted in every available space. Up to that time such methods of influencing the electorate had been employed very little in Canada. The British system of appointing different dates (extending over a considerable period) for polling in the various groups of constituencies seemed incongruous and even absurd in contrast with the Canadian system.

While in England on this occasion we availed ourselves of many opportunities to see Henry Irving and Ellen Terry in their chief roles, also William Terriss, an actor of remarkable promise whose career was cut short by assassination. Returning from England via New York, on one occasion we, most fortunately, had the opportunity of attending a performance of *The Heir at Law* with Joseph Jefferson in the role of Dr. Pangloss. Never had I seen an actor who merely by facial expression had so wonderful a control of his audience. This was my only opportunity of seeing Jefferson and I much regret that it was not my privilege to see him in the role of Rip Van Winkle.

In 1895, I consulted Mr. Treves (afterwards Sir Frederick Treves) who strongly advised me to undergo a slight operation which he thought not only desirable but essential. After my return, I prepared to follow his advice when a telegram from Sir Charles Tupper, who had retired from the High Commissionership to assume the leadership of the House of Commons under the premiership of Sir Mackenzie Bowell, requested me to institute immediate proceedings for criminal libel against the editor and proprietor of the Halifax *Chronicle*. For the time being I was obliged to abandon all thought of the proposed surgical operation (which has never been performed) and devote myself entirely to the task. There was a very long preliminary hearing but eventually the defendants offered and published an ample apology and, with the consent of the magistrate, proceedings were withdrawn.

While this issue was still in progress I was approached by prominent members of the Liberal-Conservative Party with the request that I should allow myself to be put in nomination as one of the Conservative candidates for the City and County of Halifax which elected two members to the House of Commons.[3]

During the winter the Conservative Government at Ottawa had been struggling with difficulties entailed by its policy on the Manitoba school question and as Parliament would expire by the effluxion of time in April, it was manifest that a general election was imminent.

The thought of a parliamentary career had never entered my mind. For eighteen years I had been very actively engaged in the practice of my profession, and except for a few words uttered on a public platform when called upon suddenly and unexpectedly at a meeting in support of the candidature of my cousin, Sir Frederick Borden, I had never spoken on a political platform. In 1886 I had ceased to be in sympathy with the Liberal Party by reason of the Repeal campaign in Nova Scotia at the provincial election held in that year.

At first I flatly refused. I had no political experience; no political ambitions had ever entered my mind and I was wholly devoted to my profession. At that time Halifax was represented by Thomas Edward Kenny and John Fitzwilliam Stairs. By reason of business interests and activities Mr. Stairs was about to remove to Montreal, and, as this would seriously diminish his chances of election, he was unwilling to become a candidate. The request was renewed and pressed upon me with great insistence. Finally I consented, but with the stipulation that I should not be asked to serve for more than one term. Accordingly, Mr. Kenny and I were nominated and after returning from the spring session of the Supreme Court of Canada, I put aside all other activities and devoted my whole time and energy to my candidature.

Thus, with absolute lack of experience in platform speaking

[3] The strongest and most effective pressure came from Sir Charles Tupper.

and equal ignorance of methods of political organization, I became a candidate and passed through the fierce campaign which terminated on June 23, 1896. It was to me a novel experience. Although for fifteen years I had been engaged in active practice both in Courts of First Instance and on Appeal, it was with great nervousness and diffidence that I entered this new sphere of oratorical effort.

Nova Scotia, and indeed every province was then in a condition of unusual excitement as the Manitoba school question overshadowed every other issue. The Remedial Bill, early in 1896, had been fought stubbornly to some extent by the Liberals but still more fiercely by the ultra-Protestant element of the Liberal-Conservative Party who, while asserting their allegiance to the Party, were violently opposed to any interference with Manitoba.

My colleague, Thomas Edward Kenny, who had represented the constituency since 1887, was a man of high character and fine ideals, a splendid type of Irish gentleman of the old school. He occupied a commanding position in the business life of Halifax and was highly respected. I never met anyone more sincerely and firmly devoted to the unity and welfare of the British Empire. He was handicapped by his strong support of the Government's policy in respect of the Manitoba schools, which cost him the votes of many ultra-Protestant Conservatives in Halifax.

It was a recognized convention in my constituency that one candidate on each side should be a Roman Catholic and one a Protestant. Opposed to us were Michael Keefe, a capable man who had risen from the ranks, and Benjamin Russell, a prominent lawyer, afterwards a Justice of the Supreme Court of Nova Scotia.

Nova Scotia had begun to recover from the movement for Repeal which had agitated it for at least twenty years after Confederation. In the early days of that agitation the two parties were known as the "Confederates" and the "Antis." The latter, in large majority, had an almost irresistible slogan in the battle cry that Nova Scotians had been sold to Canada, "for eighty cents a head, the price of a sheepskin."[4] While canvassing and speaking I more than once encountered people who still referred to the Liberal-Conservatives as "Confederates" and to the Liberals as "Antis." Even in very remote

---

[4] A subsidy payable to Nova Scotia under the British North America Act was at the rate of eighty cents per head of the population.

districts and among people comparatively uneducated, I found a remarkable knowledge of the Manitoba school question which had aroused an interest that permeated all classes of the population.

When the battle was over I found myself at the head of the poll, but my colleague, Mr. Kenny, was unfortunately defeated.

Sir Charles Tupper's Government met decisive defeat. Quebec, where he had confidently counted on strong support, gave the Liberals a majority of thirty-five.

3: Early Years in Public Life *1896-1901*

During the next four years I was to undergo a novel experience. Thoroughly absorbed in my professional duties, I found very little leisure between sessions of Parliament for political activities, but as soon as Parliament opened my professional duties immediately receded into the background and I concentrated my whole time and energy upon my parliamentary work. Thus, during a portion of the year I was altogether a practising lawyer and during the remainder of the year I was altogether a politician.

The combination of these two roles left little time for rest or recreation, and the strain of those four years coupled with the effects of a very strenuous life during the previous twenty years led eventually to a rather serious impairment of my health.

The nervous strain of learning to speak in parliamentary debate I found rather severe, although for many years I had been accustomed to speak in court and before juries. . . .

My early impressions of Parliament are still vivid. I had entered public life with a very high conception of its duties and responsibilities and with a rather lofty ideal of the dignity of Parliament as the grand inquest of the nation. My first impressions were disappointing as there seemed a singular lack of dignity in the attitude and behaviour of members as well as in the conduct of debate—methods were unbusinesslike and waste of time enormous. However, I soon realized that the House had an instinctive sense of dignity which was not at first apparent, and I quickly became convinced that in parliamentary government waste of time is quite inevitable.

On each side the leaders were impressive in debate. Tupper's fierce vehemence of attack was countered by Laurier's commanding eloquence and dexterity; Foster's keen thrusts were parried by Cartwright's rapier blade.

The session of 1896 opened on August 19, and my first attempt to address the House was on the twenty-eighth of that month when I spoke in a debate (on dismissal of public officials) initiated by Sir Charles Hibbert Tupper.

I deplored and attacked the evils of the spoils system and defended the right of public officials to make their voices known and the influence felt with the same freedom as other voters but subject to the necessary considerations of official duty and discipline.

Later I was asked to follow Sir Richard Cartwright in the debate upon the misuse of Governor-General's warrants. The Liberals had refused Supply at the previous session which was brought to a close by the efflux of time and now they were "hoist on their own petard" as no supplies were available except by means of such warrants. The Government relied upon the opinion of the Minister of Justice (Sir Oliver Mowat) who, probably, had strained the provisions of the statute beyond their legitimate meaning. However, the construction which he sanctioned has since been found convenient not only by Liberal but by Conservative administrations.

My effort in this debate was probably less aggressive than was expected, and I did not feel that it was a success. I was followed by James Lister, a member of the Ontario Bar, who taunted me with having used such an argument as I would address to a court. Later I had the opportunity of retorting that I could not return the compliment as neither in tone, in style, nor in character did he in the least resemble any of the eminent Ontario counsel to whom I had listened in the Supreme Court of Canada.

Before entering public life I had been somewhat affected by the prejudice against Sir Charles Tupper which, through constant assertion and reiteration, had spread itself to some extent in the Liberal-Conservative Party. It was not long before I was completely won by his indomitable courage, his broad outlook, his splendid patriotism, his inspiring optimism, and his high sense of public duty. He was then in his seventy-sixth year, but his untiring industry and keen vigilance were an inspiration to all his followers. In attack he was inclined to exaggerate every favourable fact or consideration, and he perhaps thought that I was not sufficiently aggressive as I was most careful to keep well within bounds. Often when I went to consult him before rising to address the House he would say as a parting admonition "Don't spare them on my account."

I have on occasion mentioned in public the following illustration of Sir Charles Tupper's devotion to the public interest, but it will bear repetition. During the session of 1897, I was at Sir Charles' house on a Sunday afternoon when the late Senator McKeen, from Nova Scotia, told us that the Government had definitely decided to increase the iron and steel bounties which were so important to that industry in Nova Scotia. Sir Charles could not reasonably expect to attain the premiership, which was his life's ambition, unless he should win at the next election. When McKeen communicated to him this news Tupper said with intense earnestness, "I am glad they have done it even if it gives them another five years of power." There could be no more eloquent testimony to his sense of public duty.

At first I was seated near the back of the Chamber. There were many attempts among the back-benchers to obtain seats near the front whenever vacancies occurred. I made no such effort and, very much to my surprise, the Chief Whip, in my fourth session, told me that I had been advanced to the front row where I took my seat accordingly.

The advent of the Laurier Government (1896) left the Manitoba school question still unsettled. Its solution offered the Government some embarrassment as its majority came almost altogether from the Province of Quebec. A settlement was made, the details of which it is not necessary to recount. Sir Wilfrid Laurier, who had been in attendance at Queen Victoria's Diamond Jubilee, found it convenient to visit Rome and later the Pope issued an encyclical on the Manitoba school question advising Catholics of that Province to accept the Laurier-Greenway settlement, but declaring it inadequate and expressing the hope that the province itself might in time do justice to the minority. The terms of the settlement were not entirely welcome to all the Quebec members but they were induced to sanction it. The chief difficulty probably arose with Mr. Bourassa. To Mr. Tarte was entrusted the task of persuading that fiery spirit to refrain from open rebellion. He told me that for a whole week he kept Bourassa in his house, arguing and expostulating with him lest he should light a spark that might cause inflammable material to blaze into a conflagration; but in truth the country was thoroughly tired of the Manitoba school question and quite welcomed any reasonable settlement. . . .

~ In 1897 Borden was requested to answer Sir Louis Davies, Minister of Marine and Fisheries, who was defending the government's granting of preferential tariff treatment to the United Kingdom. Borden "experienced little difficulty in successfully controverting his argument." A subsequent reference to British law officers sustained the Conservative contention that because of Britain's "favored nation" agreement, the goods of many countries thus became entitled to the preference intended only for Britain. Eventually, through agreements between Britain and European countries, an amicable settlement was reached. ~

After Mr. Tarte had resigned, as he claimed, or had been dismissed, as Sir Wilfrid Laurier claimed, he gave me interesting information as to the genesis of Mr. Fielding's preferential tariff. For several years Liberal leaders had been unsparing in their attacks upon the policy of protection. Sir Wilfrid had proclaimed on many a platform, and especially in Western Canada, that protection was no better than bondage—bondage in the same sense that African slavery is bondage. The tocsin of the Party was Free Trade or tariff for revenue only. In the campaign of 1896 it was believed and currently reported that Mr. Tarte, who was known to differ from Sir Wilfrid on this question, was authorized to give to the manufacturers of Canada the assurance that if they held their hand their interests would not be materially affected in case the Liberals should come into power. There is little doubt that such an assurance was given. Thus the new Government in preparing to formulate its tariff policy faced an embarrassing situation. On the one hand there were the pledges of Sir Wilfrid Laurier and Sir Richard Cartwright, strongly supported by Mr. Fielding and other Free Traders, to abolish every vestige of protection; on the other hand Mr. Tarte and Mr. Patterson, who were strong Protectionists, put up a very vigorous fight against any such extreme proposals as were in contemplation. It is beyond question that a serious crisis developed; according to Mr. Tarte, there was fear that the Cabinet would become disrupted. He told me that Mr. Patterson came to him in great distress and almost in tears. If I remember correctly, it was Mr. Tarte's wonderful resourcefulness that offered the solution. He suggested a tariff which would grant preference to Great Britain but would make no serious disruption in the general protective duties. This solution was accepted, and from the standpoint of the Government there was much to commend it. On the one hand, it would appeal to British sentiment in the English-speaking provinces; on the other hand, it would not seriously impair the interests of the manufacturers; and, finally, it would make a plausible case for contending that the Free Trade promise had been fulfilled so far as circumstances would permit.

During the session of 1897, Sir Charles Tupper took occasion to express, in terms as forceful as parliamentary usage would permit, his opinion of the Governor-General's conduct after the election of 1896. Lord Aberdeen had forced the resignation of the Tupper Government by refusing to accept its advice as to appointments. Sir Charles took the position that until Parliament met and by vote demonstrated its lack of confidence in his Government, he had a perfect right to remain in office; and that his advice should have been accepted by the Governor-General. There were many precedents for that view and, indeed, the right claimed by Sir Charles had been fully exercised by the Liberal Premier, Alexander Mackenzie, after his defeat in 1878. Mr. Weatherbe, my preceptor in the law, was appointed to the Bench by the Mackenzie Government after their defeat. Sir Charles supported his opinion by a long array of relevant English precedents and by reference to Mr. Mackenzie's action.

Sir Wilfrid Laurier relied on Mr. Disraeli's action in 1868, and on the similar course pursued by Mr. Gladstone in 1874; another precedent was to be found in Mr. Gladstone's resignation immediately after his defeat in 1886; however, Lord Salisbury, in 1892, had chosen to meet Parliament instead of resigning. Sir Wilfrid made a strong fighting speech and was cheered to the echo by his followers; he indulged in the extremely dubious and quite astonishing prophecy that all true Canadians would revere the name of Aberdeen for ever and for ever.

The new administration was faced with two pledges which had been put forward by its leaders in several provinces and on almost every platform and which upon their attainment of power were practically impossible of fulfilment. One already indicated was the pledge to establish in Canada Free Trade as it is in England; the other was a pledge to enact Prohibition of the manufacture, importation, and sale of intoxicating liquors if such policy should be affirmed by the people upon a plebiscite. In 1898 necessary legislation was enacted and the plebiscite was held. About 550,000 votes were recorded and the total majority for Prohibition was 12,286 – a substantial majority in every province except Quebec where a majority of 94,032 was recorded against it. The Government took the ground that as Prohibition had not received a majority of the registered vote the people had not decided in its favour; and thus no sanction for prohibitory legislation had been given. In the session of 1899, Mr. (afterwards Sir) George Foster denounced this conclusion as an evasion of the Liberal leaders' pledge; and he pointed out that few, if any, members of the Government or of Parliament sat in the House under the sanction of a majority of the total registered vote. It seems wholly reasonable that any such implied condition should have been made public before the plebiscite was authorized or held. However, I was assured by my Conservative comrades that the

Government had no cause for apprehension as Liberal Prohibitionists would still vote the Liberal ticket in time of need.[1]...

In [1899], after by-elections in West Huron and Brockville, there were indications that ballots had been tampered with, and upon investigation it was demonstrated that in certain polls ballots marked for the Conservative candidate had been destroyed and fraudulent ballots marked for the Liberal had been substituted. Affidavits were produced that at one poll in West Huron forty-three electors had marked their ballots for the Conservative candidate while at the conclusion of the poll only thirty so marked were found in the box. Sir Charles Tupper asked me to undertake a motion for Parliamentary investigation, and I consented upon condition that H. A. Powell of New Brunswick would be associated with me. Accordingly we accepted upon the stipulation that we should be permitted to devote ourselves exclusively to this task throughout the session.

On July 6, 1899, I made my motion as a matter of privilege and I had to steer a very wary course, as there was good reason to anticipate refusal based upon the consideration that all questions respecting contraverted elections had been relegated to the courts by statute. I was forced to base my motion upon the ground that returning officers and their deputies were servants of the House and that Parliament might properly inquire into their conduct although the results of any such inquiry could not legally invalidate the election. It might, of course, so influence public opinion that the sitting member would be constrained to resign.

Sir Wilfrid Laurier spoke very briefly in announcing that the Government would accept the motion. He suggested that I should have adopted a more judicial tone and he mildly reproved me for the heat with which I had set forth my case. He was followed by Sir Charles Tupper in whose speech not the slightest trace of any judicial tone was discernible; he exhausted the resources of our language in denouncing the practices which had undoubtedly prevailed at these two elections.

By Order of the House all documents relating to the election, including the ballots, were produced by the Clerk of the Crown in Chancery, and placed in the hands of the Com-

---

[1] A witty secretary of one of the Ministers was guilty of the following *bon mot*: "We promised Free Trade as it is in England and Prohibition as it is in Maine. It is true our pledge was not literally fulfilled but we did give Free Trade as it is in Maine and Prohibition as it is in England."

mittee on Privileges and Elections. Upon examining these documents Powell's quick eye soon discerned that, among the ballots at the poll in question, several (evidently fraudulent) differed distinctly in appearance from the official ballots. To make assurance doubly sure we had them examined and tested by an expert who absolutely confirmed our view. The Liberals then adopted the tactics of prolonging the investigation and did so with considerable success by aimless and protracted cross-examination of witnesses. We produced the Conservative electors who had marked their ballots at the poll in question. Among the Liberal obstructionists was Mr. B. M. Britton who invariably asked each of them whether he could recognize his ballot. The reply was always negative until a rather lively tailor from Goderich, Ontario, replied confidently in the affirmative; evidently he had imbibed some stimulant that rendered him unusually self-assertive. He was directed to indicate his ballot among those placed before him. Finding his self-appointed task somewhat difficult :"It's pretty hard," he commenced, when Mr. Britton interrupted him, "Did you not swear you could recognize it?" The witness resumed his task of examining the ballots one by one. I was watching him narrowly when I saw his face light with a happy thought. He went over the remaining ballots very rapidly and confidently, then stood up and announced triumphantly, "It is just as I expected, my ballot is not here, it is one of those that have been stolen." The witness retired victorious and Mr. Britton remained discomfited.[2]

Owing to the Liberal tactics the inquiry was not concluded and at the end of the session, and in the following year I moved to resume it as a matter of privilege. Sir John Bourinot, then Clerk of the House, was a man of great learning with an immense knowledge of precedents, but he somewhat lacked the ability to give them logical application. Under his advice the Speaker ruled that as a year had elapsed the subject was no longer a matter of privilege. Offending and corrupt servants of the House were to be protected by a fancied limitation existing only in the imagination of the Speaker and the Clerk. As appeal was useless, I put down the motion on the Order

---

[2] All our witnesses not under examination were excluded from the committee room. Mr. Britton invariably asked each of them whether he had been discussing the case while he was not in attendance; the usual answer was in the negative but one witness in the affirmative. Mr. Britton asked what had been said. The witness, apparently much confused, was unwilling to answer, but having been ordered by the chairman he replied, "Well sir, we were just saying among ourselves what terrible foolish questions you gentlemen have been asking."

paper but it soon transpired that this would be blocked. Accordingly, under the direction of Sir Charles Tupper, this motion was dropped so that I might take up the matter upon motion to go into Supply. The Government at once realized our intention and for about six weeks they did not move the House into Committee of Supply. During all that period I kept watch from three o'clock in the afternoon until midnight or later, armed with my documents and prepared to make the motion. Finally on May 11, about midnight, the House was moved into Committee. I immediately arose and spoke for an hour. A long debate ensued, but, of course, our motion was defeated. To hold some of his restless followers, Sir Wilfrid Laurier (who adroitely fastened upon an incautious observation of Sir George Foster) undertook that there would be a judicial inquiry, thorough and searching. No such inquiry was ever held. . . .

I have a vivid memory of my first all-night session. On June 7, 1899, the agreement between the Grand Trunk and Intercolonial Railways for extension to Montreal and use of Grand Trunk terminals was in committee. On May 20 the Minister of Railways (Mr. Blair) had promised me information as to the relative proportion of such use by the Grand Trunk and by the Intercolonial. But on June 7, when the discussion was resumed the information was not forthcoming. When I urged, with the support of other Conservatives, the production of the information, Mr. Blair was evasive and in the end he treated us rather cavalierly, if not contemptuously. As midnight approached and we continued to press for the information it was clear that the Minister did not intend to furnish it. Sir Charles Tupper and Sir Charles Hibbert Tupper, as well as the great body of Conservatives, had gone home and Mr. Foster was leading a small but determined group of Conservatives who would not yield—nor would the Minister. At six o'clock in the morning we put up Dr. Marcotte (member for Champlain) who asked to hold the fort for one hour. He held it for three hours and by that time (nine o'clock) reinforcements began to arrive.

Sir Wilfrid arrived on the scene about eleven o'clock and took command of the situation. In the meantime Opposition members had gathered in force and Blair realized that the game was up. He made a conciliatory and apologetic speech which relieved the tension and in doing so he warmly disclaimed any intention of treating me with disrespect. . . .

The combined effects of active professional practice and

public duties greatly impaired my health, and in the spring of 1900, I consulted an eminent physician in New York who did not give me a very reassuring diagnosis. Apart from the medical treatment which he prescribed, he insisted that I must lead a very quiet life and avoid anything that might tend to excitement, that I should do no work in the evening, and that I should spend much of my time in the open air. This advice he strongly reiterated two months later when I consulted him again. The mode of life which he so impressively enjoined under penalty of absolute loss of health was in complete antithesis to that upon which I embarked a few months later. . . .

My most important speech during the session of 1900 has already been described in my account of the investigation into the election frauds in West Huron and Brockville. Sir Wilfrid, on Junt 4, 1900, placed before the House an Order-in-Council by the terms of which Mr. Chancellor Boyd, Mr. Justice Falcon-bridge, and Judge McTavish were appointed commissioners to inquire into and to investigate fraudulent alterations, defacing and spoiling of ballots, etc., and to report thereon. On the following day Sir Charles Tupper practically approved the terms of the Order-in-Council and the personnel of the com-mission, making however certain suggestions as to the imme-diate inquiry into the West Huron and Brockville election. On the same occasion I put forward certain suggestions for the consideration of the Minister of Justice respecting the terms of the Order-in-Council.

The proposed inquiry was never proceeded with and the full history of the frauds perpetrated in the West Huron and Brockville elections has never been revealed. There is reason to believe that during the elections of 1891 certain deputy returning officers perpetrated frauds in the interest of the Liberal-Conservative Party by deliberately spoiling ballots marked for the Liberal candidate. It was said that a mark sufficient to destroy the validity of a ballot could be made by means of a small piece of lead inserted under the fingernail of a returning officer. Unless watched with the most vigilant attention the deputy returning officer could easily perpetrate such frauds. The unusual number of spoiled ballots during the election of 1891 seems to support this theory. Probably this fact dampened the enthusiasm of Liberal-Conservative leaders in Ontario for a judicial inquiry.

When a general election was impending in the summer of 1900, I went to Sir Charles Tupper and expressed the hope that he would permit me to retire from public life. I laid emphasis upon the impairment of my health and the necessity of confining myself to my professional duties. Sir Charles expressed great concern, urging that all other Conservative members for Nova Scotia would again be candidates, and that my withdrawal would be very detrimental, as I represented the metropolitan district of Halifax and had gained a leading position in our party. Upon his urgent request, although with much hesitation, I consented to accept nomination once more, but with the understanding that if my health remained impaired I should be permitted to resign.

The election did not take place until November 7, 1900. Several weeks previously, I observed in the Press that Sir Charles was about to attend the nominating convention at Sydney, Nova Scotia. At that time, this Cape Breton constituency returned two members. Observing that Sir Charles was to proceed unattended from Ottawa to Sydney, I telegraphed a message that I should be glad to accompany him if he desired. Upon receiving a cordial acceptance, I joined him at Truro, N.S., and we reached Sydney late that night. The convention met at three o'clock the next afternoon and immediately nominated Sir Charles and Hector F. McDougall. The latter first addressed the convention for about half an hour; and then Sir Charles followed with a speech of nearly three hours. It was a wonderful effort for a man in his eightieth year, vigorous, cogent, and incisive.

At its conclusion he came to me with earnest and sincere apologies for having occupied so much time that I had no opportunity to speak. I assured him with equal earnestness and sincerity that I had not come to Sydney with the least desire or intention of addressing the convention, but solely for the purpose of attending him as my leader. He protested however that I ought to speak and declared that I should have the opportunity at the evening meeting. The convention adjourned about half-past six and we proceeded to the hotel, where Sir Charles immediately went to bed and after partaking of very light refreshment received many friends in his room. At the evening meeting, after Mr. McDougall had spoken for about half an hour, the grand old man, showing no indication of fatigue, held the keen interest and aroused the warm enthusiasm of the audience in a powerful fighting speech of nearly three hours. The meeting adjourned and once more Sir Charles was conscience-stricken that he had not fulfilled his promise to have me called upon; beyond question he had really intended to do so, but his intense earnestness and astonishing vigour had carried him along so splendidly that the usual hour for adjournment had arrived before he realized it. I assured him of my profound satisfaction that he had occupied all the available time.

After prorogation, and indeed before, it was evident that the Government would appeal to the country before the end of the year. Campaign pamphlets and leaflets were abundant on both sides. The Government claimed to have accomplished tariff stability and, naturally, they took credit for improved business conditions, although there was an admission that Providence had assisted to some extent. The British preference was enlarged upon; and it was claimed that the principal tariff planks in the Liberal platform of 1893 had been effectively adopted by legislation. The pamphlets and leaflets of the Conservative Party laid emphasis upon broken pledges, waste, extravagance, the failure of the British preference, election frauds, Yukon scandals, railway deals, and many other matters. Our attack, possibly, was too discursive and lacked force in failing to concentrate on some single issue. But, in truth, there was no dominating issue; prosperity prevailed. So, on November 7, 1900, the Liberal-Conservative Party once more went down to decisive defeat.

Sir Charles Tupper, Mr. Foster, and Mr. Hugh John Macdonald were defeated. I was returned for Halifax, but my colleague, Mr. Kenny, again met undeserved defeat.

On election night Sir Charles was staying at the house of Senator McKeen in Halifax. In company with some friends I called upon him late in the evening when the results were known. He was perfectly cheerful and optimistic, saying that his personal defeat was most fortunate as, at his age, it would be impossible for him to continue in the leadership of the Opposition. Having pledged himself to speak for a Conservative candidate at a postponed election in British Columbia, he at once proceeded to journey nearly 4,000 miles across the continent in fulfilment of that promise.

Sir Charles Tupper almost immediately announced his resignation which was conveyed to the first caucus of the Conservative members on February 5, 1901. The following words may be fittingly quoted from his letter:

My feeling toward the people of Canada is one of profound gratitude for the confidence reposed in my political associates and myself for so many years; and I accept with equal readiness the adverse judgment which places our party still in Opposition. It may be that I acquiesce in this judgment the more readily that it releases me personally from duties and responsibilities too onerous for my years. I can wish my successor in leadership no better fortune than that he should enjoy the same support and the same unfailing kindness that has always been extended to me.

A resolution was passed bearing testimony to his devotion, unquestioned ability, and unfaltering courage, which during many years had won the abiding gratitude of his friends and the sincere admiration of his opponents. . . .

On Saturday, August 14, 1915, a few weeks before his death, I visited Sir Charles at Bexley Heath in England; his mind was as clear and his interest in public affairs as keen as it could have been half a century before. He dwelt upon the desirability of having the Canadian Government represented in London by one of its members as High Commissioner and he believed that this course would bring about an exceedingly valuable means of co-operation.

Returning to my narrative and to 1901, there was of course much concern in our party with regard to the leadership. While in New York, engaged in professional duties, I received intimation that the Liberal-Conservative members were to meet in Ottawa a few days before the opening of the session in order that the selection of a leader might be considered. Sir George Foster unfortunately had been defeated in St. John, N.B., by Mr. Blair, Minister of Railways. Beyond question he was the most outstanding figure in the party, although his wonderful ability in debate was not always matched by equal good judgment.

When we met in Ottawa there was much desultory discussion and finally to my amazement Sir Charles Hibbert Tupper proposed me as leader. I expressed my astonishment and told my fellow-members that I could not undertake the task. Discussion proceeded until a rather late hour. Mr. Haggart urged that the choice should fall upon Sir George Foster and that a seat should be found for him. The meeting adjourned until the following evening without reaching any decision.

At the adjourned meeting the proposal that I should be selected began to gather momentum. I endeavoured to postpone the decision and in company with Mr. W. F. McLean was engaged in drafting a proposal that would involve delay when my fellow-members became impatient and insisted that a decision should be reached then and there. They urged that inability to select a leader at an adjourned meeting would be construed as lamentable weakness. Finally, under great pressure, I agreed to accept the task for one year and coupled my acceptance with the stipulation that in the meantime a committee should be appointed to select a permanent leader of greater ability, experience, and aptitude, one who would, perhaps, desire the position from which I shrank. This stipulation was accepted but "the Sons of Zeruiah were too hard for me." After the meeting some of the older members urged me to refrain from making public the temporary character of my leadership as any such announcement would tend to diminish my authority. I yielded to their persuasions and, instead of one year, I remained twenty years in the leadership.

My selection was announced in the Press next morning and I received a charming letter of congratulations from Sir Wilfrid Laurier. When I took my seat as leader that afternoon he renewed his congratulations in very graceful terms and ended by observing with great suavity, "I am quite sure my honourable friend will believe in my absolute sincerity when I tell him that I hope with all my heart he may continue to exercise for a long, long period, the functions of leader of the Opposition." This thrust was just what I needed; and after conveying to Sir Wilfrid my thanks and expressing my appreciation of the honour conferred upon me, I retorted, "The right honourable gentleman will permit me to say, in passing, that if I should remain leader of the Opposition for as long as that joke is old, it will be wholly beyond my own expectations, and beyond the expectations of the honourable gentlemen on this side of the House." . . .

The task which I had undertaken was one of very great difficulty; the Conservative Party was at the nadir of its fortunes, and Sir Wilfrid Laurier was then approaching the zenith of his power and influence. In his Government were included many men of conspicuous ability and long political experience; not a few of them were past masters in the art of political strategy. . . .

The duties and responsibilities of a political leader in the federal arena of Canada are exceedingly onerous whether the party be in power or in opposition. In my case they were accentuated by the fact that I was a comparatively unknown man and that I was confronted with the necessity of getting into touch, really for the first time, with an electorate spread in scattered communities over a vast area, and separated not only by distance but by divergencies of interest and ideals. Moreover, the Conservative Party, having been in power for eighteen years before 1896, was without experience in the strategy and discipline of opposition. Its parliamentary representation had to begin the task of such organization, both in Parliament and in the constituencies, as would enable it to make headway against the powerful forces and the highly effective organization of the Government. In addition, there was, naturally, lack of confidence in the early success of a new and untried leader—and this made it difficult to provide the necessary financial means for organization and for the preparation and distribution of party literature. However, although I did not anticipate remaining in the leadership for more than a year, I addressed myself to this task with all the energy at my command, and at the end of the first session I felt that no serious mistake had been made.

4: Leader of the Opposition
1901 and *1902*

... Almost immediately after the accession of King Edward, a controversy developed over the Sovereign's declaration against transubstantiation which, under the Act of Settlement (1689), he was obliged to make at the first meeting of his Parliament, and which pronounced certain beliefs of Roman Catholics to be superstitious and idolatrous. On all sides it was recognized that the present Sovereign must make the declaration, but a wide movement arose for its future abolition. On March 1, 1901, an address to His Majesty was moved setting forth the provisions of the Act of Settlement, asserting that the declaration was offensive to the convictions of Roman Catholics and expressing the opinion of the House that the Act of Settlement should be amended by abolishing the declaration.

I supported the view of Sir Wilfrid Laurier that the question was above all political considerations, and, announcing my intention to vote for the motion, I said that the Protestant Succession was abundantly guaranteed by the Bill of Rights and the Coronation Oath; I pointed out that Protestants, if they were in a minority, would regard as highly offensive and improper a declaration which outraged their religious belief; and in opposing the view that the Parliament of Canada was not justified in pronouncing opinion, I said, "The compact which the King makes with his people when he ascends the Throne is a compact which he makes with us as well as with the people of the Mother Country."

I then pointed out that the resolution went altogether too far by declaring that "in the opinion of the House the Act of Settlement should be amended by abolishing the said declaration," and I proposed instead that the resolution should take the following form:

That, in the opinion of this House, from this declaration should be eliminated anything offensive to the religious belief of any subject of His Majesty.

Sir Louis Davies took warm interest in this point and I saw him in consultation with Sir Wilfrid Laurier. Having retired to my room for a short time during the debate, I had a visit from Sir Wilfrid who stated that he had discussed my proposal with some of his friends and that he concurred in my suggestion.

He submitted to me his proposed amendment of the resolution and I agreed to the form in which it was expressed; later in the debate he suggested this change which was accepted. The motion thus amended was passed by a large majority. I voted for the resolution as thus amended and was supported by the great majority of my party.

Mr. Monk, whom I regarded as an eminent constitutional authority, speaking after me in the debate made the following comment:

> The remarks made by my hon. friend the Leader of the Oposition were of such a nature that, to me, whom this question interests in a particular manner, it seems impossible either to take one word from the remarks he has made or add anything to them. . . .

During the session I criticized the fiscal policy of the administration and moved a resolution affirming that Canada required a pronounced policy of adequate protection, that the adoption of mutual trade preferences within the Empire would be of great benefit to the mother country and to the colonies and that equivalent or adequate duties should be imposed by Canada upon the products and manufactures of countries outside the Empire in all cases where such countries failed to admit Canadian products or manufactures upon fair terms. A long debate ensued and in the result my motion was defeated by the usual party majority.

The session which had begun on February 6, 1901, came to an end on May 23. Upon the whole I came through it as well as I had anticipated. It seemed to me that I was gradually gaining the confidence of my supporters both in the House and in the country, but I realized that there was a long and arduous fight before our party which, after two successive defeats, was under the chill of discouragement. Its future prospects did not seem bright in view of the wave of prosperity which had spread throughout the world and which was bringing good times to Canada.

Immediately after the session I spoke in Toronto before a great gathering. In my address I reviewed the work of the session, and dealt especially with the history of the origin and progress of British preference. The extraordinary situation that had arisen by reasons of the denunciation of German and Belgian treaties has already been explained. This offered good material for an attack upon the Government as Mr. Fielding had practically justified Germany's discrimination against

Canada. I declared that Canada should be free to give preference within the Empire without incurring hostile legislation and without the concurrence of Great Britain in such hostile action. After emphasizing the family quarrels within the administration, I alluded to Sir Wilfrid's reference to Sir Charles Tupper whom he likened to Moses, saying, "He did not carry his party to the Promised Land but he left that task to be performed some time, some day, by some Joshua still unknown and perhaps still unborn." I reminded my hearers that Joshua was the immediate successor to Moses, that when Joshua took command the wanderings of the chosen people were about concluded and that under him they entered the Promised Land, occupied and enjoyed it, and drove out the heathen.

At a banquet tendered to me the Liberal-Conservatives of Halifax on July 1, I arraigned the Government both in respect of its policies and its performances; affirmed our belief in mutual preferential trade within the Empire, challenged the attitude of the Government on German discrimination against Canada; and, dealing with immigration, declared that our attention should be given to quality rather than quantity.

After various other activities in Nova Scotia, I spoke with Mr. Whitney[1] at Toronto in the provincial campaign affirming my keen interest in the provincial elections and defending my activities in that arena by the undisguised alliance between the Provincial and the Federal Governments. . . .

On January 21, 1902, I addressed the Canadian Club at Toronto on Constitutional Development. This was followed later by an address before the Collegiate Institute of Lindsay, Ontario, in which I emphasized the influence of Canada on Imperial policy, especially in the development of Responsible Government. In securing the right of self-government in domestic affairs, Canada had taken the lead not only in its initiation but in its continued development. The most eminent British statesmen had believed that self-government for the colonies meant separation from the mother country. If it had not been granted, the Empire would have been dismembered. Canadians had claimed self-government as a gift and as a right. It had strengthened the ties that bind the dominions to the mother country and I observed that, in the future, the ties that bind self-governing nations of the Empire would probably become closer; but that any change would be slow and gradual as the circumstances required. . . .

Parliament opened on February 13, and in the debate on

[1] Then leader of the Conservative party in Ontario. [Ed.]

the address (February 14) I regretted various omissions there-from, notably with regard to Germany's prohibitory tariff, the Alaskan Boundary, the South African War, and the much-heralded fast Atlantic service. I affirmed that increase in exports was not of itself an evidence of prosperity; and, directing attention to conflicting policies enunciated by Mr. Sifton in the West and by Mr. Tarte in the East, I quoted the words of Mr. Gladstone:

> It is one of our first duties to decline to acquit any member of the Cabinet of responsibility for the announced and declared policy of another. . . .

Mr. Fielding's budget speech was delivered on March 17; and he was able to set forth a statement which, from his standpoint, was eminently satisfactory to the Government if not to the country. He presented elaborate comparative state-ments. Towards the conclusion of his speech he emphasized, although he did not elaborate, the considerations which made it undesirable to proced with any revision of the tariff at that juncture.

I took upon myself the duty of replying as there was considerable competition, if not jealousy, on our side of the House as to that privilege.

I concluded my speech by moving the following resolution:

> This House, regarding the operation of the present tariff as unsatisfactory is of opinion that this country requires a declared policy of such adequate protection to its labour, agricultural products, manufactures, and industries, as will at all times secure the Canadian market for Canadians. And, while always firmly maintaining the necessity of such protection to Canadian interests, this House affirms its belief in a policy of reciprocal trade preferences within the empire. . . .

On April 15, Mr. W. F. McLean, without notice to the Government or to the House brought up the subject of prefer-ential trade within the Empire and made a lively attack upon the Administration. The British Government had under con-sideration a proposal to impose a duty on wheat and there was a strong feeling in Canada that Canadian wheat should be exempted in full or in part from this duty.

After the Prime Minister and Mr. Fielding had spoken, I replied to Sir Wilfrid Laurier's defence of his action in declining to discuss at the Imperial Conference the defence of the Empire. Upholding the complete control by Canada of her action in that regard, I pointed out that if a Canadian subject was ill-treated in any part of the world under circumstances calling for intervention, that Canadian would be supported by every British gun and every British ship to the full extent of the Empire's resources. Thus, it seemed ungracious to refuse even a discussion of defence. . . .

As to preferential trade, I emphasized the Prime Minister's declaration that Canada wanted no preference in the mother country's markets. This declaration had secured for him the medal of the Cobden Club; and I suggested that it would be greatly to the advantage of Canada if the Prime Minister would return the Cobden Club medal and obtain an exemption from the proposed taxation on wheat. I challenged the Government to declare that they regarded the exemption of Canadian wheat from this duty as of no importance.

On May 12, I read the correspondence and again criticized the action of the Government in declining to discuss Empire defence:

> As I have pointed out before in this House and in other places, I am ready to uphold as strongly as any one, the necessity of control by Canada of the expenditure of our public moneys and of the question of imperial defence relating to Canada. But, holding this view, I see no reason why we should not be open to discuss that question with the Imperial authorities.

The proceedings of the Colonial Conference of 1902 are on record and it is not necessary to make specific allusion thereto. Canada and Australia took the ground that they must confine themselves to local defence but "in co-operation with the Imperial authorities and under the advice of experienced Imperial officers so far as this is consistent with the principle of local self-government which has proved so great a factor in the promotion of Imperial unity."

On August 14, I spoke at the annual banquet of the Canadian Manufacturers' Association at Halifax. I urged fair play for every legitimate industry under the tariff and an honest preference for the mother country, but I affirmed my belief that "a factory in Canada was worth as much to the Empire as a factory in Yorkshire."

During the session of 1902 I had arrived at the conclusion that a political tour through the Western Provinces was not only desirable but essential; and preparations for this tour were eventually consummated. The arrangement of the tour was convincing evidence of my political inexperience although it was approved by the leading members of the Conservative Party and by important Conservatives in various parts of the country. My proposal was to select representative men from each of the Eastern Provinces. I particularly desired the presence of Mr. Monk,[2] who, however, declined to be a member of the Party, making some convenient excuse as to the necessity of his presence in Quebec. His real reason was that he did not desire to be associated on such a tour with important members of the Orange party who were also influential members of the House of Commons. . . .

We were not always a happy "family party" throughout the tour which lasted from September 3 until October 20. Jealousies developed, especially among those from Ontario. It was alleged that telegrams were sent forward suggesting requests for particular speakers at certain points. There were altogether too many in the party; and the tension became so severe that one member absented himself and only returned because no notice was taken of his absence. . . .

~ In the hope that his presence would act as a "deterrent to serious dissension and tempestuous controversy" at the British Columbia leadership convention, Borden was asked to stay for the event. There was no open rupture and he enjoyed the unexpected sojourn in Revelstoke. On the Prairies he met Arthur Meighen and R. B. Bennett for the first time. ~

Our tour practically terminated with a great meeting and banquet at Winnipeg on October 13, at which Sir Charles Tupper, Roblin, Foster, and Monk spoke. However, we stopped at Fort William where I delivered an address.

Throughout the western tour, I emphasized the need of a policy of adequate protection for Canadian industries and did not in the least depart from any of the policies that had been announced in Eastern Canada. The subjects to which I gave greatest prominence in the Prairie Provinces were provincial autonomy and control of public domain. I urged that the people of the North West Territories should have the same right of self-government in respect of their domestic affairs as that which was enjoyed by the people of the older provinces. Further, as the Eastern Provinces had full control of their natural resources, the same right should be accorded to the people of Manitoba and the North West Territories. Three years

[2] Mr. F. D. Monk – then leader of the Conservatives in Quebec. [Ed.]

elapsed before autonomy was granted by the creation of the new provinces of Saskatchewan and Alberta; and more than twenty years elapsed before the troublesome question of natural resources was finally settled.

Everywhere throughout the tour we had good audiences of thoughtful, earnest people—on many occasions there was marked enthusiasm. The advent of a new party leader naturally attracted a crowd. At some of the meetings there were questions and interruptions which were always very welcome to me. One of my colleagues insisted that it would pay the Liberal-Conservative Party to hire men for the purpose of interrupting me, as in the result I was always more vigorous and more aggressive.

Immediately following the western tour, I attended a luncheon in my honour by the Junior Conservative Club of Montreal. Proceeding thence to Halifax, I was greeted by an immense popular demonstration and accompanied by a torchlight procession to my home. A similar demonstration greeted me on my return to Ottawa about October 30. . . .

5: *1903*

At the beginning of this year, 1903, I had occupied the leadership of the Liberal-Conservative Party in federal affairs for nearly two years. During that period I had apparently strengthened my position. . . . I seemed to have gained the confidence of my supporters in important aspects, although I am convinced that some of them regarded me as not sufficiently aggressive. Their confidence in my good judgment was frequently illustrated in caucus when questions arose upon which opinion was divided. The frequent procedure in such cases was to confide to me the final determination of the question; and in most cases my conclusions was loyally supported. . . .

An immense banquet was given in honour of Mr. Monk on January 29, 1903, in Montreal. Nearly twelve hundred guests assembled and practically every county in the province was represented. Mr. Monk was presented with an oil painting of himself and made the speech of the evening. Mr. Whitney and Mr. Roblin also addressed the gathering. For the first time I made a public address in French. . . .

It was a most enthusiastic gathering. In the early stages of the banquet exuberent supporters from one county would pledge the health of those from another county standing one foot on the chair and one on the table and concluding the toast with a magnificent burst of song. During my little address in French they loudly responded from all parts of the hall, "*Pas encore*," in thunderous tones and in the finale joined me in a tremendous shout of "*Pas de tout*.". . .

Throughout 1903, there was no respite from my political activities. I had donned my battle-harness early in January, and throughout the year I led the Conservative forces in the battle-arena. I spoke at several important gatherings other than those I have already mentioned. With the opening of the session my task became extremely exacting and exhausting.

The session of 1903 was the longest in the history of Canada.* It began on March 12, and ended on October 24; the later snows of one winter descended upon us after the session commenced and the early snows of the following winter greeted us before we had concluded our labours. Apart from the explanations and debate with regard to Mr. Tarte's resigna-

* The 1903 session had 155 sitting days. Three subsequent sessions were longer: 1961 (174 days), 1964-5 (248 days), and 1966-7 (250 days).

tion and the usual lengthy discussions on fiscal questions, the chief interest of the session was centred in the Government's proposals for a national transcontinental railway and in the consequent resignation of Mr. Blair who made a destructive attack thereon.

In speaking on the Address I warmly congratulated Sir Wilfrid Laurier upon the improvement in his health and assured him that however sharp our political differences might be no one would rejoice more heartily than my friends and myself at the good news of his return to health and strength.

At the commencement of his reply, Sir Wilfrid made this graceful allusion to my words:

I deem it my duty as it is my pleasure to at once thank my hon. friend for the very kind reference which he has made to myself. I also thank his friends behind him for the manner in which they have received these observations of his. I am glad to believe that this incident is a further evidence that the amenities of British parliamentary life are of so kindly a nature; and that in the hands of my hon. friend the leader of the opposition they are indeed in safe-keeping. I trust it may always be, that we can recognize honourable differences of opinion in this country, and that though we may be divided upon many questions, yet we can be united upon one, and that is mutual respect for each other.

I recall this incident because I venture to believe that as leaders of the two political parties, Sir Wilfrid and I had a not inconsiderable influence in lessening the virulence and increasing the amenities of political strife.[1]

At the very commencement of the session I invited Sir Wilfrid to explain ministerial changes. The session opened on March 12, and on March 18 Sir Wilfrid made his statement. Pointing out the necessity for solidarity between members of the same administration, he declared that if Mr. Tarte believed in the necessity of increasing the customs duties, his proper

---

[1] The fiercest political protagonists usually entertained a sincere respect and even regard for each other. On one occasion during the early years of my leadership, Sir Charles Tupper was invited by the speaker at my request to take a seat upon the floor of the House; he remained until six o'clock. No two men in public life had denounced each other more vehemently and bitterly than Sir Charles Tupper and Sir Richard Cartwright. I was a little surprised and greatly moved to observe Sir Richard who was extremely lame hobble from his seat around the Speaker's chair to greet and welcome Sir Charles before he left the precincts of the Chamber.

course, before addressing his views to the public, would have been to place them before his colleagues with the object of obtaining that unanimous action of the Cabinet which is the very foundation of responsible government. In his speech, as well as in the correspondence, emphasis was laid upon Mr. Tarte's alleged violation of this principle by his strong advocacy of increased protection in many speeches during Sir Wilfrid's absence.

Mr. Tarte, in his reply, emphatically declared that his utterances during Sir Wilfrid's absence were no stronger or fuller than those he had publicly made on several occasions in Sir Wilfrid's presence.

In the course of the considerable debate which took place, I pointed out that Mr. Sifton had made emphatic declaration that the tariff in certain respects would not be increased; and I inquired whether the Prime Minister proposed to ask for his resignation. Mr. Blair's declarations respecting another transcontinental railway and Mr. Mulock's publicly expressed views respecting tariff policy were also called to his attention with the suggestion that these gentlemen were in the very position which had brought about Mr. Tarte's retirement. I challenged Mr. Prefontaine to deny his public advocacy of Mr. Tarte's views. He did not accept the challenge. It appeared that the Prime Minister had unharnessed a "balky horse" only to place the harness on another equally balky.

The treaty for settlement of the Alaskan boundary was signed on January 24, 1903. On March 13, I contended that it ought not to have become operative until approved by the Canadian Parliament. Sir Wilfrid Laurier replied that the Government had been consulted as to its terms and had assented, not because they were perfect, but because, on the whole, they were fair. . . . Speaking in Montreal at a great political demonstration on November 10, I said:

> *I am as loyal a British subject as is to be found in Canada, but I stand first of all in matters of this kind for the rights of Canada which must be maintained. I say it was not a right or just thing for the Government to consent to that treaty without giving Parliament the right to discuss it and say whether or not its approval should be a necessary condition to the acceptance of the award. . . .*

~ Redistribution was carried out in this session. The government referred the bill with schedules in blank to a special committee. At the request of his Ontario colleagues Borden served on this committee. He found it throughly partisan with the government majority, unwilling to accept opposition suggestions either of a general or particular nature. In the House he described the use of the committee as no advance over earlier methods of redistribution and "really no more than a farce." ~

As I have said, there was no respite from my political activities during 1903. Besides the sessional and other duties outlined in the foregoing pages, I took part in many debates on important and sometimes difficult questions; and I bore the chief part of the long, drawn-out fight upon transportation and the national transcontinental railway. This question consumed most of the time of the House during the session. . . .

During the session I had broken down in health and had been obliged to leave my parliamentary duties for two or three weeks and recuperate at Caledonia Springs. There I rapidly regained my strength and ended the session in fairly good form although greatly fatigued by its protracted labours and anxieties, At its conclusion I began a tour of the Maritime Provinces. . . . My principal message to the people was a denunciation of the transcontinental railway project as ill-considered, extravagant, and unnecessary; I urged the need of adequate protection, indicated by large importations from the United States of articles that ought to be produced from our own natural resources by the labour of our own people and within our own country. Failure to protect the iron and steel industry had resulted in domination by the United States' Steel Trust which practically controlled the price of steel in Canada.

It was a trying and difficult year during the greater part of which I had been absent from my home. It had begun to dawn on me that residence at one end of the Dominion was incompatible with the efficient discharge of my duties as leader. However, we had commodious and comfortable accommodation in Ottawa at the Sherbrooke on Metcalfe Street, where out hostess, Mrs. Turner, gave us the best of care and assiduous attention.[2]

---

[2] While we were sojourning there, Lord Grey, brother-in-law of the Governor-General, had arrived in Canada, and one day while we were lunching in our private dining-room he was suddenly announced. I invited him to remain for lunch which he did. There was a delightful visit and interesting conversation. At that time he was evidently looking over the situation with a view to accepting the Governor-Generalship. In the following year he succeeded Lord Minto.

6: The Transcontinental Railway

As I have said the chief feature of the session of 1903 was the Government's proposal for the construction of a second transcontinental railway.

The country was sharing the general prosperity of the world and the West was rapidly developing under the immigration policy initiated and put into force by Mr. Sifton, Minister of the Interior. Mr. Fielding had announced a surplus of more than seven millions. Fortune seemed to smile upon Canada; and the eloquence of Sir Wilfrid Laurier in pointing out the supposed danger involved in failure to undertake forthwith the construction of another transcontinental railway stirred the imagination of the country. But the country was still more stirred by the prospect of huge expenditures about to be made by the Government and by the Grand Trunk and its subsidiary for the accomplishment of the enterprise.

Mr. Blair, in 1902, while Minister of Railways, had urged the extension of the Government railway westward to a port on Georgian Bay, and for that purpose, had advocated the purchase of the Canada Atlantic Railway. The advantage of such an extension, he said, could hardly be overestimated, and he regarded it as a certain means of putting the Intercolonial Railway on an interest-paying basis.

The Speech from the Throne at the opening of the session (March 12) set forth "the need for increased transportation facilities for the forwarding of our grain and other products to the markets of the world through Canadian channels," and announced that the whole question of transportation and terminal facilities would be referred to "a commission of experienced men to report on the subject."

On May 19, the Government by Order-in-Council declared that no satisfactory conclusion could be reached upon the question until after a thorough and comprehensive inquiry which should determine, *inter alia*, the need of more economical and satisfactory channels by land or water. This Order-in-Council further declared that one of the forces operating against the attainment of all-Canadian transport was the diversion of Canadian products through eastern outlets to Boston, Portland, and other United States' ports.

The Commission authorized by the above mentioned Order-in-Council was constituted in the first place by the appointment of Sir William Van Horne, Mr. John Bertram, and Mr. Harry Kennedy as Commissioners.

The Canadian Pacific Railway with its numerous branches in the East and in the West, its splendid organization, and its highly efficient management had acquired a commanding position and a world-wide reputation. In Ontario its branch lines did not occupy so advantageous a territory as the Grand Trunk Railway. In the Western Provinces the Canadian Northern had entered excellent territory and was strongly competing with the Canadian Pacific for traffic within certain districts. Both the Grand Trunk and the Canadian Northern Railways were under a rather severe handicap, the one having no connections in the East, the other equally destitute in the West.

Not only in the interest of the country but especially in the interest of these two companies it was obvious that they should be amalgamated, either by the purchase of the Canadian Northern or by such a close working agreement as would in effect amount to an amalgamation.

Charles M. Hays, a man of great ability and strong personality, had been brought from the United States as president and general manager of the Grand Trunk Railway Company. He realized immediately the urgent need of improving the physical condition of his railway and devoted his energies thereto with excellent results. Naturally he realized the disadvantage in the situation which made his road a feeder for the Canadian Pacific and the Canadian Northern in Western Canada, while the Canadian Pacific, having excellent eastern connections, provided only a minimum of traffic for the Grand Trunk.

On the other hand, Sir William Mackenzie could easily imagine the unfortunate results to the Canadian Northern Railway if it should be confronted in the West not only with existing competition from the Canadian Pacific but with possibly stronger competition from the Grand Trunk extension into the Prairie Provinces.

There were negotiations looking to amalgamation or purchase or a working arrangement. It is possible that Mr. Hays underrated the ability and resourcefulness of his rival and regarded amalgamation as out of the question. Probably he was willing to purchase but thought the price set upon the Canadian Northern was too high. At double the price the Grand Trunk would have been fortunate to escape its disastrous venture. The working arrangement seems to have been regarded as impracticable or unsatisfactory.

Doubtless Mr. Hays was inspired by an ambition to place the Grand Trunk in a dominating position and this could not be accomplished to the extent which he desired except by embarking upon the unfortunate project of extending the Grand Trunk into the Western Provinces and of creating another transcontinental railway.

The political advantages of vast expenditure of public money for this purpose were apparent to Sir Wilfrid Laurier with whose Government the Canadian Pacific had not been entirely sympathetic. That railway, strongly opposed by the Liberals, had proved to be an enduring monument to the foresight and enterprise of a Conservative administration. In these later days of development and prosperity it was anticipated that another great transcontinental railway, extending on Canadian territory from Atlantic to Pacific, would prove to be an even more conspicuous monument to a Liberal administration. Thus, the enterprise developed as follows.

On March 31, a petition for the incorporation of the Grand Trunk Pacific Railway was presented and the Bill founded thereon was introduced. Originally it provided for the construction of a railway from Port Simpson on the Pacific, eastward to North Bay, where it would connect with the Grand Trunk System.

In the committee to which the Bill was referred, members from the Province of Quebec insisted that the enterprise should include the extension of the proposed railway from North Bay to Quebec City. The Maritime members were not slow to follow this lead and with equal insistence they urged a further extension to Moncton. Faced by this powerful combination, the Grand Trunk Railway Company was forced to yield, but only did so after a definite understanding between Sir Wilfrid Laurier and Mr. Hays, through private negotiations carried on behind the back of the Minister of Railways (Mr. Blair).

As a result of these negotiations the Government introduced a Bill which provided "for the construction of a national transcontinental railway to be operated as a common railway highway across the Dominion of Canada from ocean to ocean and wholly within Canadian territory." The proposed railway was to comprise an Eastern Division between Moncton and Winnipeg and a Western Division between Winnipeg and the Pacific Ocean. The Western Division was further divided into a Prairie Section and a Mountain Section. By agreement be-

THE TRANSCONTINENTAL RAILWAY – 45

tween the Grand Trunk and the Government, the company was
to construct, maintain, and operate the Western Division and to
lease, maintain, and operate the Eastern Division which was
to be constructed by the Government under the charge and
control of three commissioners. Liberal aid was provided for
the company by guarantee of bonds and by payment of interest
for seven years upon the cost of constructing the Mountain
Section. This agreement was eventually approved and ratified
by the Grand Trunk shareholders. Congratulations were
showered upon the directors and especially upon Mr. Hays;
and so the Grand Trunk embarked upon an enterprise which
eventually accomplished its bankruptcy.

Sir William Mackenzie called into play his full energy and
resourcefulness to prevent an invasion of western territory that
might prove disastrous to the Canadian Northern. But Mr.
Hays' project appealed very strongly to Sir Wilfrid. Mackenzie
told me that he had the Government's promise to hear him
further before finally entering into the Grand Trunk agreement.
This promise was either forgotten or disregarded.

On July 10, 1903, Mr. Blair resigned his position in the
Cabinet, because, as he said in Parliament, he was "not in
favour of impetuously rushing into the construction of a transcontinental line from Quebec through an unknown country to
Winnipeg and the West until we have the fullest information
about it. . . . This project is one of very great magnitude and
should be dealt with only after the maturest deliberation."

Although Parliament met on March 12, the proposals of the
Government were not presented until July 30. In the meantime
on July 16, Sir Wilfrid had given to Parliament his explanation
concerning Mr. Blair's resignation. Mr. Blair gave fuller
explanations and submitted to the House his correspondence
with Sir Wilfrid.

As the Government had given its pledge to be guided by the
report of a commission of experts as to the need for increased
transportation facilities, I inquired whether the commission
had been appointed and had reported, when the report would
be presented to Parliament, and whether the Government,
without that report and in disregard of their pledge, intended
to proceed with proposals involving enormous expenditure and
relating to a national question of supreme importance and vast
complexity.

In introducing the Bill for the construction of the national
transcontinental railway on July 30, Sir Wilfrid, departing
from ordinary practice, set forth in a long speech and in glowing

colours the supposed benefits to accrue from the Government's proposal and strongly emphasized the extreme danger of delay. He dwelt on the growing importance of the West; he dilated upon past threats of the United States to withdraw the bonding privilege; and he insisted upon the need of a railway to connect Atlantic and Pacific, to lie wholly within Canadian territory and to have a port on each ocean. In this respect he seemed to regard Moncton as an ocean port. He concluded as follows:

> *To those who urge upon us the policy of tomorrow and tomorrow and tomorrow; to those who tell us, "Wait, wait, wait,' to those who advise us to pause, to consider, to reflect, to calculate, and to enquire, our answer is: "No, this is not the time for deliberation, this is a time for action. The flood of tide is upon us that leads on to fortune; if we let it pass it may never recur again."*

Sir Wilfrid did not extend the courtesy of giving me in advance a copy of the Bill which he handed across the floor of the House at the conclusion of his speech. Determined that his advocacy of the proposal should not go forth unanswered and resenting rather strongly what I regarded as unusual discourtesy, I spoke at considerable length in reply.

Recalling the Liberal opposition to the first transcontinental railway "which had been the means of binding together the people of Canada and making it the nation it is today," I adverted to the Prime Minister's statement, "We cannot wait." The transportation question had been before them for seven years. After long consideration they had deliberately declared and announced that no such conclusion could be reached without a thorough and comprehensive inquiry. In pursuance of this deliberate policy they had appointed a commission to make exhaustive inquiry into the whole question. Five months had passed and no report had been made. Although heralded as absolutely essential and even vital, the commission and its inquiry and report were absolutely to be disregarded. The attitude of the Prime Minister with regard to the United States was plaintive and indeed humiliating; Canada stood on her own strength and did not feel herself at the mercy of that country. Criticizing the agreement as tending in still greater measure to divert traffic from Canadian to United States' ports, I pointed out the vast interests of the Grand Trunk Railway Company in Portland. I challenged any minister to state the cost of the Eastern Section within ten millions. None of them accepted the challenge.

Mr. Haggart vigorously attacked the proposal to construct an additional line from Quebec to Moncton and stressed the fact that the enormous expenditure involved would shorten the route by no more than fifty miles. He also criticized the proposed route in Western Canada, pointing out that it was not designed to open up new territory but merely to compete with the Canadian Pacific and the Canadian Northern Railways in a country already well served with railways.

In Mr. Blair's attack on August 11, he affirmed that there was no need for haste and many reasons for care and caution. The Government was proposing not a second but a third transcontinental railway. The chief reason for the proposal was the urgency of the Grand Trunk Company. He (Mr. Blair) advocated the extension of the Intercolonial to the Georgian Bay by acquiring the Canada Atlantic Railway. The proposal of the Government as to the use of the line by other railways was an absolutely unworkable and senseless suggestion. The Prairie Section above all others should be constructed by the Government, and he gave an alarming estimate of the cost.

On August 18, I presented an exhaustive examination of the whole question and offered an alternative proposition. I urged the extension of the Intercolonial Railway to a Georgian Bay port by the acquisition of the Canada Atlantic Railway, the acquisition of the Canadian Pacific from North Bay around the shore of Lake Superior to Fort William,[1] and its operation by an independent commission with equal running powers over it to the Canadian Pacific, Grand Trunk, Intercolonial, and Canadian Northern railways. Assistance should be given to the Grand Trunk for a line north of the Canadian Northern and as far west as Edmonton. There was no immediate need to extend this line to the Pacific. When such need arose one line would serve the Grand Trunk and the Canadian Northern. As for the line from Quebec to Moncton, if built at all, it should be built and operated as part of the Intercolonial Railway. As for the line from Quebec to Winnipeg, the country should first be explored so as to estimate the possibilities for settlement and colonization after which such railways as conditions justified should be gradually constructed as a colonization road.

---

[1] In the meantime I had sought and obtained an interview with Sir Thomas Shaughnessy, President of the Canadian Pacific Railway, and had ascertained from him that the Canadian Pacific was willing that the Government should acquire that portion of this line for the purpose which I indicated in my speech.

I strongly advocated the development of our national waterways. "Thoroughly equip our Georgian Bay ports, our national waterways, our St. Lawrence route, and our ports on the Atlantic coast. Give them the terminal facilities which shall enable them to compete with the American ports. If necessary to effectively compete with those ports, give them free terminals . . . exploit the harbour at Montreal and make it a national port, a free port in the true sense of the term. Do the same with regard to Quebec, St. John, and Halifax."

After an extremely prolonged discussion, the Bill came up for third reading on September 29. I again reviewed the situation pointing out that the estimated cost of my alternative proposal was $47,465,000 as against $106,389,725. After reviewing the Government's objections to this scheme, I moved a resolution that the Government in accordance with the policy laid down by Order-in-Council of May 19, 1903, should avail itself of the best expert advice and assistance before seeking to commit the country to expenditure upon and national transcontinental scheme or project; that the management of Government railways and of all railways under the control or direction of the Government should be freed from political control, influence and interference. The resolution embodied certain charges against the Government in failing to lay before the House sufficient information to justify Parliament in committing the country to the agreement as a whole.

Looking back at the history of the great battle which was waged for and against the Transcontinental Bill, in Parliament and out of Parliament, one is impressed with the following considerations.

Canada, at that time, had a population of less than six millions and already had established one great transcontinental railway which was efficiently serving the territory in which it was located. The great Western Provinces were separated from the Eastern by four hundred miles of territory of such a character that it could not be expected to sustain any considerable population, although it might contain vast mineral wealth. A territory so unoccupied tended to exaggerate the divergence between the East and the West; and the cost of transporting goods and products across it greatly handicapped trade between the East and the West. The territory, through which it was proposed to build a national transcontinental railway upon high standard of construction and with a view to transportation (by a shorter line) of goods and products from East to West and *vice versa*, was almost wholly uninhabited; and any considerable population along the line of railway could not be expected for many years. The Grand Trunk, with its lines spread all over Ontario and over a considerable portion of Quebec but without western connections, was the complement of the Canadian Northern Railway which had valuable connections in the West and was stretching out toward the Rocky Mountains and the Pacific Coast. In the light of these conditions and in view of subsequent events, it seems clear that the national transcontinental railway from Quebec to Winnipeg should have been commenced as a colonization road and should have been gradually extended as settlement demanded. An amalgamation should have been effected between the Grand Trunk Railway in the East and the Canadian Northern Railway in the West; and eventually these lines, as the country developed, would have been extended to the Pacific Coast. That section of the Canadian Pacific Railway which stretched across the uninhabited area between the settled portions of Manitoba and the settled portions of Ontario should have been acquired by the Government and operated by an independent commission, to serve as a connection between all eastern and western railway lines. The Intercolonial should have been extended to the shores of Georgian Bay by the acquisition of the Canada Atlantic and should also have been operated under an independent commission. If this course had been adopted neither the Canadian Northern nor the Grand Trunk Pacific Railways would have been involved in the difficulties which subsequently arose; and when war broke out they would have been in a position to support the financial structure of Canada rather than to apply continually for further guarantees and subsidies. The western farmers who were supposed to favour Government ownership but who fought strongly for the National Transcontinental would do well to remember that increased cost of transportation on the one hand or burdensome taxation on the other is in no small measure due to the railway project of 1903.

This project, however, appealed to the imagination of the country and awakened a response which drowned the voice of prudence and caution. A prominent Conservative in Montreal, with whom I discussed the subject, and who strongly advocated it, was wholly unmoved by considerations of useless expenditure and of future burdens. He merely said, "This proposal will give us good times for at least ten years and after that I do not care." In Halifax, a Conservative of high character and excellent business capacity told me that he was strongly in favour of the project because it involved the building of a new railway line from Quebec to Moncton which would bring about expenditure of vast sums of money in the Maritime Provinces. But eventually Nova Scotia, as well as the Western Provinces, suffered from the handicap of high railway rates due in no small measure to the very project which brought temporary prosperity through enormous expenditure of money furnished by the people themselves.

On March 20, 1903, Mr. Blair had introduced a measure to amend and consolidate the law respecting railways. One of its principal features was the establishment of a railway commission invested with powers which are now familiar and which have greatly inured to the advantage of the country. The authority previously vested in the Railway Committee of the Privy Council was transferred to this commission and was greatly enlarged. We endeavoured to assist the Minister in every way. There was very little discussion on the first and second reading but there was a long debate in committee.

Mr. Blair, the details of whose resignation as Minister of Railways have already been related, was appointed Chairman of the newly constituted Railway Commission, a position which he occupied for somewhat less than a year.

... From January 11 to 16, I made a tour of the Eastern Townships. ... At two ... meetings Mr. Tarte spoke from the same platform, still emphasizing the vital need of protection for home industries to preserve them from destructive competition and to provide labour for workmen who, otherwise, would emigrate to the United States.

It had been apprehended that an election would be held before another session but the Government's announcement of proposed modifications in the Grand Trunk Pacific contract made it evident that this rumour was groundless. ...

Parliament did not open until March 10.

~ Borden spoke strongly on the railway question. He noted that none of Mr. Blair's denunciations in the previous session had been retracted. He suggested that Blair had been given the Railway Commission chairmanship in order to prevent the loss of seats in New Brunswick had the former Minister fought the Government.

Government members were annoyed at Borden's use of a stenographic report of the Grand Trunk shareholders meeting and a supposedly confidential memorandum prepared by Blair while he was Minister. Borden had received the memorandum from a government employee who retrieved it from a heap of waste paper. He refused to divulge the name of the retriever, and he and his colleagues in turn castigated the government for failing to place before Parliament such an important and timely document.

The Conservatives again advocated the railway policy which they had set forth in the preceding session and were able to draw upon Blair's memorandum to support their arguments. ~

On June 4, Lord Dundonald, G.O.C. the Canadian Militia, made a remarkable speech in Montreal at a banquet of the officers of the military district. He criticized strongly the interference of the Honourable Sydney Fisher with Militia affairs and administration. The subject created a great sensation and was discussed more than once in Parliament.

Mr. Fisher explained and defended his case and was supported in Parliament by Sir Frederick Borden, Minister of Militia, after which I attacked Mr. Fisher for his interference and lauded Lord Dundonald's work in Canada.

Sir Wilfrid followed in a speech in which by a singular *lapsus linguae* he referred to Lord Dundonald as a "foreigner," quickly adding amidst cries of dissent that he meant "stranger," to the people of the Eastern Townships.

There was much criticism both in the House and in the Press of this slip; and on June 24, Sir Wilfrid in speaking on the subject of Lord Dundonald's dismissal took the opportunity of entering into a rather elaborate explanation in which he quoted extensively from dictionaries and writings as to the use of the word "stranger." At the moment of his slip he had explained that he meant to use that word and not the word, "foreigner." Four days later in addressing the House on the same subject, I called Sir Wilfrid's attention to the fact that he had not always been ready to accept my explanation of language used in debate: "I am ready on all occasions to accept the right hon. gentleman's statement as to the word he intended to use and the manner in which he intended to use it. This is a courtesy which we owe to each other. . . . But my right hon. friend is not always so ready to extend a courtesy of that kind. When I stood up in my place during this session and stated that a certain word, reported by Hansard as having been used by me, had not been used by me and gave my word to the House as the fact, did I find my right hon. friend accepting that statement?

"No, I did not. I found my right hon. friend speaking in— well, in language that might be regarded as meaning that he was rather doubtful . . . so that I was compelled to write a letter to the chief of the Hansard staff, and to produce evidence from the original notes of the shorthand writer in support of that word of mine which I thought might have been accepted by my right hon. friend. Let not my right hon. friend be too sensitive unless he is prepared to be uniformly courteous himself. . . . The right hon. gentleman referred only the other day to a great many illustrations of the use of the words 'stranger' and 'foreigner,' and indeed in speaking on the subject he said that he regarded Lord Dundonald as a stranger only to the Eastern Townships. . . . I do not for one moment question my right hon. friend's assurance as to the sense in which he intended these words. . . . Let me however quote to him, from a well of pure and undefiled English, a few words which may be of service in interpreting what the ordinary sense of such words is:

Now therefore ye are no more strangers and foreigners, but fellow citizens with the saints.— Ephesians II, *19.*

On June 14, Dundonald was dismissed by Order-in-Council on the ground that he had failed to appreciate his position as a public official, had committed grave errors which, if ignored, would have been fatal to discipline and the due subordination of the Militia Force to constituted authority.

On June 23, the dismissal was discussed in Parliament. I moved a resolution regarding the unwarrantable interference of Mr. Fisher in appointments to the Militia by reason of political considerations.

There were many demonstrations in Dundonald's favour when he visited Toronto and afterwards when he took his departure from Ottawa. On the latter occasion, Dundonald more than once delivered the following exhortation: "Men of Canada, keep both hands on the Union Jack.". . .

On June 16, I was invited to meet a "delegation of manu-facturers," in one of the committee rooms. On arrival at the appointed hour, I found about one hundred Conservative members of the House and of the Senate gathered there for the purpose of presenting to me two handsome cabinets of silver tableware in anticipation of my fiftieth birthday (June 26, 1904). A beautiful diamond and opal bracelet was presented to my wife. The presentations were made by Sir Mackenzie Bowell, and Mr. Monk, Senator de Boucherville, E. F. Clarke, and Senator Lougheed made appreciative speeches. The pre-sentations were a complete surprise to me and in expressing our heartfelt thanks I felt and displayed genuine emotion. . . .

During 1904 public attention was frequently called to alleged irregularities in the public service and occasionally to appointments of unqualified persons to public office. One particular instance of the latter offence caused some discussion in Parliament and much comment in the Press. Mr. J. B. Jackson, K.C., a lawyer of Ingersoll, Ontario, was appointed as Commercial Agent in Leeds, England. It had been proved that Mr. Jackson had been associated with certain proceedings in attempting to unseat the Conservative member for South Oxford. Sir Richard Cartwright assumed sole responsibility for the appointment. While admitting that Jackson's "zeal had outrun his discretion," Sir Richard declared that evidently he had done nothing contrary to the law or the Conservatives would have prosecuted him. In discussing this case on July 28, I moved a resolution "that in making appointments to public offices, and particularly to those of a representative nature, party services should not alone be considered but selections should be made with regard to capacity and personal character."

I concluded my speech as follows, using what has been termed "the strongest language recorded amongst his utterances upon the pages of Hansard":

> *I say to the right hon. gentleman the Minister of Trade and Commerce, that it had been better for him as a public man in this country if he had retired to the isolation of his own parish and been heard of no more, before he made the declaration which he has made in this House. I believe, Sir, that there never was in the public life of this country or any other country a more damnable doctrine more unblushingly avowed. . . . That this man, so stigmatized by Mr. Justice Street, should be promoted to the Public Service of Canada and that the Minister of Trade and Commerce speaking for the Government should not be ashamed to stand up and justify him, is an unheard of degradation in our public life. . . .*

Throughout the session each party had been engaged in the preparation of campaign literature. The Liberal repertory was abundant and covered very cleverly every incident that could be turned to the credit of the Administration.

There was an equally active Conservative organization which dealt fully with the national transcontinental railway project, the Dundonald incident, wasteful expenditure, preferential trade, increased taxation, fast Atlantic service failure, and many other subjects.[1]

Parliament was dissolved on September 29, but in the meantime I had opened the campaign at St. John, New Brunswick, declaring that elections might be expected in November. The leading issue was the Government's project for a national transcontinental railway. I also emphasized the essential importance of purity in elections, criticized the character of appointments to the public service, and dwelt upon the Dundonald case and the Government's broken pledges, the failure of their Imperial preference policy, and other issues. . . .

On election day, November 3, the Conservative Party went

---

[1] Adam Bell, M.P. for Pictou, told me that on one occasion he conducted Sir William Mulock along the corridor of the House leading to Room No. 6, the caucus room of the Conservatives. On each side of the corridor mail bags filled with Conservative literature, ready for mailing, were piled up to the ceiling. Sir William was filled with astonishment and indignation. We told Bell that he had not used good judgment in asking the Postmaster-General to survey the extent of the output, as in view of the result of the election we felt rather confident that a considerable portion of the supply never reached its destination.

down to serious defeat. The Government's victory was almost overwhelming. . . .

In Nova Scotia we suffered a débâcle; not a single Conservative was elected in the province. I and my colleague, J. C. O'Mullin, were defeated in Halifax by more than 600 majority.

Subsequently I was informed that there was a well-concerted plan carried out by the Liberal Ministers for Nova Scotia to crush the Conservative Party in my province, to defeat me and thus drive me from public life and force the Conservative Party to select another leader. Throughout Canada the campaign fund at the command of the Liberal Party was very large but special consideration was given to Nova Scotia in this respect. A prominent Liberal, who afterwards joined the Conservative ranks, informed one of my colleagues that in each county a very large campaign fund was available and there was direction that in case any county should find its requirements for a sure victory less than the sum placed at its disposal, the surplus should be forwarded to Halifax for the purpose of ensuring my defeat. A careful estimate led us to the conclusion that not less than one hundred thousand dollars had been expended in Halifax for that purpose.

There was much exaltation; and among the smaller spirits of the Liberal Party there arose the joyful cry that no more would be heard of R. L. Borden in public life. However, the fates decreed otherwise; and less than seven years afterwards the Ministers who had planned and consummated my defeat met a similar unfortunate experience.

The Conservative Press were very kind in their references and I had the strong support of the majority of journals supporting the Party.

Many offers of a sure seat were tendered to me;* but I left with my wife almost immediately for the South as I found myself greatly fatigued from the labours of the session and the long campaign.

I returned to Montreal on December 4, and twenty-five of the more prominent members of the House of Commons and other representatives of the party met me there and urged me to continue in the leadership. I was reluctant to do so but finally consented that the question be considered by caucus to be called on the opening of Parliament. This was agreed to.

* Including one from Sam Hughes.

8: *1905*

On January 7, 1905, I addressed the following communication to the Conservative members of the Senate and to the House of Commons:

Assembled in caucus four years ago, you bestowed upon me the highest mark of your confidence when you required me to undertake the arduous duty and grave responsibility of leading the Party in the House of Commons. To the best of my ability I have endeavoured ever since to justify that confidence. I gratefully acknowledge how much you have done to strengthen my hands; and I am deeply sensible that without your loyal and generous aid freely accorded on all occasions, my task would have been infinitely more onerous.

We still firmly believe that the policy which we advocated and the principles which we upheld in the recent contest were truly in the best interests of Canada; and although we may regret temporary defeat yet we do not for one moment regret the stand which we took upon the great questions of the day.

Under the conditions which have ensued, it is necessary that you shall choose another leader. My resignation has already been given informally. I now place it unreservedly in your hands with every assurance of my hearty co-operation in the ranks of the Party. Let me add that the happy remembrance of your loyal support and comradeship will always abide with me.

At a Conservative caucus, held early in January, there was a unanimous refusal to accept my resignation of the leadership and I was respectfully requested to retain it. I was desired to attend an adjourned meeting of the caucus at the earliest possible moment. Mr. Foster, Mr. Wilmot, Mr. Roche, Mr. DeBoucherville, and Senators Perley and Ferguson were appointed a committee to convey to me this message. A resolution was then passed that, pending my return to the House of Commons, the senior Privy Councillor would lead the Opposition.

The session opened on January 11. During my absence, Sir George Foster acted as leader. After I had consented to continue in the leadership, Edward Kidd, member for Carleton, Ontario, resigned his seat and his resignation was notified to

the Speaker who announced it to the House of Commons on
January 20.

Sir Wilfrid Laurier very courteously did everything that the
law would permit to expedite the holding of a by-election for
that county and I was nominated; and, there being no other
condidate, I was declared duly elected. . . .

An interesting incident was that of May 16, when Sir Elzear
Taschereau, Administrator, attending at the Senate to give
assent to certain Bills, refused to enter the Senate Chamber
for the purpose unless the Speaker's Chair was removed so
that he, the Administrator, could sit in the chair usually
occupied by the Governor-General. This was done, but not
without vigorous protest from Senators Landry and Miller who
afterwards cited precedent against such action.

It had become increasingly evident that I could not reside
in Halifax and effectively discharge my duties as Leader of
the Liberal-Conservative Party. Accordingly, I announced in
October, 1905, that I intended to live henceforth at Ottawa. . . .

In 1901, I had been rather astonished and somewhat
dismayed at the depth of feeling evoked by the proposal to
modify the Coronation Oath; but during 1905, I was to make
acquaintance with a passion arising from prejudice and antagonism in respect of religious belief which still more surprised me.
It had far-reaching effect during that year as it caused the
formal resignation of Mr. Sifton and the practical resignation
(afterwards recalled) of Mr. Fielding, and, if Senator David
is to be credited, the desire, or at least the willingness, of Sir
Wilfrid Laurier to retire from the leadership in favour of Mr.
Fielding.

Curiously enough, the controversy, although it related to
the establishment of separate schools in the West, aroused
far more bitterness in Ontario and Quebec than in Manitoba
and the Territories. There was, however, keen interest and
some excitement in the Maritime Provinces.

The awakening of so intense a feeling was for me a novel
experience. In Nova Scotia, Protestants and Roman Catholics
lived in entire harmony. Under the Law of that province no
provision was made for separate schools, but in the city of
Halifax and doubtless elsewhere a conventional arrangement
was established by which, without infringing the provisions of
the Law, Roman Catholic teachers had charge of the instruction
of Roman Catholic children. This convention had been so long
in existence that no one thought of questioning it. Moreover
several Roman Catholics in Halifax preferred to send their

children to the public schools rather than to the conventional separate schools.[1]

Although Sir Wilfrid Laurier seems to have been astonished at the storm created by his proposals for separate schools in the new provinces, yet he must have apprehended that they would create strong antagonism in certain quarters, and further, there was always the danger, which doubtless he foresaw, of failing to go as far as the more extreme elements of the Roman Catholic Church might desire. He may have been warned by his colleagues and supporters as to the double danger and it was probably for this reason that for at least three years after conditions were ripe for the creation of the new provinces the Government refrained from taking up the question.

While the situation was difficult for Sir Wilfrid Laurier, it involved still greater hazards for me. However, my tour through the West in 1902, had convinced me that the time had even then arrived for granting to the virile and enterprising population of the North West Territories the same rights of self-government as those enjoyed by the provinces. When the time came, I had no difficulty in making my decision; and, basing my attitude on constitutional grounds and on considerations of public policy, I strongly urged that the people of the new provinces like the people of Nova Scotia might safely be entrusted with the duty of making provision for the education of their children. I am still convinced that this would have been the wiser and safer course.

Sir Wilfrid Laurier introduced the Autonomy Bill on February 21, 1905. It had been arranged that I should receive a copy on the previous evening but through some unfortunate misapprehension I did not receive it until a few minutes before Sir Wilfrid spoke.

Apart from the financial arrangements, the two principal features of the Bill were the provisions for separate schools and the control and disposition of the public domain. As to the first, Sir Wilfrid placed chief reliance upon the fact that under the Act of 1875, separate schools had already been established in the North West Terrtories; as to the second, he contended that in order to encourage and control immigration it was desirable that the disposition and management of un-patented lands should remain with the Dominion.

In replying briefly to Sir Wilfrid, I expressed my opinion

---

[1] My colleague, Adam B. Crosby, told me he preferred to do this as he desired his children to grow up in intimate acquaintance with their Protestant companions and not to regard them with distrust.

that the question of separate schools had better be confided to the people, as in Nova Scotia and New Brunswick where less difficulty and controversy had arisen than in Ontario and Quebec. The new provinces should have the management and control of their public domain; although the boundaries of Quebec and Ontario had been greatly enlarged, it had not been thought desirable to restrict in any way provincial control of the added territories.

The second reading of the Bill did not take place until March 22.

Meantime in the Press and on the platform there had been extremely excited and controversial discussion of the educational features of the Bill.

On March 1, Sir Wilfrid Laurier announced that Mr. Sifton, finding himself unable to agree with the terms of the Bill, had tendered his resignation on February 27, and that it had been accepted on February 28. Mr. Sifton then rose to explain that, upon reading the Prime Minister's speech on the introduction of the Bill, he found some principles enunciated with which he was unable to agree. Then, having procured a copy of the Bill, he discovered in Clause 16 provisions which he could not endorse or support.

This clause provided that the provisions of Section 93 of the British North America Act, 1867,[2] should apply to the new

---

[2] In and for each Province the Legislature may exclusively make Laws in relation to Education, subject and according to the following Provisions:

1. Nothing in any such Law shall prejudicially affect any Right or Privilege with respect to Denominational Schools which any Class of persons have by Law in the Province at the Union:

2. All the Powers, Privileges, and Duties at the Union by Law conferred and imposed in Upper Canada on the Separate Schools and School Trustees of the Queen's Roman Catholic Subjects shall be and the same are hereby extended to the Dissentient Schools of the Queen's Protestant and Roman Catholic Subjects in Quebec:

3. Where in any Province a System of Separate or Dissentient Schools exists by Law at the Union or is thereafter established by the Legislature of the Province, an Appeal shall lie to the Governor-General-in-Council from any Act or Decision of any Provincial Authority affecting any Right or Privilege of the Protestant or Roman Catholic Minority of the Queen's Subjects in relation to Education:

4. In case any such Provincial Law as from Time to Time seems to be Governor-General-in-Council requisite for the due Execution of the Provisions of this Section is not made, or in case any Decision of the Governor-General-in-Council on any Appeal under this Section is not duly executed by the proper Provincial Authority in that Behalf, then and in every such Case, and as far only as the

provinces and further that the Legislature of each province should pass all necessary laws in respect of education and that it should therein always be provided "(a) that a majority of the ratepayers of any district or portion of the said province or of any less portion or sub-division thereof, by whatever name it is known may establish such schools therein as they think fit, and make the necessary assessments and collection of rates therefor, and (b) that the minority of the ratepayers therein whether Protestant or Roman Catholic, may establish separate schools therein, and make the necessary assessment and collection of rates therefor, and (c) that in such case the ratepayers establishing such Protestant or Roman Catholic separate schools shall be liable only to assessment of such rates as they impose upon themselves with respect thereto." It was further provided in the same Section that in the appropriation and distribution of public moneys in aid of education, there should be no discrimination between public schools and separate schools. . . .

In the interval between the first and second reading of the Bill, which was very prolonged owing to the resignation of Mr. Sifton and the threatened resignation of Mr. Fielding, both Sir Wilfrid and I were assailed from different angles in the most virulent manner. I have a distinct recollection that in some quarters I was termed a fanatic; and by extremists of the opposing type I was characterized as a coward.[3]

When the Bill came up for second reading on March 22, Sir Wilfrid Laurier, in a skilful speech, upheld his position by quotation of many authorities and endeavoured to square his present position with that which he had assumed in relation to the Manitoba school question. He alluded to my statement that the subject should be approached with calm and moderation and he declared that the Press which supported me had spared no effort to inflame the public mind upon an ever-delicate subject.

In my reply I attacked Sir Wilfrid for misleading the House as to the attitude of Sifton and Fielding; and so far as my own

Circumstances of each Case require, the Parliament of Canada may make remedial Laws for the due Execution of the Provisions of this Section and of any Decision of the Governor-General-in-Council under this Section."

[3] Even an eminent cleric of the Anglican Church was kind enough to refer to me in very sarcastic terms through his deplorable ignorance of parliamentary procedure. Between the first and second readings there was no opportunity for me to set forth my policy upon the proposed provisions of the Bill; and this ignorance led my ecclesiastical critic to indulge in sarcastic comment.

followers were concerned I said that each might act as his conscience and judgment would dictate. I urged that the control of lands should be confided to the new provinces and expressed the opinion that they might safely be entrusted with this control since they were as much interested in immigration as was the Dominion. Further, any danger might be obviated by a provision as to free homesteads and the price of lands for settlement.

Continuing, I pointed out that the Prime Minister had gained power as the result of passion and prejudice on the question of separate schools. As to the educational provisions, I proposed to stand upon the firm rock of constitution as I understood it. For this reason I opposed the provision for separate schools and equally I would oppose with the same vigour a provision against the establishment of separate schools. I maintained that such matters were for the provinces themselves and any controversy liable to arise should be confined to the limits of the province: "Let the minorities trust the majorities and the result will be the same as in Nova Scotia and New Brunswick."

One passage from my speech might be quoted:

The Prime Minister first declared that this questions is not one of separate schools, and then he proceeded to give us a long argument with regard to the value and necessity of such schools. I shall not follow him along that path. It is not, in my opinion, a question of separate schools, but a question of provincial rights. It is not a question of separate schools but a question of provincial self-government. It is not a question of separate schools but of constitutional home rule. It is a question of those privileges and liberties of which the right hon. gentleman, up to the present at least, has claimed to be a champion and exponent. No one apreciates or respects more highly than I do the moral and ethical training which the Roman Catholic Church bestows upon the youth of Canada who were born within the pale of that church. I esteem at the highest the value of the moral training of the children of this country; and I am free further to confess that I appreciate more highly than some others the consistency and devotion of Roman Catholics in this and other matters of their faith, wherein they give to the Protestants of this country an example from which the latter might well learn valuable lessons.

Finally I moved the following resolution, explaining that it did not defeat the Bill but laid down the principles upon which the Bill should be founded:

Upon the establishment of a province in the Northwest Territories of Canada as proposed by Bill (No. 69) the Legislature of such province subject to and in accordance with the provisions of the British North America Acts 1867 to 1886, is entitled to and should enjoy full powers of provincial self-government including power to exclusively make laws in relation to education. . . .

My motion was defeated by a very large majority as thirteen of my followers supported the Government. . . .

During this session (1905) a self-constituted committee of the Liberal-Conservative Party, acting with my approval, took up with a similar committee of the Liberal Party the question of increased sessional indemnity, increased salaries for the Prime Minister and Ministers, and pensions for ex-Ministers.

It was reported that members on both sides of the House were unanimous in signing what is commonly known as a "round-robin"[4] with respect to the increase in the sessional indemnity. Having learned that this document contained a proposal for an increased indemnity to the Leader of the Opposition, I sent for our Chief Whip and informed him that such inclusion was entirely against my wishes and without my authority; and I requested its elimination. Accordingly, that proposal was eliminated.

As a result of the conference of the committees alluded to, the Government introduced two Bills, one providing an increase

---

[4] Speaking in the House of Commons in the following session (1906), with respect to the round-robin, and the initiation of the proposal for a special indemnity to the Leader of the Opposition, I set forth my position in the following words: "I never saw the round robin, but I heard that it contained an allusion to a proposed salary to the leader of the opposition. I insisted that that reference thereto should be eliminated and afterwards I asked that that particular matter, when it was mooted in the House, should be referred, and it was referred, to a committee of Conservative members to take it into consideration. The committee consisted of gentlemen representing every province of Canada except, unfortunately, two provinces from which we have no representatives. That was our misfortune and not our fault. We endeavoured to make the committee representative and as wide as possible. Those gentlemen took that matter into consideration, and arrived at the conclusion that the measure might fairly be put on the statute book. I have heard rumours in my own province, I do not know from what source they emanated, that not only did I initiate and insist upon this, but that I threatened to oppose the other measures of last session if a salary were not provided for myself. I desire to take this public opportunity of stating that no more infamous falsehood was ever uttered about any public man than that same statement."

to $2,500 in the sessional indemnity for members, an increase
in the salary of the Prime Minister and a special indemnity for
the Leader of the Opposition; the other making provision for an
annuity or pension of one-half their salaries to ex-Cabinet
Ministers who had served as such for not less than five years.

As these Bills were introduced very late in the session, the
discussion was necessarily inadequate. So far as the increase
of the indemnity for members was concerned, there was practically no discussion whatever on the merits of the increase.

There was, I think, a real necessity for removing anomalies
and inequalities and creating more adequate safeguards with
respect to the sessional indemnity.

The sufficiency of ground for the legislation authorizing
the increase was set forth in my speech during the following
session upon the proposal to repeal it. My reasons may be
summarized as follows: After speaking of the scandals that
were possible and that had occurred under the former system,
I dwelt upon the increasing length of the sessions. That of 1903
had begun on March 12, and had lasted until October 24 and
there seemed every probability that the length of future sessions
would extend to five months.[5] The destructive influence of
attendance for so long a term was especially evident in the
case of professional men and men whose business required
their active personal attention. From 1867 to 1872 the average
length of the session was eighty days, from 1873 to 1890, the
average length was 93 days, from 1899 to 1905, the average
length was 155 days. A comparison with the length of the
session in Ontario, Quebec, and other Provinces indicated that
$2,500 was a reasonable and moderate indemnity.

I had found extreme difficulty in persuading representative
men to enter public life.[6] An indimnity of $2,500 was not too

[5] The session of 1907-8 commenced on November 28th, 1907 and
terminated July 20th, 1908, a period of nearly 8 months, seven days
longer than the session of 1903.
[6] In writing to the late Charles A. Pentland, of Quebec, July 10th, 1905,
I said: "Those who are opposed to any increase of indemnity might
have their views altered if they had undergone my own experience in
endeavouring to get representative men to enter public life. This is
rapidly becoming impossible under present conditions. Men from
Ontario and Quebec spend two or three days per week at Ottawa and
devote the rest of their time to their personal affairs. This lengthens
the session by at least 25 per cent, for men from the Maritime
Provinces and the West whose business affairs remain wholly neglected during a period of many months. I have privately discussed
with Sir Wilfrid Laurier a proposal to have the fiscal year end on
March 31st instead of June 30th and to begin the sessions of Parlia-

much for one who attended faithfully and constantly to his public duties. A member who makes a mere pretence is worth nothing, but the remedy lies with the people. In Australia, members received an indemnity of £400, in the United States a member of Congress received $5,000 together with certain other allowances. "I do not know that we can reasonably say that a representative Canadian citizen, serving the Canadian nation in the Parliament of Canada, is to be pronounced a robber and a thief because he accepts a sessional indemnity of $2,500, or less than half what is received in the United States."

Continuing, I said that it would have been better to postpone the effect of the legislation until after the election but constant and consistent practice in Canada from 1867 had been with the policy of the Government in the present instance.

With respect to the increase in the salary of the Prime Minister there was complete unanimity, on both sides of the House.

The proposal for a special indemnity to the recognized Leader of the Opposition was discussed by Mr. Stockton, Sir Wilfrid Laurier, Mr. Fielding, and Sir Charles Fitzpatrick. All of them warmly supported it.[7] Mr. Stockton pointed out that the office of Leader of the Opposition had already been recognized by Statute in Ontario. Sir Wilfrid Laurier spoke as follows:

In this country we have no men of leisure or of means; we are all bound to work for the bread of every day and we must recognize this, and we are simply recognizing it. The leader of the opposition under our system is just as much a part of the constitutional system of government as the prime minister himself. We acknowledge that it is better for the country, that it is indeed essential for the country that the shades of opinion which are represented on both sides of this House

ment in November so that public affairs might be disposed of in Parliament during the winter months. This would be of some assistance. The present sessional indemnity is quite large enough for many – it is even too large for some. There are lawyers in Montreal who do not spend ten days of the session in Ottawa and who draw the whole of their sessional indemnity. On the other hand, there are many men eminent in commercial, business and professional life whose presence in Parliament is attended with very great personal sacrifice."

[7] The advisability of such an increased indemnity had been previously discussed in the Press; and, as far back as March 6th, 1901, Sir James Whitney had suggested it in a letter to me and had pointed out that the position of Leader of the Opposition had been recognized by the Statutes of Ontario.

*should be placed as far as possible on a footing of equality and
that we should have a strong opposition to voice the views of
those who do not think with the majority, and moreover that we
should have that legitimate criticism, not only legitimate criticism, but necessary criticism which is essential to good government in any land. I have thought for a long time that it is not fair
that the person who holds the position of leader of the opposition
should be called upon to give his services to the country without
any remuneration at all. It is not to be expected that he can give
to the discharge of his important duties the attention which they
need and demand, it is not to be expected that if he has to
pursue his ordinary vocation as well as attending to his public
duties he can do the two things at one time; either his public
duties must suffer or his private duties must suffer, and under
such circumstances I think the country is rich enough to pay
the services of the gentleman who for the time being is
discharging the important functions entrusted to him. The idea
is not a new one. It has been before the public for a good many
years but as in all British countries these things do not come
to maturity in a moment; they are discussed and discussed and
it is only after public opinion has become, as I may say, overwhelming that at last parliament gives it expression and in so
doing I think we are only doing what is fair and right and what
will be approved by all shades of opinion in this country.*

Mr. W. F. MacLean expressed anxiety lest a provision for
a special indemnity might restrict the prerogative of the Crown
in selecting a head of an administration. Sir Wilfrid Laurier
made light of this suggestion which was characterized more by
absurdity than by substance. . . .[8]

It was with the greatest goodwill that I had expressed in
advance my approval of an increase in the salary of the Prime
Minister who, under the proposed legislation, would receive
five thousand dollars per annum in addition to his salary as a
Minister. I would have been willing also to support an increase
in the salaries of the Ministers, but the Government were not
prepared to carry this out.

[8] Our chief Whip informed me that a conference of Government and
Opposition members had decided that there should be a special
indemnity of $5,000 to the Leader of the Opposition. I told him at
once that I would not assent to any such proposal. If there was to be
a special indemnity for the Leader of the Opposition it should be not
less than the salary of a Cabinet Minister. His labours were certainly
as arduous as those of any member of the Cabinet and his position
was as responsible as that of any member of the Government with the
exception of the Prime Minister.

Considerable excitement soon developed over these enactments. The principal attack was upon the provision for pensions
to ex-Ministers and it was also rather violent with regard to
the increase of the sessional indemnity. I was not spared in
connection with the special indemnity to the Leader of the
Opposition. W. F. MacLean began a vicious attack immediately
after the session with the evident desire of advancing on the
crest of a great wave of public indignation. The movement
was much greater in noise than in substance although two or
three Conservative Associations passed resolutions condemning
me.

The Liberal Press, and in some cases, the Conservative
Press spoke of me as the "hired man" of the Government;
and even moderate men seemed to consider that the sessional
imdemnity was paid by the Government and not by the country.
I found it necessary to issue a statement, summarized as follows:

1. *Neither the Prime Minister nor the Opposition Leader
   is known to the Law, as such, except by the statute
   paying a salary to one and a special indemnity to the
   other.*

2. *I never suggested or initiated in any way the proposal
   of an increased indemnity to myself and I had the
   suggestion taken out of the round-robin as soon as I
   heard of it being there.*

3. *A committee of Conservative members finally dealt with
   and approved the Government's proposals in this connection and I then acceded to their wish.*

4. *Before this legislation, an Opposition Leader had either
   to be a rich man, to accept gifts from his party and be
   under obligation to its wealthy members, or sacrifice
   his personal interests and family's welfare.*

5. *The Leader of the Opposition under the new arrangements is paid by the country—not by the Government—
   just as the judges are; and there is no more reason in
   his case than in theirs for the charge of dependence or
   subserviency.*

6. *I would be very glad to have this and all other portions
   of the measures re-considered and I deprecate now, as
   I did in the House, the haste with which the measure
   was put through. . . .*

A system of payments to the Leader of the Opposition was
subsequently adopted by several of the Canadian provinces
and it is now the rule rather than the exception in Canada.

. . . I assailed the Government for passing over Mr. Haultain and selecting Mr. Scott as Prime Minister of Saskatchewan; and I attacked Mr. Oliver (Minister of the Interior) for the political activities of his officers in defiance of the unanimous resolution of the House.

On the same day, I introduced four Bills. The first, I briefly explained, was practically the same as one introduced by me toward the close of the previous session. It was designed to accelerate the bringing on of by-elections in case the administration of the day did not see fit to act within a given time. The second Bill, to amend the House of Commons Act, was supplementary to the first. I thought it desirable for the purpose of accomplishing results that the two statutes should be amended and separate Bills introduced for the purpose. I introduced the third Bill (Criminal Code 1892 Amendments) in fulfilment of a promise which I had made during the previous session to introduce legislation with respect to the practice of members of Parliament and of Legislatures receiving rewards for their services in Parliament or in a Legislature or in departments of the Government. I understood that the Minister of Justice proposed to introduce a Bill along similar lines; and I explained that the Bill dealt with several other matters. It provided that members of the Board of Railway Commissioners are persons holding judicial office within the meaning of Section 131 of the Criminal Code and that Section 133 should apply to and include the Commissioners of the Transcontinental Railway and persons holding the office of such Commissioners from time to time.

In introducing the fourth Bill (to amend the Dominion Controverted Elections Act) I explained that the immediate occasion of this measure was a recent decision of the Supreme Court of Canada by which the existing law had been interpreted as preventing further proceedings upon an election petition if it was established upon preliminary objection that the petitioner had been guilty of hiring a team for the conveyance of voters to the polls. I pointed out the curious anomaly of the law as it existed; under a judgment of the Supreme Court of Canada and under the Law, as interpreted by it, a petitioner who had been guilty of bribery, personation, or very much grosser corrupt practices was not disqualified from carrying on a petition; but if he committed the less serious offence of paying to convey a sick voter to the poll he was absolutely debarred from becoming a petitioner. I expressed the hope that this Bill might be referred to a committee, of which I had given notice on the Order Paper, and that the whole question of corrupt practices and of further amendments to the Act should receive the attention of the House and of the Government before the conclusion of the session.

Thus, on March 15, I asked in the House by Resolution, for a Select Committee to "inquire into the Acts relating to elections to this House and the prevention of corrupt practices thereat, and the procedure and practice upon petitions relating to such elections, and to report to this House if any changes are desirable therein."

My motion was, in effect, superseded by a motion which the Minister of Justice had placed upon the Order Paper; and I requested that debate upon my motion might be adjourned until the motion of the Minister of Justice had been disposed of.

As I was not in a position to become a member of the committee, I took the opportunity of making a few suggestions which I thought might be of value to its members. Briefly, my suggestions were that, if possible, there should be non-partisan returning officers and deputies; a limitation of expenditure somewhat as in Great Britain, stringent provisions in regard to payments or assistance by political organizations; and above all, there should be created some independent authority charged with the enforcement of Law and I advocated the appointment of a public prosecutor whose duty it would be to see that the law was carried out whenever a petition was filed or whenever there was grave reason to suspect that corrupt practices had prevailed on a great scale.

Following me, the Minister of Justice stated that he had been instructed by the Prime Minister to prepare a measure which would require a committee such as I proposed. On the next day (March 16) he announced the personnel of the committee.

On March 21, I moved second reading of the four Bills alluded to. I made a further explanation of the measure to amend the Criminal Code and I emphasized my desire to make it an indictable offence for any member of the House, whether a member of the legal profession or not, to accept money or reward for any services performed with regard to legislation before a committee of the House or before the House itself. On my motion the Bills were referred to the committee for consideration and report.

On July 5, I asked whether the committee was likely to make a report before the close of the session concerning the Bills respecting electoral law and independence of Parliament. The Minister of Justice (Mr. Aylesworth had become Minister of Justice the preceding month) replied that, owing to the amount of work in the House and in the various committees, it had been practically impossible for this committee to give the necessary consideration to the matters submitted and that no report could be expected during the present session.

The Bill to amend the Criminal Code was read for the third time and passed without debate on July 11. . . .

On May 29, Mr. Foster arose to a question of privilege and called attention to an article written by Mr. Cinq-Mars under the pseudonym "Blaise" in *La Presse* newspaper of May 26, 1906. The article is too long to recall, but the words to which, eventually, Sir Wilfrid Laurier himself attached importance were as follows:

He (Mr. Foster) has but one principle, that of self-interest. He has only one desire, the desire to insult. He belongs to the school of lying, hypocrisy, and cowardice. In his eyes the person to whom civic and political virtue are not vain words is an imbecile and a hot head. It is useless to discuss these questions with him; he would not understand them.

Mr. Foster emphatically denied the libellous statements attributed to him by Mr. Cinq-Mars and gave notice that, at the first convenient opportunity, he would present a motion to the House with regard to the matter. Mr. Foster had discussed the subject with me and I had endeavoured to dissuade him from his proposal to have the writer called to the Bar of the House. My method of meeting such scandalous statements was by emphatic public denial and I had always felt it unnecessary to go further. However, Mr. Foster felt the attack very keenly and notwithstanding my advice he persevered with his motion.

Accordingly on June 6, he read the article to the House and moved that Mr. Cinq-Mars be ordered to attend at the Bar of the House on June 7. Some debate took place. The outstanding incident of the occasion was the attitude of Mr. Aylesworth who, with the support and co-operation of a number of members from the Province of Quebec, endeavoured to treat Mr. Foster's motion with derision and contempt. During the debate Sir Wilfrid Laurier felt called upon to deny that *Le Soleil*, of Quebec, was his personal organ and he quoted unfair and unjust criticism of him which had appeared in

L'Evénement, the Conservative organ of Quebec. In characterizing as absolutely false and malicious certain statements in
Le Soleil respecting myself, I took occasion to quote to Sir
Wilfrid the following telegrams which had passed between him
and the Hon. P. A. Choquette, of Quebec, in February, 1906:

> *I have refused up to the present to intervene in the munici-*
> *pal contest in Quebec, but in view of the complication of the*
> *situation I think that in the interests of the party generally it*
> *would be better that you withdrew your candidate.*
>
> *(Sgd.)* WILFRID LAURIER

> *At your request, and as you say, in the interest of the party,*
> *I retire from the municipal contest. I desire also to return to*
> *you the control and direction of* Le Soleil.
>
> *(Sgd.)* P. AUG. CHOQUETTE

These messages, I suggested, had naturally created a
reasonable impression that the Prime Minister controlled the
organ in question.

An unfortunate debate upon the general question of racial
difficulties and Press attacks was precipitated, chiefly by Mr.
Armand Lavergne; finally, Mr. Foster's motion was agreed to.

On the following day (June 7) Mr. Cinq-Mars appeared
at the Bar of the House and upon motion of Mr. Foster the
journals of the previous day, as well as the article complained
of, were read. Again Mr. Aylesworth, supported by a number
of members from Quebec, endeavoured to throw contempt and
ridicule upon Mr. Foster and his proposal.

Mr. Cinq-Mars admitted that he was the correspondent of
La Presse and asked for an adjournment of one week which
was granted.

The proceeding was continued on June 14. In such matters
the methods of the House are unavoidably clumsy as no
question can be put unless it has been ordered by vote of the
House. Mr. Aylesworth, seconded by Mr. Duncan Ross of
British Columbia, and practically all the Liberal Quebec members, carried on his previous tactics and endeavoured to turn
the proceedings into ridicule. It seemed that he expected to
defeat Mr. Foster's attempt to subject Mr. Cinq-Mars to the
censure of the House. Referring to Mr. Foster, Mr. Aylesworth
observed, "The hon. gentleman has never heard of a case being
laughed out of court." Following Mr. Aylesworth, I ironically
congratulated him on the "eminently judicial" character of his
speech which was, in my view, partisan, narrow, and technical.

After Mr. Cinq-Mars had made his statement which included much hearsay matter, Mr. Ross, presumably under the direction of Mr. Aylesworth, took up the parable and moved, seconded by Mr. Beauparlant, that the House should proceed to the Orders of the Day. This motion if carried would have dismissed the proceeding and apparently was in accordance with an arranged programme.

But they had reckoned without Sir Wilfrid Laurier. No Canadian statesman was ever inspired by a higher sense of the dignity of Parliament than Sir Wilfrid, and in no degree did he permit his responsibility to be interfered with by party animus. Moreover I felt at the time, and I still believe that he was somewhat annoyed at Mr. Aylesworth's attempt to take charge of the proceedings, to laugh Mr. Foster out of court, and to answer his motion merely by derision and contempt. Immediately after Mr. Ross had taken his seat, Sir Wilfrid rose and the course which he pursued was properly regarded as a distinct snub to his Minister of Justice. He reviewed the authorities and, while he did not agree with Mr. Foster as to certain portions of the article, he declared that the language already quoted was not within the bounds of fair criticism and he moved the following amendment:

That all the words after "that" be struck out and the following substituted: That the passages in La Presse *newspaper complained of pass the bounds of reasonable criticism and constitute a breach of the privileges of this House; that Mr. Cinq-Mars, the writer of the article, has incurred the censure of the House; that he be recalled to the Bar; and that Mr. Speaker do communicate this resolution to him.*

Following Sir Wilfrid, I supported his view and cited British authority to indicate that the House could properly take action in the matter and that it was its duty to do so.

Sir Wilfrid's amendment was carried unanimously. Members from Quebec were greatly angered but they dared not raise their voices against the decision of the Prime Minister. In due course Mr. Cinq-Mars was brought before the House and reprimanded in the terms of Sir Wilfrid's amendment. . . .

10: *1906-1907*

After the overwhelming defeat of the Liberal-Conservative Party in 1904, I undertook, about 1906, a systematic organization of the Opposition in the House of Commons. For each department of the Government a committee was formed under the direction of a chairman. The duty of each committee was to examine thoroughly the proposals of the Government in respect of each department and to scrutinize with great care the estimates of that department and obtain, by correspondence or by personal visit, full information as to the need of the various expenditures proposed and generally to criticize whenever necessary the proposals, the work, and the expenditure of the department concerned. In this way the various members were taught to develop a sense of responsibility and they were encouraged to give the closest possible attention to the duties assigned to them. The system had great merit and in the result, between 1906 and 1911, the Opposition became a well-directed and effective fighting force, so that few of the many opportunities for criticism and attack were overlooked. In this organization I had effective co-operation from many of the leading Conservative members, and among them George (later Sir George) Halsey Perley, who had entered Parliament in 1904, gave invaluable assistance. He had wide business experience, was very systematic, and pursued with wonderful thoroughness any duty assigned to him.

The session of 1907 began on November 22, 1906. This early date was in pursuance of a proposal much favoured by Mr. Fielding. It was hoped that if the session began in November it would be possible to prorogue in April, or in May at the latest. Eventually the experiment proved completely unsuccessful. It was particularly disliked by members from a distance, especially by those from the four Western Provinces. Very little progress was made before the Christmas holidays and the session virtually began in January instead of November. The members residing at a distance were faced with the necessity of a long journey to their homes or with the alternative of spending Christmas in Ottawa.

The Speech from the Throne alluded to Lord Grey's visit to the West. In some instances his enthusiasm outran his judgment,[1] and on this occasion his utterances at various points which he visited in British Columbia were so glowing that they proved extremely useful for advertising purposes. . . .

Speaking in the debate on the Address, I urged once more the extreme importance of reform in the laws relating to elections and mentioned the Bills which I had introduced in the previous session and which had not received consideration for reasons already stated. . . .

On November 22, 1906, the Speaker announced that Hon. C. S. Hyman, who had been under attack in connection with a recent election in London, Ontario, which had been conducted with unparalleled corruption according to disclosures made in the courts, had sent in his resignation. The Speaker stated, however, that the resignation was not quite in proper form. The Prime Minister had not accepted it or presented it to the Governor-General, and the subject was brought up by question and in debate on several occasions. On February 15, 1907, I asked for information as to the validity of Mr. Hyman's resignation as a member of the Commons. On the eighteenth I moved that it be referred to the Committee on Privileges and Elections, and that Committee subsequently reported that the resignation was not valid. Eventually, however, the resignation was put into proper form and Mr. Hyman ceased to be a member of Parliament and of the Administration. . . .

The charges and insinuations made against several Conservative members as a result of the insurance investigation finally aroused Mr. G. W. Fowler, member for King's, N.B., to a pitch of fury which inspired the following outburst:

I want this House and the Right Hon. the First Minister, and the Government to understand that if matters in connection with my private business are to be discussed in this House, I shall take an opportunity to discuss the private character of members of this Administration and members on that side. I want to say to the hon. gentlemen opposite that I shall discuss those without fear or favour, that I shall call a spade a spade, and when I speak of the indisposition of an hon. minister which keeps him out of the House, I shall tell exactly what it was and how it was brought on. I shall allow no man to make an attack on me or my character without retorting. I shall discuss the

---

[1] After Lord Grey had visited Hudson Bay, where he experienced very mild weather, he designated that inland sea as "the Mediterranean of Canada."

characters of hon. members opposite, whether they be Ministers or private members, and their connection with women, wine, and graft.

This speech gave rise to widespread comment in the Press and was taken up in Parliament by Mr. Bourassa on February 21 with a view to future full discussion. In a brief speech Mr. Bourassa dealt with the honour of the House, the reputation of the Government, and the evil results of such insinuations as Mr. Fowler had set forth. On March 26 he initiated a lively debate on the subject and concluded with a long motion in which he set forth the attacks made upon Messrs Foster, Fowler, Bennett, Pope, and Lefurgey, the observations of Messrs. Carvell, Ross, and Devlin to the effect that these gentlemen were unworthy of seats in the House, and the observations of Mr. Fowler already alluded to. He declared that these statements had become a matter of general comment and had become a scandal throughout the country so that an immediate inquiry had become imperative. He moved for a special committee "to conduct a strict inquiry as to whether any Ministers of the Crown or members of Parliament had improperly made use of their positions as such for their private gain or have otherwise been guilty of personal misconduct under such circumstances or of such character as to justify the intervention and censure of this House.". . .

Sir Wilfrid Laurier in reply to Mr. Bourassa declared that it was absolutely unprecedented in any British Parliament that the House of Commons should investigate a mere rumour. Such an investigation should only be ordered upon a definite charge which the man against whom it was levelled could face and to which he could make answer. He utterly denied Mr. Bourassa's allegation that there was a "saw-off" between the two sides of the House and he cited my denial twice repeated that there had been any such arrangement.

In following the Prime Minister, I alluded to the circumstance that he had failed to arise after Mr. Bourassa and had signalled to Mr. Carvell to take the floor, and I suggested that this had been done in pursuance of an arrangement which assigned to Mr. Carvell the task of attacking Mr. Foster. I recalled the language of the Prime Minister on February 21 (1907) in which he had declared that the session would not pass without this matter being brought to the attention of the House. I concluded in the following words:

I have pledged myself to two things in this House and I

propose to stand by them to the end. I have pledged myself that I have not made and that I would not make any arrangement with hon. gentlemen on the other side of the House upon any matters touched upon in the discussion during the past session which have been commented on by the hon. member for Labelle and I have pledged myself also that if any hon. gentleman in this House took steps to forward an inquiry touching the position of hon. gentlemen on this side of the House, who are my colleagues and associates, I would give my best efforts to probe the matter of that inquiry to the bottom. Therefore, I am not disposed for the sake of any Parliamentary precedent, for the sake of any hair-splitting, or for the sake of anything that has been uttered by the Prime Minister, and especially in view of the construction which I put upon this resolution, I am not disposed to vote against this motion and I shall record my vote in favour of that resolution although I wish that the procedure suggested had been different and that the resolution had been couched in somewhat different terms.

Mr. Bourassa's motion which was supported by the Conservatives, and for which I voted, was defeated by 109 to 55. . . .

The subject of strikes, lock-outs, and labour disputes in general was fully discussed during this session. On January 9, I moved the following resolution:

That in the opinion of this House more effective legislative provision should be made for the prevention and settlement of disputes between employers and workmen, to the end that strikes and lock-outs, sometimes resulting in loss of life, and always entailing privation and suffering, may be prevented. That a select committee of nine be appointed to inquire into the matters aforesaid and to consider and report what further enactments are desirable or necessary. That the committee have power to send for persons, papers and records, and to examine witnesses on oath. That three be a quorum of the committee.

I went fully into the subject and reviewed Canadian legislation affecting trade unions. I explained the purpose and effect of New England legislation, and I dealt with the difficulties and disadvantages of international labour organizations. In concluding my speech, I emphasized the importance of giving to employers, as well as to the working men, the opportunity of being heard, of giving their suggestions, and of stating their objections, if any, to the Bill previously introduced by the Minister of Labour (Mr. Lemieux) and eventually enacted. I claimed that the working men themselves realized that public utilities ought not to be paralyzed by strikes; they realized, or at least some of them did, that supplies of necessary commodities, such as coal and other similar articles must not be cut off by reason of controversy between capital and labour.

There was considerable discussion upon this motion but eventually it was side-tracked by an amendment.

Mr. Lemieux's Bill passed after a discussion in which I participated. The motion which I had proposed had been treated by Government supporters from a rather partisan standpoint, and I thought it worth while to point out that, in 1872, twenty-four Toronto printers, including the late Edward F. Clarke, had been prosecuted under the common law of England for conspiracy, because they had combined together to strike—not for any violence or molestation, or threats, but simply because they combined to leave their employment by reason of alleged unfair treatment. Thereupon, in the same year, Sir John A. Macdonald had placed upon the statute book of Canada an enactment permitting men to strike. I reviewed at great length the provisions of the Bill introduced by Mr. Lemieux and made many suggestions for amendments while supporting the general principle of the measure.

During the debate, Mr. Lennox raised a question as to the jurisdiction of Parliament to enact such legislation. Mr. Lemieux produced an opinion by the Deputy Minister of Justice, in which the Minister of Justice concurred, affirming the competence of Parliament. But in 1926 the Judicial Committee of the Privy Council pronounced it *ultra vires*; this decision was extremely unfortunate as the measure had served an excellent purpose. The judgment of the Judicial Committee was probably due in great measure to Lord Haldane whose subtlety of intellect was not always combined with wide vision in the construction of Canadian enactments.

On January 15, 1907, a debate arose on the second reading of a Bill, introduced by Mr. Aylesworth, respecting The Revised Statutes of 1906, and to provide the French version thereof. Chapter 61 of the Acts of 1903, which created a commission to revise the statutes, directed that a certified roll of the consolidated statutes should be deposited with the Clerk of the Parliament and that such roll should be held to be the original of the said statutes.

Section 133 of the British North America Act enacts that:

Either the English or the French language may be used by any person in the debates of the Houses of the Parliament of Canada, and of the Houses of the legislature of Quebec; and both those languages shall be used in the respective records and journals of those Houses . . . and either of those languages may be used by any person or in any pleading or process in or issuing from any court of Canada established under this Act, and in or from all or any of the courts of Quebec.

The Acts of the Parliament of Canada and of the legislature of Quebec shall be printed and published in both those languages.

I took the ground that the Act of 1903 required the records of Parliament to be printed in both languages, as provided by Section 133 of the British North America Act. The Minister of Justice supported the opposite view; thereupon I inquired whether he was of opinion that the law would be complied with by depositing the roll in the French language alone, and I observed that this would be quite as valid as its deposit in the English language alone. Neither the one language nor the other was mentioned in the statute authorizing the deposition of the roll, and, as the constitution under which records of Parliament are printed required that the record should be printed in both languages, I maintained that the roll was not complete until it was expressed in both languages. . . .

The view of the Minister of Justice, supported by Sir Wilfrid, prevailed upon a division. With twenty-eight of my supporters I voted for the French language but many of the English-speaking Conservatives were not impressed by the arguments I had adduced which, however, in my opinion, were well founded.

On January 28, 1907, Mr. J. J. Hughes, in a vigorous speech, moved a resolution that the British North America Act should be amended so that the three Maritime Provinces should not at any time have fewer representatives in the House of Commons than the number assigned to each when it entered Confederation. He was supported by the Maritime members and was answered by Mr. Aylesworth who took a rather narrow technical view of the subject. As was aptly remarked by Mr. A. A. Stockton: "The Minister of Justice entrenched himself entirely within the limits of the constitution as expounded by the Judicial Committee of the Privy Council." He (Mr. Aylesworth) had argued, what no one disputed, that Prince Edward Island was not entitled as of right to the proposed measure of representation. A considerable debate ensued in which the

Prime Minister spoke at some length. He addressed himself to the subject in a broad spirit and replied to Mr. Stockton's contention that the recent addition of a large territory to the Province of Quebec had in itself altered the basis of representation as originally established. Answering Mr. Crocket, he declared that Confederation was a compact and urged that it should not be altered except for adequate cause, and after the provinces themselves had been given the opportunity to pass judgment thereon; and he claimed that all the provinces had agreed to the Government's proposal to alter the financial terms of Confederation.

In following the Prime Minister, I commented on the narrow spirit in which Mr. Aylesworth had approached the question as compared with the view which the Prime Minister had set forth. I saw no distinction between amending the constitution in relation to provincial subsidies and amending it in respect of the representation allotted to each province. I pointed out that the Prime Minister was inaccurate in his claim that the proposal to increase provincial subsidies had commanded the consent of all the provinces. It was true that British Columbia had agreed to a revision but not to the terms of this revision— and terms meant everything in such a case. The Prime Minister had spoken sympathetically but there was danger of manifest injustice to the three Maritime Provinces and, while sympathy was appreciated, a safeguard would be much more helpful. . . .

On January 29, 1907, I moved adjournment of the House to discuss the great delay in filling the vacancy on the Bench of the Supreme Court of Nova Scotia which had existed since March 29, 1906. The Minister of Justice, in reply to my question on November 28, 1906, had declared that the administration of justice had not suffered from the delay and that no complaint in that behalf had been made. On January 27, I had received very urgent letters and telegrams and on that day (January 29) two telegraphic messages arrived informing me that no quorum of the court *in banco* was available to hear an important matter relating to special litigation then before the Judicial Committee. The Prime Minister had said that the Government was suffering from an embarrassment of riches and I characterized that answer as extremely unsatisfactory. Within a few minutes after receiving the telegram alluded to, I had notified the Prime Minister that I would bring up the question, and I declared that the Government had been absolutely derelict in its duty in failing to fill the vacancy.

A considerable debate ensued. The Minister of Justice

explained that the Attorney-General of the province had not thought the situation of such gravity as to necessitate a communication with the Department of Justice. As a matter of fact the Attorney-General, Hon. Arthur Drysdale, was subsequently appointed, March 13, 1907, and for reasons of political convenience had desired to delay the appointment.

On March 27, 1907, I initiated a debate with regard to the then approaching Colonial Conference. In the course of the debate I made a rather caustic comment upon certain observations of Mr. Lloyd George in the British House of Commons and characterized his utterances as indicating lack of dignity, pettiness of outlook, and deplorable ignorance of political conditions in Canada. Alluding to the Australian proposal that a system of preference within the Empire should be inaugurated and recalling the pronouncement of the Government in 1902, I inquired whether they still adhered to their declaration that of Great Britain should not grant preference to colonial products, Canada would be free to take such action as might be considered necessary in the presence of such conditions. This was a clear intimation, indeed a threat, that unless Canada received preferential treatment in British markets, the British preference would be withdrawn in whole or in part. In his reply, Sir Wilfrid Laurier used the following language:

If the people of Great Britain are prepared to extend to us preferential treatment for the products and manufactures of the colonies, we have already stated that we are prepared to meet them and to go one step deeper into the preferential system and to discuss what more we can do in order to meet that view. The answer must come from them and I repeat that it would be unseemly on our part, not to use a stronger expression, to try to force the views of the colonial governments upon the people of the motherland.[2]

I had touched upon the question of Empire defence as to which Sir Wilfrid expressed himself in the following terms:

I think I must adhere to the view I expressed five years ago that for no consideration would Canada be induced to be drawn into the vortex of European militarism. . . . The conditions which prevail today in Europe are deplorable to a degree. The condition which prevails in Europe is an armed peace, almost

---

[2] The proposals of Mr. Bennett which resulted in the economic Conference called for July of the present year (1932) are clearly in line with Sir Wilfrid Laurier's language of 1907.

as intolerable as war itself. This cannot last forever; it seems to me the date is not far distant when these nations, the wisest, the most advanced, the most civilized in the world, will recognize the folly that has been carried on for centuries and will come back to a more humane system such as we have on this continent.

Unfortunately the reasonable and humane anticipation which Sir Wilfrid set forth in these eloquent words had a bitter disappointment in the storm of war which burst upon the world seven years later. . . .

It became apparent that, notwithstanding the existence of a widespread scheme of corruption and bribery which had made itself manifest in many constituencies, the Government proposed no such amendment to the electoral laws as would secure enforcement, correct abuses and anomalies and lead to more wholesome conditions in federal elections. Accordingly on April 16, I brought up the subject on motion to go into Committee of Supply.

In the Speech from the Throne, the Government had given its pledge that during the session, amendment of the Electoral Laws would be submitted to Parliament. We had now reached the closing days of the session and no such measure had been submitted. I dwelt upon the extraordinary system of electoral bribery, corruption, and ballot switching which had been exposed in West Huron, in St. James, St. Antoine, and Ste. Anne's divisions of Montreal, in West Hastings, in London, in Queen's, and Shelbourne. After reviewing the failure of the Government to enforce the existing law, through the punishment of the expert criminals employed by the Liberal Party, I produced an affidavit from James Farr who explained in great detail the process of ballot switching in which he had been instructed and which he had carried out in West Huron. He had been provided with money by James Vance, a Liberal organizer, to maintain him in the United States while he was evading the service of a subpoena. I contrasted the extraordinary apathy of Mr. George F. Shepley in pursuing criminals in West Hastings with his extreme diligence during the Insurance inquiry to find material for casting discredit upon Mr. Foster and other Conservative members of Parliament. . . .

I urged that responsible men, not party heelers, should be appointed as deputy returning officers and that there should be full publicity in respect of campaign funds and contributions by corporations should be prohibited. I pointed out, as I had already done in the preceding session, that in Great Britain a public prosecutor intervened in case of suspected collusion between parties to an election petition; and I urged the enactment of a similar measure in Canada. I emphasized the extraordinary delays available by means of preliminary objections which, in the case of the Halifax election petition, had occupied more than two years and I again called attention to a recent decision of the Supreme Court of Canada that the petitioner and not the respondent was first to be tried; that is to say if it was alleged by preliminary objection that a petitioner had been guilty of hiring a team, the first proceeding was the trial of the petitioner upon that issue.

A long debate ensued, and my motion was defeated by the usual party majority. However, this exposure had its effect and undoubtedly led to the measure, introduced at the following session, for the amendment of the Electoral Laws.

On April 24, 1907, I raised a question as to the proposal of the Federal Government to expropriate a large area of Ontario public lands at Petawawa. The proposal was to take over and vest in the Federal Government, for the purpose of the Department of Militia and Defence, about 55,000 acres of land without compensation and without much regard to the rights of timber licensees. The proceeding was taken under Section 117 of the British North America Act which is as follows:

The several provinces shall retain all their respective public property not otherwise disposed of in this Act, subject to the right of Canada to assume any lands or public property required for fortifications or for the defence of the country.

The land was taken for the purpose of a training camp and I expressed a doubt as to whether this purpose was within the meaning of the Section.

The Province of Ontario took strong exception to the Government's action and urged that under the Ontario regulations licensees were entitled to a renewal of their licences from year to year upon payment of a ground rent and Crown dues at rates fixed by regulations. Ontario claimed that the Federal Government had no right to take the property without compensation both to the province and to the licensees.

My summary of the situation, as I viewed it, was as follows:

The situation is this. The Government of Canada says to the Province of Ontario: "We will not pay you one dollar

*compensation although you have an interest to the extent of
one-fourth the value of all the timber standing upon that land
under arrangements, partly by virtue of law and partly by
virtue of convention, which exist between you and your licensees." It says to the licensees: "We will pay you compensation
but, inasmuch as you have no absolute legal right as against
the province of Ontario to renew your license at the end
of the year we will give you compensation up to the end of
this year only, and from that time on you will not get one
dollar"—although but for this action of the Government of
Canada those licensees would have continued in the enjoyment
of the property, in the enjoyment of their right to cut upon
payment of the proper dues, and in that way were possessed
of a property of very considerable value.*

A long debate ensued but the Government persisted in its
attitude although there was much doubt as to the constitutional
validity of their action.

The session of 1907, which terminated on April 27 of that
year, was emphatically a fighting session and many attacks,
long since forgotten, were launched against the administration
in respect of alleged scandals.

It would be useless to recall these attacks as their value
was ephemeral. Possibly they may have contributed something
to the discredit of the Government just as, in the session
immediately preceding 1896, the attacks of Mr. James McMul-
lan and a small band whom he led with great adroitness called
attention to supposed extravagances of the Conservative Administration with respect to Rideau Hall (the Ottawa residence
of the Governor-General) and the High Commissioner's
residence in London.

There was an amusing story of such an attack in a rural
district. It was the custom to read a list of articles provided
for furnishing the High Commissioner's house. One Liberal
campaigner, in reading the list, came across an item, "dinner-
wagon." Someone in the audience asked what a dinner-wagon
was. The orator had not the slightest idea of its purpose but
this did not deter him from the following vivid explanation:

*I am glad that question was asked. This man, Tupper,[3] in
London gives great dinner parties, paid for by your money and
mine, to which he invites the swells of London. At these dinners
every kind of wine is served, paid for by your money and mine.*

---

[3] Sir Charles Tupper was then High Commissioner. [Ed.]

*In great flowing goblets, it is passed around and the toffs whom
Tupper invites to his dinners drink it until they can drink no
more. Finally one of them slips off his chair and falls under
the table. Then two of Tupper's flunkeys, paid for by your
money and mine, haul the guest from under the table, place
him on the dinner-wagon, take him to the front door, call a
cab, and send him home. Then another goes under the table
and the flunkeys bring the dinner-wagon again and so on until
all the guests are disposed of. That, ladies and gentlemen, is
the purpose and use of this dinner-wagon, paid for by your
money and mine.*

The audience, marvellously enlightened, went home full of
indignation at this scandalous and iniquitous misuse of public
funds.

It is probable that similar supposed iniquities of the Laurier
Government were used in the same way to edify Conservative
assemblages.

During this (1907) and the previous session I had given
much thought and consideration to an announcement of policy
and had discussed with my supporters in Parliament, with
eminent journalists, and with men high in the councils of the
Party, the lines upon which such pronouncement might be
made in the public interest and to the advantage of my party.

After the close of the session, I proceeded to Halifax and
on August 20, I delivered a speech in which I set forth the
following platform:

1. Honest appropriation and expenditure of public moneys
    in the public interest.
2. Appointment by merit: *Appointment of public officials
    upon considerations of capacity and personal character
    and not of party service alone.*
3. Honest elections: *More effective provisions to punish
    bribery and fraud at elections; to ensure thorough pub-
    licity as to expenditures by political organizations; to
    prevent the accumulation of campaign funds for corrupt
    purposes; and to prohibit contributions thereto by
    corporations, contractors, and promoters; to expedite
    the hearing of election petitions, and to prevent collusive
    arrangements for the withdrawal or compromise there-
    of; to provide for a thorough investigation of corrupt
    practices, and if necessary to appoint an independent
    prosecuting officer charged with that duty to simplify*

the procedure therefor and to enforce the laws so amended.

4. Civil Service Reform: *A thorough and complete reformation of the laws relating to the Civil Service so that future appointments shall be made by an independent commission acting upon the report of examiners after competitive examination.*

5. Reform of the Senate: *Such reform in the mode of selecting members of the Senate as will make that Chamber a more useful and representative legislative body.*

6. Immigration: *A more careful selection of the sources from which immigration shall be sought, a more rigid inspection of immigrants, and the abolition of the bonus system except under very special circumstances and for the purpose of obtaining particularly desirable classes of settlers.*

7. Public Lands and Franchises for the People: *The Management and development of the public domain (in which are to be included great national franchises) for the public benefit and under such conditions that a reasonable proportion of the increment of value arising therefrom shall inure to the people.*

8. Non-Partisan Management of Government Railways: *The operation and management of our government railways by an independent commission free from partisan control or influence.*

9. National Ports, Transportation and Cold Storage: *The development and improvement of our national waterways, the equipment of national ports, the improvement of transportation facilities and consequent reduction of freight rates between the place of production and the market, whether at home or abroad, and the establishment of a thorough system of cold storage.*

10. A Public Utilities Commission: *The reorganization of the present Railway Commission as a Public Utilities Commission with wider powers and more extended jurisdiction, so as to establish thorough and effective control over all corporations owning or operating public utilities or invested with franchises of a national character*

11. Public Telegraphs and Telephones: *The establishment, after due investigation of a system of national telegraphs and telephones under conditions which shall be just to capital already invested in those enterprises.*

12. Improved Postal Facilities: *The improvement of existing postal facilities, especially in newly developed portions of the country, and the inauguration, after proper inquiry as to cost, of a system of free rural mail delivery.*

13. Tariff Policy: *A fiscal policy which will promote the production within Canada of all useful articles and commodities that can be advantageously produced or manufactured from or by means of our natural resources, having due regard to the interests of the consumer as well as to the just claims of our wage earning population.*

14. Imperial Preference: *The promotion by negotiation, legislation, and other constitutional means of a system of mutual preferential trade within the Empire.*

15. Justice to the New Provinces: *The restoration of the public lands to the provinces of Alberta and Saskatchewan upon fair terms.*

16. Provincial Rights: *The unimpaired maintenance of all powers of self-government which have been conferred upon the provinces of Canada under the Constitution.*

Each of these articles I endeavoured to support by arguments which would commend them to the people of the country as being essential in the public interest.

In concluding my speech I alluded to the probable return of the Liberal-Conservative Party to power at the next election and expressed in the following terms my conception of what victory would mean:

Let the people send to our aid at the next election a reinforcement of sixty men, the best that Canada can produce, pledged to stand for a progressive policy, to maintain the rights of the people, to uphold honest Government and no other, to enforce decency in public life. In return you have my pledge that any administration which I am called upon to form shall be so constituted that it will not be unworthy of the great country which it is to serve.

A vast audience listened to my address and among them were several United States visitors. One of them, a strong Republican, came to congratulate me at the conclusion of my speech. He observed that if I were a citizen of the United States, I would undoubtedly be a Republican. Immediately after, another American extended his congratulations and assured me that if I were a citizen of his country I would certainly be in the Democratic ranks.

This speech attracted widespread attention in the Conservative and in the Liberal Press as well, and I believe it had considerable effect upon public opinion. We did not win in the following year, but except for an incident for which I was not responsible and which I would have denounced had I known of it in time, the Government, if it triumphed at all in 1908, would have won by an exceedingly narrow majority. I am convinced that this incident cost us at least ten and probably twenty seats.

My Halifax speech was the opening meeting of an All-Canada tour which was continued to October 30. During this tour I was assisted by many of my colleagues, including Messrs. Foster, Bergeron, Tanner, Marechal, Monk, Sévigny, Dr. Reid, and many others. I traversed every province and spoke at nearly one hundred meetings. It was a most arduous campaign as we had not the convenience of a private car and used the trains as best we could. In many cases the tour involved very early rising with perhaps a change which kept us waiting at some junction for an hour or more. On several occasions the only available accommodation was a seat in the second-class car; and once in Saskatchewan, we rode for several hundred miles in the caboose of a freight train. This was not by any means uncomfortable as we were treated to a bountiful luncheon, and from the seat in the upper part of the caboose we had an excellent view of the country through which we were passing. Before being permitted to enjoy the privilege of travelling in this way we were obliged to sign the usual agreement, that in case we should be maimed or killed, no complaint would be made.

From Halifax I proceeded to Middleton in Western Nova Scotia where, on August 24, I addressed a gathering of about twenty-five hundred people in the open air. After meetings at several points in New Brunswick, I arrived at Quebec on August 28, where Messrs. Bergeron and Sévigny spoke with me. The Quebec Bridge had fallen that afternoon and the Liberal Press subsequently had the bad taste to issue campaign literature headed "Bad Luck Borden" with the implication that my arrival was connected with the fall of the structure. Fortunately the Conservative Press refrained from the retort that the bridge had been called "Laurier."

At Quebec I entered into a discussion of the Autonomy Bills of 1905, declaring that I came from a province where such questions were settled in a broad and generous spirit and in that spirit I would endeavour to approach the question. The Manitoba school question had had its day. A Conservative Administration, firm in its determination to adhere to the constitution, was defeated by unworthy appeals and by Laurier's promise that if he came to power the rights of the minority in Manitoba would be maintained and upheld. Clifford Sifton, speaking in the House of Commons March 24, 1905, said that the Conservatives failed to give effect to the constitutional rights of the minority of Manitoba, "because the right hon. gentleman who leads this Government stood in the way." Eleven years have passed and Laurier's promise remains unfulfilled. I then proceeded to a defence, upon constitutional grounds, of the course adopted by the Opposition in Parliament; and I concluded by reminding my hearers that to the Province of Quebec, more than to any other province, it was of supreme importance that the constitution be adhered to.

In Ontario I emphasized the circumstance that in three recent appointments to the Cabinet (Aylesworth, Graham, and Pugsley) the Prime Minister had again overlooked his docile supporters in Parliament. At Port Hope on September 11, I alluded to the remarks of Mr. Aylesworth, who was reported in the Press to have said that "Some day somebody would give evidence that would disqualify Borden from holding a seat in Parliament,"[4] and challenged him to bring forward his evidence and he would find me ready to meet him at any time or place.

Aylesworth's insinuations were absolutely and utterly without foundation. I had gone to Halifax to meet my accusers, and had submitted to examination in court, but they had sought refuge in the contention that the court had no jurisdiction to proceed further with the case.

At Dunnville I urged the importance of national telegraph and telephone lines and alluded to the Toronto *Globe's* support of this policy, "Since the *Globe* is with me, where stands the Liberal Party on this question?"

My campaign in Ontario was concluded at Beaverton. I had held in all ten meetings in that province, the success of which had been aided considerably by Mr. Aylesworth's personal attack upon me and by the *Globe's* support of public ownership.

I arrived in Winnipeg on September 17. Mr. Roblin, the Prime Minister of the province, asked me privately why I was

---

[4] Mr. Aylesworth afterwards claimed that he had been misreported.

opposed to a general convention of the Party. I replied that I was not at all opposed to any such convention but that the Quebec Conservatives would decline to attend and I inquired whether he believed that a convention, in which the Quebec Conservatives declined to take any part, would assist our cause.

I then met provincial and federal members and I frankly discussed with them the difficulties of the situation. The question of a convention was again raised and it was urged that the Liberal-Conservative Party should hold a convention for the purpose of announcing a definite policy upon which we would go to the country at the ensuing election. This statement aroused my wrath and I spoke in very emphatic terms. Were they not aware that in the previous month I had put forward at Halifax the most advanced and progressive platform ever placed before the people in Canada by any party in federal affairs? That policy had been carefully thought out and prepared. It was based upon consultation not only with the Conservative members but with leaders of the Party throughout Canada. The ablest journalists supporting the Party had been called in and consulted. The platform had been received with warm approval by the Conservative and the independent Press; it had evoked enthusiasm and applause at more than a score of meetings which I had since addressed.

My rather unusual outburst on this occasion seemed to suppress further inquiry as to a convention or policy and I proceeded on my journey to Vancouver.

Arriving at Vancouver on September 20, I was the guest of the Board of Trade at a banquet where I made a non-political address in which I dwelt upon the importance of co-operation between the East and the West. In Victoria on the following day I spoke to the Canadian Club on the responsibilities of citizenship and addressed a political meeting that evening. In British Columbia I addressed further meetings at New Westminster, Kamloops, and Nelson, stressing principally the Oriental question and the transcontinental railway. Throughout British Columbia I found the audiences both appreciative and receptive.

In Alberta I spoke first at Lethbridge, advocating the transfer of the public domain to the Province. Throughout my western tour I emphasized the importance of provincial autonomy, civil service reform, public ownership, rural free mails, and the need of a public utilities commission. Indeed throughout the tour I put in the forefront the articles of the Halifax platform and I took the same ground in the West as in the East.

During my campaign in Alberta I spoke at a small town in the Red Deer constituency which was the home of our candidate, George F. Root, who claimed to be a distant relative of the Hon. Elihu Root. At our meeting he set forth a very advanced programme of an extremely socialistic character, which was not at all in accord with my views nor indeed with the articles of the Halifax platform. Before the meeting we called at his house and in the drawing-room I was attracted by a beautifully framed motto hanging on the wall; I went over to inspect it and found that it purported to set forth the ranchers' rule of daily conduct. It read as follows:

So live this day that you can look every damn man straight in the eye and tell him to go to hell.

The sentiment was excellent but the form of expression rather lurid.

Mr. Root's opponent was Dr. Michael Clark, for many years an outstanding member of Parliament, a man of great ability, an excellent debater, and a fine platform speaker. However, the vote was comparatively close—Dr. Clark, 3,481; Mr. Root, 3,421.

At one stage of the tour in Saskatchewan I was threatened with pneumonia. However, I felt able to address a meeting that evening. It was proposed that I should speak only fifteen minutes. I intended to act upon this advice, but, becoming interested in speaking to a very responsive audience, I went on for an hour, fortunately without any ill effects.

With the exception of a meeting at Port Arthur on October 30, my tour ended at Winnipeg on October 28, where I addressed an immense gathering in the Walker Theatre. The building was crowded to overflowing with an audience of not less than three thousand in the body of the building; invitations for one thousand had been issued for the stage, while hundreds thronged the streets outside.

Mr. Roblin was chairman of the meeting, and supporting him was a great group of the leading Conservatives of Canada, including Sir Charles Tupper and Sir Hugh John Macdonald. We returned from this remarkable gathering with strong confidence in Manitoba's support at the next election.

To illustrate the difficulties of a long political tour, I recall two incidents. It was necessary for me to leave Toronto at seven o'clock in the morning in order to arrive at about one o'clock at Owen Sound where I was to hold an evening meeting. En route I was joined by Dr. Sproule, and a question arose whether we should take luncheon on the train or wait until we arrived. Finally we concluded to postpone it until our arrival as we anticipated that we should be expected to lunch with members of the committee. On arrival we were greeted by a large gathering and a procession was formed which proceeded to pass through some of the principal streets after which we turned toward the outlying portions of the town. I inquired whether the hotel was situated in that direction and was informed that we were not proceeding to an hotel but to a building (I forget whether it was a drill hall or a skating rink) where there was to be a meeting at two o'clock. We had not been informed of any such meeting and, expressing my surprise, I was told that the farmers could not wait until evening and therefore an afternoon meeting had been arranged. Accordingly, without having luncheon, we proceeded to the scene and a meeting, lasting until nearly five o'clock, was held. It was a rather trying situation as when one is to speak at an evening meeting one must abstain from anything but the lightest refreshment and in the meantime we had become horribly hungry.

In the same campaign, at a town in Western Canada, a meeting lasted until nearly eleven o'clock and at its conclusion we adjourned to an hotel. Following my usual practice I had abstained from a meal before the meeting and at its conclusion my thought was of supper. I was therefore rather surprised that the room to which we were taken did not seem especially convenient for that purpose; it was a long room equipped with very large tables in the centre and subsequently I learned that it was used as a sample room for commercial travellers. The local committee were present in considerable numbers and, shortly after we had seated ourselves, the chairman produced from his pocket a typewritten document which he proceeded to read and which set forth reasons impelling the committee to urge that a general convention of the Liberal-Conservative Party, to frame a policy, should be held forthwith. This proposal had been pressed upon my attention more than once and I have already set forth that I had declared with much emphasis that my Halifax platform which had been accepted by the party throughout Canada embodied the most advanced and progressive policy ever put forward in federal affairs, in Canada. On this occasion I expressed myself with justifiable warmth; the discussion lasted until about midnight. As soon as I got rid of the committee I resorted to the hotel management for the purpose of procuring food; to my sorrow and indignation I learned that everything was locked up and that any refreshment was out of the question until morning.

During this tour, Mr. Bergeron usually spoke at the conclusion of each meeting and was extremely effective. His magnificent voice, his slight accent, his ready wit, and his dramatic power brought him great success, especially when he dwelt upon the departure of the Liberal Administration from the platform laid down at their Ottawa conference in 1893. So graphically did he describe the incidents of that conference and so vividly could he portray an imaginary person writing down the articles of their policy upon the blackboard, that I have repeatedly seen an audience turn their eyes toward the wall upon which this imaginary blackboard was supposed to be affixed, while Bergeron indicated the particular article which was then being written down. He gathered many stories of his compatriots who had settled in the West and of course the French-speaking citizens in the Western Provinces thronged to hear him. One of his stories is worth recalling. A French-Canadian residing in the West had driven into an adjacent town and entered the bar-room of the hotel where he observed upon the wall a beautifully framed and engraved inscription, "*Ici on parle français.*" Delighted to have an opportunity of using his own language, he immediately proceeded to address the barman in French. He was coldly received by the latter who said: "Young fellow, if you want anything around this place the English language is good enough for me and it will have to be good enough for you." "But," said the astonished visitor, "I spoke French only because that inscription tells me that French is spoken here." "Young man," said the barman, "you can't tell me anything about that motto. I bought it from a commercial traveller and paid five dollars for it—it's Latin and means 'God Bless Our Home'."

The domestic ties between Bergeron and his wife were extremely strong and their very warm attachment continued throughout their married life. Before accompanying me on my western tour, Bergeron had procured from Dr. Reid a carefully prepared itinerary which gave most exact and explicit instructions to Madame Bergeron as to the days on which she should address to her husband a letter which would reach him on the day of our arrival at the various cities or towns. He hated to be separated from his wife and could not endure the thought of not hearing from her each day. Unfortunately the mail service was defective or his instructions were not sufficiently accurate; day after day as we traversed through the West he rushed eagerly to the post-office for the expected letter. He became so excited and nervous at their failure to appear that he threatened to leave us and return to his home; with great difficulty we dissuaded him from taking this course. Eventually at some town (I do not recall the name) a long series of letters reached him; this, however, only served to exasperate him and he employed his fine vocabulary in fierce denunciation of so wretched a postal service inflicted upon suffering humanity by an inept and corrupt Administration. . . .

In December, 1907, Joseph Israel Tarte passed away. He had been for twenty years a great figure in the public life of the country. When I first entered Parliament he was Minister of Public Works and I was fascinated by his dynamic energy and immense resourcefulness in putting through his estimates. He was subjected to fierce criticism and sometimes to bitter attack but he never lost his balance and never lacked a keen retort.

It is probable that in 1902 he believed Sir Wilfrid Laurier would not long survive and his ambition led him to place himself before the country in such a light as would secure the support of industrial and financial interests and give him the succession to the premiership.

Sir Wilfrid found him immensely useful during the first six years of his administration. It was Tarte who was called on to quiet Bourassa after the so-called settlement of the Manitoba school question. On one or two occasions I had him under examination before a Committee of the House and I found him as resourceful there as in the House of Commons. . . .

11: *1907-1908*

The session opened on November 28, 1907 and the hearts of Conservatives were greatly cheered that evening by tidings of John Stanfield's election for Colchester, N.S., by a majority of 223. The constituency had been opened by the appointment of Hon. F. A. Lawrence to the Supreme Court of Nova Scotia. Thus the "solid eighteen" of 1904 was broken.

The Speech from the Throne was long and discursive. It laid emphasis upon the expansion of trade and the consequent increase of revenue and it made allusion to the financial stringency prevailing throughout the world which had also affected Canada, notwithstanding the Government's best endeavours. In former years the prosperity of the world, in which Canada had had her full share, was attributed by the Government and its members to the existence in Canada of the best Government that the world had ever known. However, it was necessary to change the song to suit the occasion and thus the influence of world conditions was invoked. References were made to the Imperial Conference, the commercial treaty with France, the Hague Tribunal, the controversy with the United States respecting the fisheries convention of 1818, the progress of the transcontinental railway, the collapse of the Quebec Bridge, and Mr. Lemieux's mission to Japan. . . .

Oriental and especially Japanese immigration into Canada had been alluded to in the Speech from the Throne and I had commented upon it. Subsequently, on December 16, Mr. Ralph Smith* initiated a debate in which he was followed by several members from British Columbia; an adjournment of the debate was moved and it was not reached again on the Order Paper.

On December 18, I took up the subject in moving that Orders-in-Council, correspondence, and other documents relating to Japanese immigration into Canada should be laid upon the table of the House. I deprecated the Prime Minister's statement that as Japan was a great military and naval power and China was not we should discriminate between them. Canada had been insistent that she should be permitted to accede to the treaty with Japan (1906) which accorded to the citizens of that country absolute and full right and liberty to enter, travel, and reside in this country. The danger of excessive

* M.P. for Nanaimo.

immigration was apparent, but the Government defended itself by a supposed understanding under which the Japanese Government would limit emigration to Canada. In this respect Sir Wilfrid evidently felt that he was upon insecure ground as the only safeguard against a Japanese influx was vested in the Government of Japan and not in the Government of Canada.

During the debate initiated by Mr. Smith, no member of the Government had ventured to intervene; and I quoted once more the language of the Minister of Agriculture in 1903:

> *The Government there, in accordance with negotiations with our Government, issued orders . . . that for the future no permit should be given to the Japanese except the classes I have mentioned to come to Canada, and that has been strictly maintained to the present time. I had the assurance of the Government there, personally, and in writing, that this policy would be maintained.*

It transpired eventually that Mr. Fisher had been quite inaccurate in stating that he had this assurance in writing; and eventually he was obliged to admit this inaccuracy.

Later in the session, January 28, 1908, I again reviewed the question; under the admitted facts, the control of Japanese immigration into Canada was vested, not in the Canadian but in the Japanese Government. Quoting despatches from the Colonial Secretary, dated July 14, 1905, I pointed out his warning against the policy announced by the Minister of Agriculture (June 22, 1905) which practically declared that there would be no discrimination against Japanese labourers entering Canada, and that Canada was prepared to accede absolutely to the treaty without reserving control of immigration from Japan.

Finally, I concluded my moving the following resolution:

> *This House, while expressing its profound appreciation of the friendly intentions and courteous assurances of the Japanese Government, and while declaring its sincere desire for the most cordial relations with the Japanese people, desires nevertheless, to record its strong protest against a policy under which our wage-earning population cannot be protected from destructive invading competition except by entreating the forbearance and aid of a foreign country.*

There was considerable debate upon the Bill approving and carrying into effect the Franco-Canadian Trade Treaty, negoti-ated by Mr. Fielding and Mr. Brodeur. The stipulations of the treaty respecting trade were fully dealt with by Mr. Foster, and I intervened only on two points. On February 20, 1908, I punctured the bubble which had been blown by the Prime Minister and the Minister of Marine and Fisheries with regard to the supposed tremendous advance in treaty-making powers by the negotiation of this treaty. Many years previously, Sir Charles Tupper had been invested with the same status in trade negotiations with the Spanish Government. . . .

A prolonged and sometimes acrimonious debate arose upon the Government's Bill to amend the Dominion Election Act. The principle laid down by Sir Wilfrid Laurier in 1885, adopted as an article of the Liberal platform of 1893 and acted upon by the Government in 1898, declared that the lists to be used at federal elections should be those under which members of the provincial Legislatures were elected in the various provinces. "This is the position we have taken from the beginning; this is the position we maintain at the moment." Such was the pronouncement of Sir Wilfrid in 1898 and it was reiterated and emphasized by him on many occasions. This system continued in force until after the Conservative Party had come into power in Ontario, Manitoba, and British Columbia. Then for the first time the Liberal organizers began to regard it as unsatisfactory.

The Bill which was introduced by the Minister of Justice contained provisions which were altogether inconsistent with this principle. The provinces principally affected were Manitoba and British Columbia, but the Bill also dealt with the unorganized districts of Ontario. There was a plausible pretence of adherence to provincial and municipal lists but the effect of the Bill was to place the preparation of the lists in the control and under the direction of officers appointed by the Federal Government. There was no such provision for the right of appeal to a judicial tribunal as would ensure the preparation of fair lists.

In replying to Mr. Aylesworth, I went quite fully into the subject, cited about a dozen pronouncements of the Prime Minister in deadly opposition to any such proposal, and illustrated the situation by quoting the following declaration of a prominent Liberal in 1885:

> *Give us the power of appointing the revising officers and we can determine beforehand who will command a majority in this House.*

Later in the debate (May 7), which continued for many days, Dr. W. J. Roche gave an elaborate explanation of the situation in the Province of Manitoba and moved the following amendment:

This House affirms that the Dominions Elections Act should be effectively amended during the present session in order to prevent corrupt practices and ensure honest elections, but that the discrimination against the provinces of Manitoba and British Columbia created by the first section of the proposed Bill is not founded upon any inquiry, evidence, report or sufficient information, is a radical departure from the principle of acceptance of provincial voters' lists and is invidious and unjustifiable.

The next day Mr. Monk intervened in the debate and used the following language:

For my part, I say frankly and sincerely that the Bill seemed harmless when I first read it; but after having listened to this discussion, I look upon it as one of the most pernicious, most mischievous, and most wicked pieces of legislation that has come under my notice since I have had the honour of a seat in this House.

At the conclusion of his speech, Mr. Alcorn had declared, with my consent, that if the objectionable sections should be maintained, the Opposition would exhaust their constitutional rights in opposing the Bill.

The situation became very tense and for about five weeks very little progress was made either upon the Bill or in the general business of Parliament. The majority of my followers were disposed to adopt extreme measures and absolutely prevent any progress whatever. This view I over-ruled, as I pointed out the probability that in such case the Government would resort to closure, although I knew that Sir Wilfrid Laurier was disinclined to adopt that course. However, I vehemently protested to him against the Government's proposals and informed him that we would fight throughout the summer if necessary.

There were innumerable conferences between Sir Wilfrid and myself on the Bill; I would report to my followers what he proposed and he, in turn, would confer with his supporters respecting my suggestions. Misunderstandings arose so frequently under this method that finally I told Sir Wilfrid that any proposals, on the one side or the other, must be put in writing. This had a good result and its usefulness was proved on one occasion when Mr. Fielding dissented from my statement as to some matter in relation to the Bill and I was able to produce written evidence that I was right.

During these alarums and excursions, Mr. Roblin, Prime Minister of Manitoba, and his colleague Mr. Rogers arrived on the scene to urge that we should stand firm and not permit the provincial lists to be over-ridden. Mr. Roblin had an interview with Sir Wilfrid and returned with a vivid account of the Prime Minister's language respecting the extremists who had forced upon him a measure with which he had little or no sympathy; according to Mr. Roblin, the Prime Minister's description of these gentlemen was extremely forcible and picturesque and by no means complimentary.

Eventually a compromise, which was not satisfactory to the extreme factions of either party, was arranged. We fought the Bill both by speech and amendment until the end, but its most obnoxious features were eliminated and we had a reasonable degree of satisfaction in the result of our fight.

One extraordinary provision of the Bill, proposed by Mr. Aylesworth, was the proviso that no ballot paper should be rejected on account of any writing, number, or mark placed thereon by any deputy returning officer. Pointing out that the deputy returning officers were almost invariably strong partisans, I criticized this proviso in the following words:

If it is desired that the vote of any elector shall be known, and the manner in which he marks his ballot shall be known, any partisan deputy returning officer can mark upon it, "This is John Smith's ballot," and that will be an absolutely good ballot. I see no justification for any such amendment.

Fortunately this proposed amendment did not become law.

The Bill, as passed, contained some excellent general provisions which were a decided improvement, especially the enactment respecting contributions by corporations to party funds.

There was much debate upon a Bill introduced by the Minister of Interior to amend the Dominion Lands Act. On June 26, I took exception to the powers conferred upon the Minister by Section 12 of the amendment; it read as follows:

The Minister shall settle disputes between persons claiming the right to entry for the same land.

I suggested that such a question should not be decided by the Minister but by a competent tribunal. Mr. Oliver replied that in many cases the dispute was of a trifling character; that neither party had a legal right, i.e., a right established by law; in other cases the right was so indefinite and in many cases of such a trifling monetary value that reference to the courts would be a denial of justice.

I suggested that the words which gave the Minister power to settle trifling disputes in a summary manner necessarily gave him power to deal with matters of great moment; and of this I gave two illustrations that had already given rise to discussion. Every citizen was entitled to the ordinary remedies of the courts, and to substitute for that, in respect of matters that may involve very large amounts of money, the summary and sometimes rough methods of departmental inquiry is a very serious thing. I urged the Minister to add to Section 12 the proviso that he might, in respect of any dispute or difficulty of importance, refer the question for determination to the courts.

Throughout the debate I gave very close attention to the provisions of the Bill and made an earnest, sincere, and not altogether ineffective effort to aid the Minister in placing a good measure upon the statute book.

Later in the session (July 4, 1908) a question arose as to an amendment proposed by Mr. R. S. Lake; the Speaker ruled that it was out of order because it proposed alienation of public lands and therefore could not be moved by a private member without the consent of the Government. The Speaker was supported by Sir Wilfrid Laurier, whom I reminded that many motions of the same character had been proposed and considered to be in order in 1905, during the discussion of the Acts creating the Provinces of Alberta and Saskatchewan. I argued that, if the Prime Minister was correct, the House of Commons had not acted regularly in 1905, but had transcended its powers. The Speaker reserved his decision which he subsequently gave on July 8.

If Mr. Lake's amendment was out of order, certain provisions of the Bill were clearly out of order. The Speaker felt constrained to decide to the contrary, as the Government was obviously in an embarrassing situation. It is extremely doubtful whether his decision was correct.

From time to time many alleged scandals were brought to the attention of the Committee on Public Accounts and fierce controversies frequently ensued as to the right to probe such matters. Three or four Liberal members had been constituted or had constituted themselves into an informal committee for the purpose of opposing, and if possible thwarting, every attempt to investigate subjects that might develop into a scandal. They attained such notoriety that in parliamentary circles, and sometimes in the Press, they were designated as "The Blockers' Brigade."

Some dispute arose as to limiting the admission of evidence by technical rules prevailing in the courts, sometimes with regard to the refusal of a witness to answer a dangerous question and sometimes upon other important incidents. The Conservative members of the Committee asserted their right to appeal to the House from the action of the majority in excluding evidence or restricting inquiry.

A lengthy and acrimonious debate ensued, in which Sir Wilfrid Laurier endeavoured to defend the practice of the Committee. In replying to Sir Wilfrid, I pointed out that the course pursued might be very convenient for the Government as it would frequently stifle investigation. The right of appeal had always been recognized until that session—the right to appeal to the House and by the publicity thus given to appeal from the House to the country. Otherwise the Government were taking away from the minority not only an undoubted right but a great safeguard of the public interest.

Mr. Fielding and Mr. Foster became involved in a lively controversy in the course of which Mr. Fielding went to the extreme length of declaring that the minority in the House or in committee had absolutely no rights whatever, except such as the majority saw fit to concede. Mr. Fielding even made the somewhat absurd declaration that the majority had power to deprive the Opposition of the right to speak and therefore of the right to vote.

The discussion attracted wide attention in the Press and had a perceptible influence on the proceedings of the Committee.

On February 12, Mr. Lancaster introduced, for the third or fourth time, a Bill to amend the Canadian Shipping Act and in the course of the debate a question was raised as to whether its provisions were within the powers of the Dominion Parliament, having regard to the Colonial Laws Validity Act and to certain recent enactments of the Imperial Parliament.

Supporting the view of the Minister of Marine and Fisheries, I expressed the following opinion:

In such matters it should be the duty of the Imperial Parliament always to consult the Government of Canada with respect to any amendments which concern this country. Constitutional writers, as the Minister of Marine and Fisheries and every lawyer in the House who has paid attention to constitutional law knows, affirm that there is a vast difference between the legal power to pass a statute or to perform a legislative act and the constitutional right to do it. The King in Great Britain, as part of the Imperial Parliament, has the technical right, the legal power, to disallow any statute of Great Britain since the reign of Queen Anne, and it may be said to have fallen into desuetude. Other instances could be given. While the Imperial Parliament has the absolute technical right to repeal the British North America Act, pro tanto, in respect to legislation affecting this country, I would respectfully submit that it has not the constitutional right to do so, without first consulting the Government of this country and ascertaining whether or not the proposed legislation will meet and fulfil the wants and requirements of the people of Canada; so I think it might well be stated to the Imperial Government that in respect of any proposed future amendments of the Merchant Shipping Act which concern or affect this country the Government and Parliament of Canada ought to be consulted in the first place before bringing about any such state of confusion as that which apparently does exist at the present moment. I would suggest that a respectful despatch along those lines would possibly prevent instances of this confusion being brought to our attention in future. The Parliament of Great Britain gave this Parliament, by the terms of the British North America Act, power exclusively to make laws with respect to this particular subject. That word "exclusively" has been construed by some authorities as relating to the distinction between Dominion jurisdiction and provincial jurisdiction. Other authorities have construed it more widely. Whether that be the case or not, it is certainly only constitutionally right that we should be consulted before any acts of the Imperial Government are passed which conflict with the opinion of the people of this country as expressed in their parliamentary enactments affecting the inland waters of Canada. . . .

During this session, which opened on November 28, 1907, and closed on July 20, 1908, the Government had put into force three articles of my Halifax platform, namely Civil Service reform, re-organization of the Railway Commission, and the placing of telegraph lines under the Railway Commission. . . .

On September 3, I began my campaign, as it was evident that a general election would take place before the end of the year. My opening meetings were in Nova Scotia, Mr. A. B. Crosby and I having been nominated for Halifax on August 19. The campaign was continued, almost without interruption, until October 23; the election took place on October 26.

In the seven weeks of the campaign I addressed more than sixty meetings and covered a very wide sweep of country from Halifax to Western Ontario. Time did not permit me to speak in the four Western Provinces which I had visited during the previous year.

In general I spoke upon the lines of the Halifax platform and laid emphasis upon the article which I regarded as most important. Especially did I emphasize civil service reform, state ownership and control of public utilities, improvement of the Intercolonial Railway, and a more efficient postal service with free rural mail delivery. I did not hesitate to express a frank and strong opinion with regard to the scandals that had been exposed since 1904, and the wasteful expenditure of the Government.

In Nova Scotia I addressed eight meetings in all; the main meeting was at Halifax on September 14, where I was assisted by Messrs. Roblin, Hanna, and Hazen; it was a large and enthusiastic gathering. I analyzed the Liberal platform of 1893 and showed its effect, and I expounded the Halifax platform, assuring my auditors that if we were returned to power it would be enforced. Defeat in a clean fight was better than triumph by corrupt or dubious methods.

I emphasized the effort of Government supporters to prevent disclosure of corruption and scandal in public affairs. If returned to power I would compel restitution, so far as practicable, from those who had pilfered from the public treasury.

Mr. Roblin, Mr. Hazen, and Mr. Hanna made eloquent and effective speeches and the enthusiasm of the audience indicated that Halifax would not repeat in 1908 its verdict of 1904. . . .

Perhaps the most important meeting of my tour was in Montreal on September 19. A strike by the employees of the Canadian Pacific Railway was in progress and the strikers thought it important to arrest public opinion by organized interruption at my meeting and by preventing me from speaking. A report of an independent paper, *The Toronto News*, describes the meeting as follows:

A determined, premeditated, and pre-arranged effort was made tonight to howl Mr. Borden down and to refuse him a hearing. It was not that he said things which displeased his audience, and from which it dissented; the effort to break up the meeting began before he arose to speak, and it simply was an attempt to prevent him from presenting his facts and arguments before the public of Montreal. The attempt failed signally. Mr. Borden fought and beat the interrupters; and his meeting was by far the better for the incident. It might be as well to set forth the more significant circumstances connected with the affair.

It was the work of a minority and not of a large minority. The meeting as a whole was strongly, heartily, and enthusiastically in favour of Mr. Borden. An ingenious device of the managers of the meeting proved this; when the disturbance was at its height the chairman called for counter-cheers for Mr. Borden, and the overwhelming bulk of the audience rose and cheered furiously. Here and there men retained their seats, showing them Liberals who had come to listen to him. . . .

The effect was that Mr. Borden showed himself as a fighting man. His unusual courtesy and his somewhat methodical and formal method of speech perhaps convey the impression to some that he lacks fire. Tonight he showed that his temper is high, and that his quiet means reserve of strength. It was interesting to see him before he was called upon, and while the disturbers were making a deafening din, which showed what his reception would be. Usually he leans far back in his chair when awaiting the chairman's call to speak. Tonight he was leaning forward, ready to spring to his feet, and his face lit up with animation and positive pleasure, evidently the prospect of the fight had stirred him up and was agreeable to him. Once he had plunged in, he faced his enemies, matched his one voice against their many, told them he would wait there till midnight, said that if necessary he would make his speech to the reporters, worked doggedly through and finally by degrees got the attention, and finally the quiet of the crowd. It was a prolonged struggle; he began at 8:45 o'clock; soon after nine o'clock it was evident that he was getting the crowd; by 9:10 or 9:15 he had won, all was quiet, and he was pursuing his argument, the only sign of combat, so far as he was concerned, being his unwonted animation and spirit. The gallery was policed later in his speech, but he had won before the extra constables arrived. . . .

I opened my Ontario tour at Pembroke on September 21. After emphasizing the points of the Halifax platform, I alluded to Sir Wilfrid's quip in which he paraphrased the words of King Charles II to his brother, afterwards King James, "They'll never kill me to make you King." Sir Wilfrid had likened himself to King Charles and I reminded my hearers that under Charles' reign the constitution was violated, the public revenues were squandered to maintain a dissolute court, the public domain was misappropriated, and conditions were set up which resulted in revolution. . . .

In twenty days I held thirty-seven meetings in Ontario.

In Halifax, not only leaders but the rank and file of our party had been thoroughly aroused by the wholesale purchase of votes in 1904. In addition, there was a strong force of independent opinion which was equally aroused and fully determined that every possible effort should be put forth in 1908, to prevent a repetition of the corrupt methods which had disgraced the constituency (Halifax) four years previously.

My former partner, W. B. A. Ritchie, K.C., took personal direction of measures for this purpose. Within the city limits a telephone was installed close to every polling booth; a capable lawyer with blank forms of warrants for arrest was stationed in each booth. Elaborate steps were taken to prevent personation and in addition, the Independent Citizens' Committee, under the presidency of the late Sir Frederick Fraser, did very active and effective work.

No great attention was paid to the offence of conveying voters to the polls, as this was considered inevitable. But, apart from that infraction of the Electoral Law, I believe that on both sides, the election of 1908 was as clean and free from bribery and corruption as could possibly be attained having regard to the infirmities of human character.

One gentleman, whose activities in 1904 were well known, was closely watched throughout the day, and there was considerable alarm when he suddenly disappeared; there was hurrying to and fro and it was strongly suspected that he was engaged in some nefarious work. It transpired that, for some unknown reason, he had betaken himself to a moving-picture show and had remained there about two hours.

The unusual character of the election was illustrated by a conversation between a commercial traveller and a well-known coloured man who hailed from a settlement near Halifax. Each party had been in the habit of holding meetings in this settlement, and after the meeting it was usual to provide a supper at which the party adherents enjoyed themselves with cold ham, biscuits, cheese, and beer. During this election the practice was discontinued; and Peter had come to Halifax to ascertain the regrettable cause of the discontinuance. A commercial traveller who met him in the market knew that he would obtain some amusement from the renowned "darky" and the following conversation took place:

C.T. *"Well Peter, have you come into town to see about the election?"*

PETER. *"Yes, suh, that's what I come to see about."*
C.T. *"Well, this is a different election from any other we have ever had."*
PETER. *"How come you say that, suh?"*
C.T. *"This year, Peter, there are to be no suppers."*
PETER. *"No suppahs, suh?"*
C.T. *"No, Peter. No ham, no biscuits, and no beer."*
PETER, *astonished and reflective—"No ham, no biscuits, no beer. Well, ah'll tell you, suh, if dat's so, there ain't gwine to be nobody elected."*

I was elected for both Halifax and Carleton but the general result was by no means what we had anticipated. In a House of 221, the Government had 6 seats less than in the previous House of 214. We gained 14 seats and reduced the Government's majority from 65 to 45. Outside Quebec, we had a small majority; and in the House the Government was practically without a majority except that derived from Quebec.

From 1904 to 1908 the Government had made an unfortunate and indeed evil record; extravagance and corruption had run riot in some of the departments. Public opinion had been profoundly disturbed, and the Halifax platform had appealed to a large body of independent electors. At this election (1908), the Liberal-Conservative Party would probably have made such gains as to deprive the Government of a sufficient working majority, except for the incident I am about to describe.

The most effective assistance to the Government came from a Liberal-Conservative quarter. The *Ne Temere* Decree of 1907 was agitating many minds about this time. A Roman Catholic gentleman has given to me the following explanation of the *Ne Temere* Decree:

It was an exclusively Catholic and exclusively theological matter. It was designed to remedy, within the Catholic Church, certain real evils arising from clandestine marriages of Catholics. Prior to the Decree of the Council of Trent, marriage not in face of the Church, e.g., marriage by common consent, in the absence even of witnesses, contracted per verba de praesenti, *was valid although subject to censure. The Council of Trent required, for validity, marriage in face of the Church, but provided that the decree should not have effect canonically unless promulgated by or with the consent of the civil power in the domains of such civil power. In consequence of this provision, until the* Ne Temere *Decree, canonically these clandestine marriages were good in England, Germany, United States (except Louisiana territory), Canada (except Quebec), the Scandinavian countries, Turkey, etc.* Ne Temere *provided for Catholics a common marriage law, designed to operate canonically and without any influence or reliance upon the law of any state. Its terms show this.*

Some members of the Orange Order, who were also members of the Liberal-Conservative Party and whose zeal outran their discretion, prepared and published in large numbers a pamphlet entitled *The Duty of the Hour*. The proposal to issue it was not made known to me; it did not have my sanction and I should have unhesitatingly forbidden its preparation and publication had I known of it. When it was first brought to my attention by a Liberal speaker who denounced its publication, I had no idea to what he was referring; later I made inquiries in Halifax where nothing seemed to be known of it. Thus, I was quite unable to deal with the situation which it created on the day of the election. The pamphlet exhorted the Protestant electors to vote against Sir Wilfrid Laurier becaues he was a Catholic and French. Probably it served no purpose whatever, so far as Protestant electors were concerned. But Liberal organizers saw their opportunity. They reproduced the pamphlet by thousands and circulated it, as if coming from the Liberal-Conservative Party, throughout the Catholic sections in many constituencies. I was told, after the election, that at many polling booths, Catholic priests, who had hitherto supported the Liberal-Conservative Party, stationed themselves with this pamphlet and besought members of their flock to cast their vote against a party that had resorted to such unworthy appeal.

In this election, we lost several prominent men, including W. H. Bennett, G. W. Fowler, A. A. Lefurgey, W. F. Cockshutt, J. G. Bergeron, A. E. Kemp, and others. On the other hand, there were some notable additions to our ranks, including Arthur Meighen, C. J. Doherty, Alexander Haggart, T. W. Crothers, W. B. Nantel, E. N. Rhodes, C. A. Magrath, J. D. Taylor, Wm. Price, A. S. Goodeve, Martin Burrell, J. W. Edwards, Glen Campbell, J. W. Maddin, G. H. Barnard, and Clarence Jameson.

Between 1904 and 1908, I had developed through experience, had become a more effective speaker, and had gained in large measure the confidence of my parliamentary following. During the same period, I had got into touch with the people of the country through constant campaigning and in this way, as well as through my work in Parliament, I had acquired increasing influence, and, in some measure had won the confidence of the rank and file of my party, and of many men not actively affiliated with either party.

We met in caucus very frequently whenever questions of policy, methods of attack, and the general outline of our course in Parliament were to be considered and discussed. There was lengthy consideration given on many occasions to the exact phraseology of the resolutions to be moved. Frequently, there were pronounced differences of opinion and in such cases the phrasing of the resolution, or the course to be adopted was left to my decision. This action of caucus involved, perhaps, too great an appreciation of my political sagacity and resourcefulness and sometimes it proved embarrassing.

During the next three sessions, from time to time, there was intrigue against me both within and without Parliament, as there had been against Edward Blake and Sir Wilfrid Laurier; Blake retired after his defeat in 1887 and Laurier, with great reluctance, accepted the leadership at the close of the first session in that year. It is certain that after Sir Wilfrid's defeat in 1891 he decided to retire and if he had not won in 1896, another leader would undoubtedly have been selected.

Failure is the unforgiveable sin of a political leader and it is not to be wondered at that a change should have been sought after the Conservative defeat in 1908.

However, the great majority of my followers were very loyal. The intrigue was chiefly instigated and carried on by three men,* one of them a new member, a man of great wealth, of strong opinions, and enormous self-confidence. He had conceived the idea that he could master the political situation within a few months after entering the House of Commons. Two old members of the party from Ontario came very much under his influence; it is known that their intrigue against me resulted in several singular and sometimes fantastic proposals. Less than two years later when we came into power these experts in political intrigue faced a situation which they had not anticipated and of which I was master. However, I realized that although their conduct had been short-sighted, mischievous, and maladroit, nevertheless they were sincere. Recalling Sir John A.

* [William Price, who was knighted in 1915; W. B. Northrup who was appointed Clerk of the House of Commons and J. D. Reid, who became Minister of Customs in 1911.]

Macdonald's maxim that one should never select a colleague by the standard of one's personal likes or dislikes, I admitted one of the intriguers as a colleague in the Cabinet and throughout my premiership I found him absolutely loyal on every occasion; another I appointed to an important post in the public service; and the third I recommended for knighthood.

We faced the session of 1909, encouraged by the reduction of the Government's majority but disappointed that the result had not been so favourable as we had anticipated. At the election of 1908, Sir Wilfrid Laurier received the first check since his accession to power in 1896. His majority had been reduced. . . . In a public vote of 1,150,000 he had a majority of less than 25,000; the tide of increasing success and popularity had begun to ebb.

Charles Marcil, member for Bonaventure, had been elected Speaker, and in supporting Sir Wilfrid Laurier's proposal in this regard, I called attention in a delicate way to Mr. Marcil's methods of campaigning. He had appealed for support upon the ground that he had secured very large appropriations for his constituency. I denounced this system of bribing constituencies by such appropriations and declared that it should be prohibited by statute. Alluding to the judicial quality of the speakership, I expressed the hope that Mr. Marcil would realize that a person filling so high an office could not, with dignity, be a suppliant for such favours.

The Speech from the Throne contained little of note beyond a reference to the International Waterways Treaty. Instead of a boastful reference to the prosperity of the country and the implicit claim that this was due to the Administration, there was a reference to the commercial, industrial, and financial depression upon which the entire civilized world was said to have entered. To this was added the rather mournful admission that this depression which had seriously affected Canada, had occasioned substantial shrinking in revenue, and called for exceptional caution.

In the debate upon the Address, I alluded at some length to the pamphlet called *The Duty of the Hour* (to which I have already referred), of which I had first heard on October 21 (five days before polling day) when it was being circulated among electors of a certain religious belief. After denying in most emphatic terms the innuendo that I was responsible for the pamphlet, I declared that any statement that it had emanated from or had been circulated by the Conservative Party or by any Conservative organization was a malicious and deliberate falsehood.

Sir Wilfrid had reviewed the results of the recent election, speaking particularly of British Columbia where his Government had sustained severe losses. He attributed these losses to attacks upon the Government's policy respecting Japanese immigration, and he denounced me for sending a telegram to Mr. Barnard, member for Victoria, which he quoted as:

> *Your message received. The Conservative party stands for a white Canada, the protection of white labour and the absolute exclusion of Asiatics.*

I immediately interposed and declared that I had sent no such telegram. Sir Wilfrid replied that he would put upon the table the facsimile of my alleged message. I retorted that he might put it on the table or under the table, but that I never sent a telegram in those words.

The message which I sent was not to Mr. Barnard, but to the *Victoria Colonist* and was as follows:

> *Your message received. The Conservative Party stands for a white Canada and the absolute protection of white labour.*

After its receipt it was fraudulently altered by a reporter, a copy thus altered was taken to Mr. Barnard who was then addressing a public meeting and it was read by Mr. Barnard in good faith.

~ In noting that the Waterways Treaty was before the American Congress but not the Canadian Parliament, Borden suggested that treaties should have a clause to the effect that they will not become binding on His Majesty until they have been ratified by the Parliament of Canada. Laurier agreed with the suggestion. ~

On January 22 Mr. Justice Cassels tabled his report of the investigation he had been conducting into the affairs of the Department of Marine and Fisheries. A number of high officials of that department were severely criticized; the political patronage system of the past was analyzed and condemned, and suggestions were offered and recommendations made for the more efficient conduct of the affairs of various departments of the service.

~ Later in the session the Cassels report was vigorously debated, with an argument between Laurier and Foster which led to the "most violent and stormy scene" within Borden's memory. After a calming intervention by Borden, Sir Wilfred withdrew the remarks (in reference to manipulation of stock funds) which had aroused Foster.

The Conservatives had moved for "a thorough and un-trammelled investigation by a competent business commission into the workings of all the great spending departments of the Government."~

In 1907 I had begun to make a study of the natural resources of Canada and I was surprised at the paucity of available information respecting their variety and importance.

On February 1, 1909, I moved the following resolution:

That in the opinion of this House it is advisable to appoint a select standing committee on natural resources who shall have authority to inquire into and consider and report upon all matters appertaining to the conservation and development of the natural resources of Canada, including fisheries, forests, mines, minerals, waterways, and water powers, and to whom may be referred from time to time any report, document, or matter touching the subject which they are appointed to consider.

I spoke upon this resolution at considerable length and the general tenor of my remarks may be summarized as follows: there was a Committee on Agriculture which was undoubtedly the principal basis of the country's wealth but it was necessary to consider also our fisheries, forests, mines, minerals, water-ways, and water-powers, the extent of which was not then realized. The development and conservation of these resources were of immense importance. Conservation did not mean non-use but was consistent with such reasonable use as was necessary for development. On the other hand development did not imply destruction or waste but should be of such a character as to transmit to future generations a continuing heritage.

After referring to the Forestry Congress, convened three years previously by the Prime Minister, and to the work of the Forestry Branch of the Interior Department, I laid emphasis upon the excellent work carried on in the United States by the Forestry Service of that country over which Dr. Gifford Pinchot then presided. He had recently delivered an inspiring address in Ottawa and I quoted at some length therefrom.

Referring to the importance of our fisheries I expressed my belief that they were not carried on as thoroughly and efficiently as would be possible. On both Atlantic and Pacific coasts there were many species of fish not utilized but which would eventually be utilized for food. The fisheries of the Atlantic should be made to supply Quebec and Ontario.

Coming to the forests, I pointed out the remarkable results attained in Saxony by the development, under state control, of about 430,000 acres of rough mountain land which yielded a gross revenue of nearly seven dollars per acre and a net revenue of nearly four and a half dollars per acre. Estimating the forest areas of the United States and Canada, respectively, I reached the conclusion that the actual area in each country would not exceed 250,000,000 acres; and that, notwithstanding the enormous denudation of United States' forests, that country still possessed reserves slightly greater than those of Canada. After pointing out that fire had destroyed more of our forests than lumbermen had utilized, I urged the need of forest protection.

Coming to the waterways and water-powers, I declared that water-powers would eventually prove a more valuable asset to the people of Canada than all our coal and other minerals, all our iron, all our gold and silver combined. They should be investigated, estimated, and scheduled. They should not be subject to exploitation for purely individual profit, but should be conserved as an asset held in trust by the state for the benefit of the whole people.

Dealing then with the advisability of appointing a committee, I emphasized the decreasing influence of Parliament as compared with the increasing influence of the Cabinet. This development I did not regard as healthy. Such a committee as I proposed would bring Parliament into closer touch with matters of urgent moment. In this connection, I spoke of the immense export of our pulp wood for which we were receiving six or seven dollars per cord, while labour bestowed upon it in the United States made it worth about ten times as much in the eventual market.

Finally I declared that the initiative as to conservation and development should come from Parliament, without regard to party. And, striking out all partisan considerations, we should take up this all-important work.

Some discussion arose and eventually Sir Wilfrid Laurier, expressing himself as fully in accord with the principle which I had put forward, suggested that more than one committee might well be established and, subject to this amendment, he proposed that my motion should be adopted.

Accordingly, my resolution carried; and it bore excellent fruit in the legislation introduced by Mr. Fisher which provided for a permanent commission on the conservation of natural resources and appears as Chapter 27 of the Acts of 1909.

~ In discussion of a bill to incorporate a power company, Borden took issue with Laurier's contention that Parliament had power to expropriate land belonging to a provincial government. ~

... On March 4 the Secretary of State introduced a Bill to establish a Department of External Affairs; he proposed that this Department should be the common centre for all communications relating to matters other than those of purely internal concern, that it should be presided over by the Secretary of State, and that the Governor-in-Council should appoint an officer to be the deputy head. It was passed without division on April 16.

Sir Wilfrid explained that the purpose was three-fold: (a) to allot and distribute despatches; (b) to prepare and keep up from day to day a history of each question to which reference could be made; and (c) to prepare for submission to the Minister or to Council a memorandum or reply to any communication from abroad.

An interesting discussion ensued. Following Sir Wilfrid, I agreed that these objects were both desirable and necessary, but I was at a loss to understand the necessity of a new department in order to achieve them. In the United States there were only nine departments, one of them being the Department of the Secretary of State which dealt with all foreign relations, and I emphasized the fact that the foreign relations of Canada were very limited in comparison to those of that country. I suggested that the present Administration needed better organization rather than more machinery. The new department should be under the direction of the Prime Minister as was the case in Australia. Matters of a confidential character, some of which possibly could not be disclosed even to the Cabinet as a whole, should come in the first instance to the Prime Minister.[1]

The question of Canada's contribution to Imperial Defence was the subject of an important discussion during this session. On March 29, Mr. Foster moved the following resolution:

That in the opinion of this House, in view of her great and varied resources, of her geographical position and national environments, and of that spirit of self-help and self-respect which alone befits a strong and growing people, Canada should

---

[1] In 1912 the administration of the Department of External Affairs was transferred to the Prime Minister.

*no longer delay in assuming her proper share of the responsi-
bility and financial burden incident to the suitable protection
of her exposed coast line and great seaports.*

He made a powerful and eloquent speech in support of his
motion and was followed by Sir Wilfrid Laurier who paid him
a generous tribute. Sir Wilfrid declared that his only objection
to the motion was its lack of definite policy. He took strong
exception to the implication that Canada had been remiss in
the duty she owed the Empire and finally he submitted the
following as a substitute:

*This House fully recognizes the duty of the people of
Canada, as they increase in numbers and wealth, to assume in
larger measure the responsibilities of national defence.*

*The House reaffirms the opinion, repeatedly expressed by
representatives of Canada, that under the present constitutional
relations between the mother country and the self-governing
dominions the payment of any stated contribution to the
imperial treasury for naval and military purposes would not,
so far as Canada is concerned, be a satisfactory solution of the
question of defence.*

*The House has observed with satisfaction the relief afforded
in recent years to the taxpayers of the United Kingdom through
the assumption by the Canadian people of considerable military
expenditure formerly charged upon the imperial treasury.*

*The House will cordially approve of any necessary expen-
diture designed to promote the organization of a Canadian
naval service in co-operation with and in close relation to the
imperial navy, along the lines suggested by the admiralty at the
last Imperial Conference, and in full sympathy with the view
that the naval supremacy of Great Britain is essential to the
security of commerce, the safety of the empire, and the peace
of the world.*

*The House expresses its firm conviction that whenever the
need arises the Canadian people will be found ready and willing
to make any sacrifice that is required to give to the imperial
authorities the most loyal and hearty co-operation in every
movement for the maintenance of the integrity and the honour
of the empire.*

Following Sir Wilfrid, I emphasized Canada's full control
of her own affairs and maintained that this absolute autonomy
had strengthened the ties which bound our country to the
Empire. The evolution by which self-government had been

accomplished was due to the fact that the constitutional law of the Empire was, for the most part, an unwritten law.

I alluded to the power of custom superimposed upon law, to the limitation of constitutional law by the growth of custom. In Great Britain the King's veto, although not formally abolished, had ceased to exist; similarly the legal power of the British Parliament to alter our constitution without our consent had disappeared, if it ever existed.

Contrasting our considerable expenditure for military with our lack of expenditure for naval purposes, I pointed out the magnitude of Canada's sea-borne commerce and urged that our effort should be devoted in greater measure to the development of naval defence. Our best course was to establish a Canadian naval force. Fully concurring in the Prime Minister's eloquent words respecting the necessity of maintaining the integrity of the Empire, I urged that we should act in conjunction with and by the advice of the British Admiralty whose experience and expert knowledge would be indispensable.

Coming to the terms of the Prime Minister's proposed resolution, I invited him to consider that the day might come, "tomorrow, next week, or next month," when the only aid we could afford would be a contribution. Therefore, I suggested that the second paragraph of the resolution should be so amended as to provide for such a possibility. It seemed inappropriate and unnecessary to set forth in such a resolution by Canada a mere negation by declaring that no contribution ought to be made under any circumstances. Further, the third paragraph ought to be omitted. Canada's contributions to the defence of the Empire were inconsiderable in comparison with the enormous amounts paid by British taxpayers for many years past. Such a reference was altogether too trivial in so important a resolution. Then I urged the inclusion of words in the fourth paragraph to indicate the intention to act promptly. I concluded as follows:

> You say that we may rest contented to depend for our naval defence on Great Britain. Well, if we have assumed the status of a nation in one respect, shall we adhere to the status of a Crown colony in other and still more important respects?
>
> You speak of a Monroe doctrine, but that doctrine would not defend our coasts, our cities, and our commerce from the attacks of any foe; and it is idle to suggest that we could, in the case of a great naval war, obtain any measure of comfort from the Monroe doctrine. . . . We desire that this resolution should

*go out as the unanimous resolution of the parliament of Canada
to the whole world.
. . . It should go in such terms as would entitle the Canadian
people to the gratitude of the empire and do much to restore
to the people of this country that self-respect in which, it seems
to me, we have been somewhat lacking in these days when
others have done so much, and we so little, for naval defence
so absolutely essential to the integrity and the maintenance of
our great Empire.*

Rather a lengthy discussion ensued and at its conclusion
Sir Wilfrid announced that the suggestions which I had made
would be accepted by that side of the House and he modified
the terms of his resolution as at first proposed so that it would
read as follows:

*This House fully recognizes the duty of the people of
Canada, as they increase in numbers and wealth, to assume in
larger measure the responsibilities of national defence.
The House is of opinion that under the present constitutional relations between the mother country and the self-governing dominions, the payment of regular and periodical
contributions to the imperial treasury for naval and military
purposes would not, so far as Canada is concerned, be the most
satisfactory solution of the question of defence.
The House will cordially approve of any necessary expenditure designed to promote the speedy organization of a
Canadian naval service in co-operation with and in close relation
to the imperial navy, along the lines suggested by the admiralty
at the last Imperial Conference, and in full sympathy with the
view that the naval supremacy of Britain is essential to the
security of commerce, the safety of the empire, and the peace
of the world.
The House expresses its firm conviction that whenever the
need arises the Canadian people will be found ready and willing
to make any sacrifice that is required to give to the imperial
authorities the most loyal and hearty co-operation in every
movement for the maintenance of the integrity and honour of
the empire.*

The motion as amended was unanimously agreed to.
On October 26, there was a banquet at Winnipeg in honour
of Mr. Foster at which I was not present. Mr. Roblin made a
strong appeal for a contribution to the Imperial navy and
against any "toy navy." The Press seemed to indicate an

immense body of opinion in favour of a similar policy; and doubt was expressed as to the efficacy of the proposals set forth in the resolution of the previous session. Mr. Roblin's view was supported also by a number of prominent men in our party, including Mr. McBride, Mr. Rogers, Mr. Haultain, Mr. Hazen, and several others.

On October 29, I issued the following Press statement in connection with Naval Policy:

So far as the Conservative Party is concerned, the question of Canada's participation in the organization and maintenance of Imperial naval defence rests today exactly where it did when the unanimous Resolution of Parliament was passed on the 29th March last. That Resolution was so modified as to permit of a special contribution in time of emergency. Whether such emergency existed then or is imminent today is within the knowledge of the British Government and of the Canadian Government. The report of the procedings of the recent Imperial Conference when laid before our Parliament will doubtless throw some light on the subject; Canada should take no action which does not receive the unqualified approval of the British naval experts.

On November 1, I spoke at Toronto with Mr. Foster. We did not go into details as to the Conservative attitude respecting the naval question but I said:

It is my own belief that a Canadian unit of the Imperial navy may be made powerful and effective. I also believe that our own natural resources and raw material, and above all, our labouring population, ought to be considered and employed so far as may be reasonably possible. That course is incident to the policy of protection. The advice of the best naval experts of the Empire should be secured and nothing undertaken without the full approval of the Admiralty. Our action should be inspired and characterized by neither hysteria nor indifference, but by a solemn and abiding sense of national responsibility. . . .

~ In the debate on a bill authorizing a loan to the Grand Trunk Pacific, Borden was sharply critical of the government's railway policy. "Sir Wilfrid had estimated the cost of the Mountain Section at $18,000,000. The actual expenditure would be $67,500,000. Mr. Fielding had estimated the cost from Moncton to Winnipeg at $71,156,000; the actual expenditure would be $124,403,000." He recalled his own 1904 proposal that since nine-tenths of the financial support was being supplied by the Canadian people, the Government might well go one step further and assume complete ownership. ~

Parliament was prorogued on May 19. The Opposition had strengthened its position in some respects and had continued to impose its policies upon the Government. Another plank of my Halifax platform—free rural mail delivery—had been adopted.

The important disclosures made by the First Lord of the Admiralty in the British House as to Germany's naval plans, which threatened Great Britain's supremacy on the seas, had changed the whole tone of Empire politics, and had turned the thoughts of all to the question of Empire defence. These disclosures had been productive of the resolution unanimously agreed to by the Canadian Parliament; and the question began to be the subject of wide discussion and heated controversy in our country. An Imperial Defence Conference was to be held in London in July and Canada was invited to participate. Sir Wilfrid Laurier named as Canada's representatives to that Conference Sir Frederick Borden and Mr. Brodeur.

On September 18, the official report of the conclusions of the Imperial Defence Conference was tabled at Ottawa.

The Admiralty presented a memorandum in which it was clearly set forth that:

The greatest output of strength for a given expenditure is obtained by the maintenance of a single navy with the concomitant unity of training and unity of command;

and that

The maximum of power would be gained if all parts of the Empire contributed, according to their needs and resources, to the maintenance of the British navy.

This was the first proposition. The second, which had relation to the desire of some of the Dominions to create local navies, was as follows:

In the opinion of the Admiralty, a Dominion Government desirous of creating a navy should aim at forming a distinct fleet unit; and the smallest unit is one which, while manageable in time of peace, is capable of being used in its component parts in time of war.

The Canadian delegates would not accept either suggestion, but asked the Admiralty for two plans, one designed for an annual expenditure of £600,000; and the other for an annual expenditure of £400,000. The Admiralty, accordingly, prepared such plans; finally the first plan was the basis of the Navy Act of 1910. . . .

~ In late June Borden made his first trip to Britain in fourteen years.

At a Dominion day dinner he said: ~

Some feeling was created in the British Isles owing to the fact that Canada did not by Resolution, or by speech from the Prime Minister, vouchsafe the offer of one, two or three dreadnoughts. I think the Resolution in the form in which it was passed, while its terms might not upon their surface seem as significant at the moment as the offer of one or two dreadnoughts would have been, laid down a permanent policy for the Dominion of Canada upon which both parties united and which would serve a more practical purpose than any such offer of dreadnoughts. The Resolution which was the outcome of a conference between myself and Sir Wilfrid Laurier, entered into before the remarkable utterances of British statesmen of all parties, was designed to show to the world Canada's unanimity of desire to take her full share, when necessary, in securing the safety and integrity of the Empire. . . .

While in England I gave an interview in which I especially dwelt upon the character and responsibilities of immigration into Canada. In speaking of the influx of United States citizens, I said:

The Americans make excellent settlers. But we have not yet learnt how to deal with non-British emigrants as the Americans do with their new citizens. In the United States the greatest pains are taken to train the children of foreign settlers to become good American citizens, and to respect and revere the Stars and Stripes.

Some restriction of emigration is necessary. I know little of the method of enforcement. It is useless to attempt to send Canada men of twenty-five or thirty fears of age who have led vagabond or criminal lives, and who have acquired tendencies which cannot easily be combated at that age even in a new country. If, however, children of the submerged class are taken at an early age and sent to Canada, brought up in homes provided for the purpose in decent surroundings and with proper influences and education, the problem solves itself. . . .

While in England I met for the first time Mr. Bonar Law at a dinner given in my honour by Mr. (later Sir) Fabian Ware.

The methods of parliamentary government were discussed and I asked Mr. Law as to the use in Great Britain of the caucus system, explaining that in Canada measures as to which differences of opinion might arise within a party were usually discussed at a caucus of members and senators, so that the proposals might be fully explained in advance, criticisms answered, and an estimate of the situation obtained. I also observed that members with grievances were afforded in caucus the opportunity of "exploding" which was far better than to have internal differences discussed on the floor of the House. Mr. Law said that no such system prevailed in Great Britain but that on occasion when some important question or policy had to be determined, Mr. Balfour would call ten or a dozen of his leading supporters into conference. "But," said Mr. Law, "the only result, so far as I could observe, was this: each one of us endeavoured, by the exercise of his best ingenuity, to ascertain what was Mr. Balfour's opinion and then proclaimed himself entirely in favour of that view." . . .

After my return from England, I announced my decision to retire from the representation of Carleton County and to sit again for Halifax. On October 4, Opposition members of both Houses of Parliament tendered me a banquet in Ottawa at which practically every Conservative representative was present. Mr. Monk presided and introduced me in most enthusiastic terms. In my speech, referring to the expenditures of the Government, I said:

> *They have murdered economy who swore loyalty to it, but still they are hardened and unrepentant. Like the three famous witches invoked by the Thane of Cawdor the three demons, Extravagance, Folly, and Corruption, swing joyously hand in hand, in wildest dance around the Government cauldron.* . . .

On October 15, I spoke at the Halifax County Convention; discussing Canada's future in connection with the Empire, I asked:

> *How shall we stand in the future within this Empire? Shall we, as Mr. Goldwin Smith desires and predicts, become part of the great American Republic? Shall we follow the aspirations of Sir Wilfrid Laurier who hopes and believes that Canada will sever her connection with the British Empire as a ripe apple drops from a tree?*
> *Or, shall we follow the ideal of Sir John A. Macdonald who foresaw and predicted a cordial and healthy alliance with the*

mother country by which Canada would become a powerful nation owning allegiance to the British sovereign and flag and maintaining the advantage of connection with the greatest Empire of the World?

Speaking on naval defence I said:

The House of Commons last session laid down a certain policy touching naval defence in which both political parties united. It may not have satisfied the aspirations of all Conservatives; but it seemed our bounden duty to place, if possible, above the limits of partisan strife a question so vital and far-reaching and to attain the standard which has for many years governed both political parties in Great Britain with respect to foreign relations.

How the present Administration will work out the policy which was outlined by the resolution to which I have alluded, remains to be seen. One governing principle at least should control, namely, that out of our own materials, by our own labour, and by the instructed skill of our own people, any necessary provision for our naval defence should be made so far as may be reasonably possible.

I also announced that a convention would he held in the early part of 1910; this convention, in view of subsequent events, did not take place.

13: *1909-1910*

The session of 1909–10 opened on November 11. After reference to prosperity and growth, the Address alluded to the commercial treaty with France, progress in the construction of the transcontinental railway, the plans for reconstruction of the Quebec Bridge. But the most interesting announcement was the proposal to establish a Canadian naval service. . . .

Speaking on the Address I observed that while the rapid growth and general prosperity of Canada had been alluded to, no reference had been made to the equally rapid and remarkable growth of the national debt. Dealing with naval defence, I said that I neither opposed nor denounced the proposals of the Government for the reason that as yet I did not know what they were. I promised that reasonable and fair consideration would be given to these proposals and I urged that they should be brought down as soon as possible. I congratulated Mr. Mackenzie King upon his accession to the Cabinet and I reminded the House that this was the sixth occasion upon which the Prime Minister had gone outside the House of Commons for a Cabinet Minister.

In his reply, Sir Wilfrid remarked that he could not discuss all the questions I had raised. As to expenditure, he believed that the people of Canada were quite content with the Government's policy. He repudiated Mr. Monk's charge of unnecessary secrecy as to the report of the Defence Conference and he drew attention to the rule that when a conference takes place the report of it is not made public without the consent of all the parties to it. He added, however, that he thought it proper to have a word on the subject before the papers were brought down. He then alluded to rumours that the Conservative Party was seriously divided in opinion on the subject of naval defence. He understood from recent Press reports that several prominent members of the Opposition had come out openly with declarations that nothing would satisfy them except a contribution in money from Canada into the British treasury and of such an amount as would at least build a dreadnought. He recalled that the question of naval defence was not a new one but that it had been considered in 1902 and tha the resolution at that time had been precisely the resolution adopted by the House in the previous March. He said further:

if the British Empire is to remain strong as it is today, it will not be by compelling the daughter nations to revolve as satellites around the mother country but by allowing every daughter nation to develop herself to the fullest extent possible so that it may add to the strength of the whole.

He then referred to what he terms the "stand-patters" among the Opposition members, designating Mr. Monk as chief of that class and he proceeded to attack that gentleman for a speech which he recently made at Lachine. He claimed that Mr. Monk, in stating that the Government's proposed project would cost annually $20,000,000, had deliberately appealed to prejudice and that the statement was made without knowledge; further that Mr. Monk's assertion to the effect that were we to build a Canadian navy we would thereby be drawn into every European war was another deliberate appeal to prejudice.

Need I say to my hon. friend that whether we have such a navy or not, we do not lose our right to self-government; if we do have a navy that navy will go to no war unless the Parliament of Canada, including the hon. gentleman, choose to send it.

On January 5, 1910, I announced the personnel of the preliminary committee of the national Liberal-Conservative Convention to which allusion had been made in the previous October. A meeting took place at Ottawa on January 24, at which it was unanimously agreed that the convention should be held. Mr. Perley was elected chairman and Mr. Blount, secretary; and it was decided that the Convention should be held at Ottawa on June 15. However, on March 1, Messrs. Lacoste, Chase Casgrain, Beaubien, Emard, Coderre, and others came to discuss matters with me. Quebec Conservatives, under the leadership of Mr. Monk, were refusing to follow my lead on the naval question. Mr. Monk had allied himself with M. Bourassa in opposition to any naval action for the time being, either by naval construction or contribution, and they were loudly proclaiming this view throughout Quebec. A party convention without the Province of Quebec would have been a farce and thus the Convention was put off.

The attitude thus announced by Mr. Monk indicated a serious difference of opinion between the Conservatives of Quebec and those of the English-speaking provinces. The situation was full of embarrassment. On the one hand, Quebec Conservatives affirmed with vehemence that I had gone altogether too far; on the other hand, many Conservative leaders in the English-speaking provinces were firmly of opinion that I had not gone far enough.

It seemed to me that the position I had taken was reasonable in not being extreme. I had supported the proposal of establishing a Canadian naval service which, in the event of war, must necessarily constitute an integral part of the Empire's naval defence. On the other hand, I had induced Sir Wilfrid Laurier so to modify his resolution that in the event of emergency, Canada could make an immediate and effective contribution to that defence. . . .

14: The Naval Service Bill *1910*

In dealing with the proposal for naval aid to Great Britain, Sir Wilfrid Laurier was obliged to have regard to constitutional considerations, to the conclusions of the recent Imperial Defence Conference, and to political and sympathetic prejudices that would inevitably be aroused in Quebec and in Ontario. There were elements in the situation that could not be reconciled. Undoubtedly there was pressure from his colleagues in the English-speaking provinces that urged immediate and effective action. On the other hand, there was undoubted antagonism in Quebec to any considerable expenditure for the purpose of Empire defence. There is no doubt that Sir Wilfrid would have been glad, if political conditions had permitted it, to refrain from any immediate action which necessarily would involve embarrassment, possible detriment, or even disaster.

As I have explained, I was equally embarrassed; the resolution to which I had agreed, with some reluctance, in 1909, was regarded by extremists in the English-speaking provinces as setting forth a dilatory, ineffective, and unsatisfactory policy. The cabal or cabals that were intriguing against me had endeavoured to arouse in the English-speaking provinces strong criticism of my course. Then, in the Province of Quebec, Mr. Monk had deliberately broken with us on the question and had denounced in vehement terms any proposal for expenditure in aid of the Empire's naval forces.

The debate initiated by Sir Wilfrid Laurier in introducing the Naval Service Bill on January 12, 1910, was by far the most important episode of the session. In the absence of Mr. Brodeur, Sir Wilfrid introduced the measure and briefly explained its provisions. He declared that the Government had not seen fit to accept, for the present, the Admiralty's suggestion for a naval unit on the Pacific. The decision was to have part of the Canadian force on the Atlantic and part on the Pacific. At the conference of 1909, two alternatives had been suggested, one of seven and the other of eleven ships. The latter proposal had been accepted by the Government whose intention it was to commence construction immediately and, if possible, in Canada. In résumé the Bill provided for the creation of a naval force comprised of three classes—permanent, reserve, and volunteer forces—and the naval service might be placed at the disposal of His Majesty in case of war. Answering Mr. Sproule's question whether "war" referred to war in any part of the Empire or in Canada only, Sir Wilfrid stated:

War everywhere. When Britain is at war, Canada is at war; there is no distinction.

One passage in his speech was in somewhat strong contrast with his attitude upon the Military Service Bill in 1917:

Under the Militia Act it is provided that the whole male population of Canada, from the age of 18 to the age of 60, is liable to military service. Should an emergency arise the whole male population within these ages may be called upon for service. Some discretion is vested in the government under the law. The first class is composed of men from 18 to 30 years of age, the second class of men from 30 to 45, and the last class of men from 45 to 60 years of age, and should the volunteer force in its different classes not be sufficient there may be an enrolment and balloting under the law. Nothing of that kind is to take place under the present Bill, no man in this country, under the Naval Service Act or any other, will be liable to military service on the sea.

Following Sir Wilfrid I emphasized Canada's debt to the Empire for protection of her commerce, the security of her shores upon every sea and in every land, and for the benefits and prestige which were hers on account of that connection. I congratulated the Prime Minister on his recession from the view previously expressed by him: "If we do have a navy that navy will go to no war unless the Parliament of Canada choose to send it." I vigorously asserted the principle that upon the high seas in times of war all British fleets were one. The proposed force should be regarded as a unit of the British navy under Canadian control and autonomy in management during peace times. I expressed my conviction that Great Britain would never engage in war without consulting the Dominions and I founded this belief on her action in the case of the South African War.

In dealing with the outcry against militarism I said:

I am opposed to militarism. . . . The fact that war exists today, the fact that preparation for war is maintained upon so gigantic a scale upon the continent of Europe is the best possible evidence that what we call the civilization of the twentieth century is only a very thin veneer over a certain underlying barbarism which has always prevailed throughout the world. . . . There is no doubt about the evil of war.

I strongly advocated that a Defence Committee, composed of men from both parties in Great Britain as well as from the self-governing nations of the Empire, should be given some control over the organization of Imperial Defence, and that as an outcome of such a committee or conference, Great Britain would engage in no great war without knowing beforehand that she had the support and sympathy of the Dominions:

This would give to these dominions a voice in the control of war, because I thoroughly agree that if we are to take part in the permanent defence of this great empire we must have some control and some voice in such matters.

I was not of opinion that the establishment of a Canadian navy would have any separatist tendency provided that co-operation and close relation to the Imperial navy were observed.

Dealing with the suggestion that there should be an annual contribution to the mother country for the purpose of naval defence, I said:

I am free to admit that from the strategical point of view, I would be inclined to agree with the view of the admiralty that this would be the best way for the great self-governing dominions of the Empire to make their contributions. But, from a constitutional and political stand point, I am opposed to it for many reasons. In the first place I do not believe that it would endure. In the second place it would be a source of friction. It would become a bone of partisan contention. It would be subject to criticism as to the character and the amount of the contribution in both parliaments. It would not be permanent or continuous. It would conduce, if anything could conduce, to severing the present connection between Canada and the Empire. . . . Permanent co-operation in defence, in my opinion, can only be accomplished by the use of our own material, the employment of our own people, and the development and utilization of our own skill and resourcefulness, and above all by impressing upon the people a sense of responsibility in their share in international affairs.

However, my contention was that, in view of the German situation, an emergency contribution should be forthcoming from Canada. This, I contended, in no way affected our autonomy:

Have we not given subsidies to cable companies, to railway companies, to steamship companies? Have we not sent contributions to San Francisco and to Italy in times of disaster?

I emphasized the German peril in the following words:

The right hon. gentleman says the British navy is supreme today. I do not dispute it; there is not a man in the Empire disputes it. But the question is not of today, but of tomorrow; the question is of next year and the year after that. Britain, through the mouths of her wisest, sanest and ablest sons has told us within a few months that her hour of peril is fast approaching. Take the facts and nothing but the facts as they are known today, and no one can dispute that the naval supremacy of Great Britain which, as we declared in March last, is absolutely essential to the integrity of the Empire, is openly and avowedly challenged as it has not been challenged for more than a century.

I emphasized the growing military power and the progress of industry and naval strength in Germany and I spoke of the challenge issued by that country to the supremacy of the naval power of Great Britain:

If the Germans prove themselves the greater race, if they have greater resourcefulness, higher skill, superior organizing ability, and more sincere and self-sacrificing patriotism, they are entitled to be supreme on the sea as they now are on the land. We have no right to resent the challenge, but unless the ancestral blood flows less red in our veins we shall meet it with a heart no less firm than that with which our forefathers encountered the shock of the "Invincible Armada."

Further, I said:

No one pretends that the British navy is not supreme today, but the continuance of that supremacy will cease within the next two or three years at least, unless extraordinary efforts are made by the mother country and all the great dominions.

Referring to the Prime Minister's contention that the situation in Europe was not so serious as had been announced, I remarked:

These statements (statements of the Prime Minister to the Secretary for Foreign Affairs and to the First Lord of the Admiralty) pointed to a crisis and an emergency and a peril which might face the British Empire within two or three years at the outside. Has that peril passed? No, Sir, we are nearer to it by nearly a year. Has Germany's policy been modified in the meantime? No, on the contrary Germany has since put forward

*the greatest naval budget in her history: $105,434,000, $60,-
000,000 of which are to be devoted to construction and armament alone. My right hon. friend may dismiss all this with a
wave of the hand and an eloquent phrase and he may say there
is no danger and no peril. . . . I do not say there will be war; I
do not know nor does the Prime Minister know. I trust, I hope,
I pray there will not be war. But, without war, without the
firing of a shot or the striking of a blow, without invasion,
German naval supremacy would bring the Empire to an end.
It is idle to assure that there will be no war. The war has already
begun, the war of construction, and victory will be as decisive
there as in actual battle.*

Upon Canada's position in this general connection I said:

*I can understand the man who advocates independence.
In that case with ten thousand miles of coast line and a great
sea-borne commerce, we must of necessity become a naval
power at enormously increased expense or else remain the
plaything and laughing-stock of the world. I can understand
the man, if such there be in Canada, who conscientiously
advocates the union of this country with the great neighbouring
republic, but let him remember that such a union would be
followed by naval and military charges of from twenty to
twenty-five millions per annum. I cannot, however, understand
how any man receiving and accepting the protection of the
British flag, the advantages of British citizenship, the safe-
guarding of our coasts, the security of our shores, the benefits
and advantages of the diplomatic and consular service throughout the world can reconcile it with our self-respect to have
every dollar of the cost paid by the over-burdened taxpayers
of the British Islands. . . . If my country, one of the richest
in the world, in proportion to its population, should accept the
humiliating, the degrading, the pauperizing position of receiving
future protection and safety at the hands and cost of the British
taxpayer without contributing one dollar in aid or assistance,
I would say that the sooner the Empire was rid of her the better
for all.*

I concluded as follows:

*When the battle of Armageddon comes, when the Empire
is fighting for its existence, when our kinsmen of the other
great dominions are in the forefront of the battle, shall we sit
silent and inactive while we contemplate with smug satisfaction*

*our increasing crops and products, or, shall we pauper-like seek
fancied but delusive security in an appeal to the charity of
some indefinite and high-sounding political doctrine of a great
neighbouring nation? No, a thousand times no. There will be
no such outcome. It may be that the Canadian people absorbed
in the development of their marvellous natural resources, have
paid little heed to the wideworld activities of the Empire and
have realized but imperfectly the responsibilities and duties
of their country as one of its greatest dominions. But they do
not lack the intelligence, the vision, the courage, the patriotism
necessary to realize those duties and accept those responsibilities. So, if Canada be true to herself she will not fail in the day
of trial, but stand proud, powerful and resolute in the very
forefront of the sister nations. But she must not stand unpre-
pared. I say to my right hon. friend the Prime Minister, so far
as my words have any weight with him: "Go on with your naval
service. Proceed slowly, cautiously and surely. Lay your proposals before the people and give them if necessary opportunity
to be heard, but do not forget that we are confronted with an
emergency which may rend this Empire asunder before the
proposed service is worthy of the name. In the face of such a
situation immediate, vigorous, earnest action is necessary. We
have no dreadnought ready, we have no fleet unit at hand.
But we have the resources and I trust the patriotism to provide
a fleet unit or at least a dreadnought without one moment's unnecessary delay. Or, and in my opinion this would be the better
course, we can place the equivalent in cash at the disposal of
the Admiralty to be used for naval defence under such
conditions as we may prescribe. In taking this course we shall
fulfil, not only in the letter but in the spirit as well, the resolution
of March last, and what is infinitely more important we shall
discharge a great patriotic duty to our country and to the whole
Empire."*

Mr. Monk followed; he admitted that he differed in opinion
from many of his party; however, he claimed the privilege of
expressing his own view. He believed that the situation in
England had been much exaggerated and that there had been
temporary panic. He claimed that the Prime Minister's amendment to Mr. Foster's resolution of March 29 had entirely
changed the sense of the original motion. His understanding
of the motion as agreed to was that it conveyed to the mother
country an assurance that Canada would take her part should

the mother country be threatened by a powerful enemy. He seriously doubted whether Canada was in a position to build and maintain a navy worthy of the name.

The Bill came up for second reading on February 3; Sir Wilfrid, in an able, eloquent, though somewhat discursive speech, reviewed the Liberal attitude toward defence in 1902.[1] He recalled that at the Imperial Conference in that year Great Britain had suggested a yearly contribution from the Dominions beyond the seas. To this suggestion most of the Dominions represented agreed. However, Canada had dissented, putting forth the view that as our country increased in wealth and population it would go further in the matter of defence and that in everything undertaken in that direction there would be maintained the strictest co-operation with the Imperial authorities, but "Always and ever under the control and responsibility of the Canadian authorities, in accordance with our right to self-government in this as in all matters." This policy, he declared, was again affirmed at the Conference of 1907. . . .

He characterized the attitude of the Conservative Party as "Divided in counsel and divided in action." He asserted that the proposed measure had received open commendation from the best and most experienced minds in the Party outside of the House. He scored the criticism of the measure by those within the Conservative Party who:

Carry abroad upon their foreheads the Imperial phylacteries, who boldly walk into the temple and there loudly thank the Lord that they are not like other British subjects, that they give tithes of everything they possess, and that in them alone is to be found the true incense of loyalty.

He accused Conservative members of appealing to the passions and prejudices of audiences in various parts of Canada. He declared that there were three distinct and entirely different schools of thought among Conservatives:

The Leader of the Opposition agreed to the principle of this Bill but thought it did not go far enough. My hon. friend from

[1] One expression of Sir Wilfrid dwells in my memory. In speaking of responsible government he said: "It was not until there was sent from England a man as broad in genius as Lord Durham himself–Lord Elgin–that with the assistance of Baldwin and Lafontaine, we had responsible government in this country. *And it was from that date that the British Empire started upon its triumphant march across the ages.*"

Jacques Cartier (Mr. Monk) . . . is opposed to this Bill and to everything of that kind. My hon. friend from Digby (Mr. Jameson) . . . wanted to have a referendum . . .

Sir, all these forms of opinion are simply different forms of a respectable, though misguided imperialism.

Referring to himself he remarked:

I do not pretend to be an Imperialist. Neither do I pretend to be an anti-Imperialist. I am a Canadian first, last, and all the time.

Paying a glowing tribute to the prestige of British institutions, he emphasized his desire for Canadian autonomy within the Empire. He quoted at length Lord Milner's views in support of the Government's policy.

He maintained that the Parliament of Canada should reserve the right to say when and where the navy should go to war. Reiterating his previous statement that if England is at war we are at war, he added that he did not say that we should take part in all the wars of England.

He was of opinion that Canada's chief consideration was public works and the development of her resources. He upheld the right of the Government to call the navy into action in an emergency without the consent of Parliament. Quoting Lord Charles Beresford's opinion favouring cruisers instead of dreadnoughts to assist in Imperial Defence, he announced the Government's intention to provide eleven ships, built if possible in Canada. It would take about a year to complete a plant for the building of the ships and probably about four years for the completion of the eleven ships proposed. The cost was estimated at $11,000,000.

Regarding my proposal that we should also make an emergency Contribution he said:

For my part I do not see any cause of danger to Great Britain at the present time. Let me say further that if Great Britain were engaged in such a contest, a wave of enthusiasm to assist her would sweep over this country and all other British countries. It is true Germany is creating a navy but I see no reason whatever for supposing that Germany is creating a navy for the purpose of attack or that England is increasing her navy for the purpose of attacking Germany. . . . I was impressed by one statement of my hon. friend the Leader of the Opposition, though I do not share in the conclusions which he implied from it. He said that if war came between England and Germany it would come within the next three or four years.[2]

He argued that there was no cause for war between England, and Germany, and he declared that as democracy advanced the prospect of war decreased.

He then turned his attention to those members in the Province of Quebec who fought the Government policy on the ground that any action regarding naval defence was unnecessary at the time.

Do they forget that our country extends from one ocean to the other and from the American boundary to the Arctic ocean, not on the map only but in actual and ever-increasing settlements? . . . Do they forget that Canada is expanding like a young giant, simply from the pressure of the blood in its young veins? Are we to be told . . . that we do not require a naval service? Why, Sir, you might just as well tell the people of Montreal, with their half-million population, that they do not need any police protection.

Concluding he said:

Again on this occasion, as in the days of Lafontaine and Baldwin, we appeal to moderate men in all parts of the community. We appeal as they did appeal, in a spirit of amity, of union, of fraternity; we appeal, as they appealed, in the highest conception of the duty which we owe to our country and to the Mother Country. It is the tradition of these great men, which is our supreme inspiration today in turning this page of the history of Canada.

Following Sir Wilfrid, I reminded him that this was not the year 1837 and that we were not engaged in a discussion as to whether this country should have autonomous rights and privileges. I commented on the fact that whenever the Prime Minister found himself in difficulties with his own party he invariably went back to the days of 1837 and quoted at length from Lord Durham, Lafontaine, and Baldwin. . . .

Recalling the Prime Minister's declaration on first reading of the Bill that when Great Britain was at war, Canada was at war, and noting with regret his recession from that principle of international law, I emphatically declared that "So long as the English flag floats above Canada, Canada is at war when that flag is attacked."

---

[2] This anticipation proved to be well-founded.

I maintained that this measure was not the outcome of advice or suggestion by the Admiralty at the conference of 1909, and emphasized the declaration of the Admiralty that there must be unity of control in time of war.

Are we to be face to face with the condition which the hon. gentleman says is demanded by our autonomy that Great Britain being at war we shall declare that we are not at war and that our fleet shall not take any part in it?

Certainly Clause 18 of the proposed measure conveyed just that meaning.

If, either by declaration or simply by inaction, the Government of Canada failed to place the Canadian navy under the control of the Imperial authorities during a time of war, such declaration or inaction could be interpreted only as a declaration of independence.

Further, so far as the Bill provided, there was little likelihood of unity of training or organization. The highest naval authorities prescribed a training period of six years as necessary —our training period was to be three years and that not in the British service but in schools to be established for the purpose.

I enumerated the requirements for a fleet unit, and doubted the value, in war, of the proposed cruisers:

They might be useful as scouts, or be of some advantage to this country in protection of our fisheries. But what would be the result in time of war? . . . An Australian or a New Zealand dreadnought would be called on to protect these Canadian cruisers from attack by the enemy. Surely that would be a very proud position for the people of Canada to occupy in the day of stress and trial.

The effective organization of a Canadian naval service could not be brought about in less than fifteen to twenty years. The people of Canada should be given an opportunity of deciding whether they desired such a measure:

What the people of this country desire is immediate and effective aid to the Empire, and to have any proposals of a permanent character very carefully considered and matured, as they ought to be considered and matured, before any such policy is embarked upon. . . .

I believe they (the people of Canada) are ready to assume their full share of meeting any peril that shall assail the Empire, come when it may. Their hearts and their hands are as strong to will and to dare as were those of their fathers before them, and I do not doubt, as my right hon. friend has eloquently expressed it, that the men of French descent in this country will be as prompt and ready to do their share with the English-speaking citizens of Canada, as they have proved themselves in days gone by. Thus, let our aid be prompt and generous, so that it may bring to the Motherland the assurance not only of material support but of a courage, a faith and a determination which shall proclaim alike to friend and foe that whether in peace or war, the Empire is one and undivided.

In conclusion I moved the following resolution:

That proposals of the Government do not follow the suggestions and recommendations of the Admiralty and, in so far as they empower the Government to withhold the naval forces of Canada from those of the Empire in time of war, are ill-advised and dangerous.

That no such proposals can safely be accepted unless they thoroughly ensure unity of organization and of action without which there can be no effective co-operation in any common scheme of Empire defence.

That the said proposals while necessitating heavy outlay for construction and maintenance will give no immediate or effective aid to the Empire and no adequate or satisfactory results in Canada.

That no permanent policy should be entered upon involving large future expenditures of this character until it has been submitted to the people and has received their approval.

That in the meantime the immediate duty of Canada and the impending necessities of the Empire can best be discharged and met by placing without delay at the disposal of the Imperial authorities as a free and loyal contribution from the people of Canada, such an amount as may be sufficient to purchase or construct two battleships or armoured cruisers of the latest dreadnought type, giving to the Admiralty full discretion to expend the said sum at such time and for such purpose of naval defence as in their judgment may best serve to increase the united strength of the Empire and thus assure its peace and security.

Mr. Monk followed in a lengthy speech in which he claimed that the creation of a Canadian navy was only another means of annual contribution to the defence of the Empire and that the whole policy of the Government did nothing more than put into effect a political union of the Empire with a view to reducing the dependencies to mere municipal institutions. Maintaining that we had no control over the Government and no representatives in the Parliament which "makes and unmakes wars and controls our destiny," he declared that the whole scheme was largely the work of the Imperial Federation Society and the British Empire League and he termed both these associations "anti-Canadian." He questioned our indebtedness to the mother country and declared:

Whatever we have in this country in the way of economic development or in the way of free political institutions is our own work. We built it up ourselves . . . and in the early days we had to wrest concessions from the mother country.

He stated that in many instances the British Government had sacificed Canadian territory for diplomatic interests, and he vigorously denounced the Canadian Government for its policy of giving everything and demanding nothing when attending conferences in England. He moved an amendment to my resolution that "This House, while declaring its unalterable devotion to the British Crown, is of opinion that the Bill now submitted for its consideration changes the relations of Canada with the Empire and ought, in consequence, to be submitted to the Canadian people in order to obtain at once the nation's opinion by means of a plebiscite.". . .

The debate was resumed on February 8. Notable and eloquent speeches setting forth the varying personal and party views were heard from members on both sides. In general the Conservative members stressed the importance of an emergency contribution and denounced the Government for its failure to carry into effect a measure more actively in co-operation with the suggestions and wishes of the British Government as expressed at the Defence Conference.

Government members were equally emphatic in expressing their loyalty to the Empire and their desire to maintain British naval supremacy. It was their general opinion that the need for emergency aid had been greatly exaggerated and that we should use our autonomy to develop our country in a national aspect.

On February 10, Mr. Foster made a vigorous fighting speech. Alluding to several Liberals who had dwelt with satis- faction upon division of opinion in Conservative ranks and particularly to Sir Wilfrid Laurier's remarks thereon he said:

Let me say to my right hon. friend, when he talks about unity and diversity of opinion, that I would rather have diversity and difference of opinion coupled with manhood and individual independence than uniformity of opinion coupled with servility and loss of independence.

He reviewed at length the recommendations and suggestions of the defence Conference and denounced as "pitiable" Canada's position in the debates of that Conference. . . .

The debate continued at great length. On March 9, Mr. Meighen in a short speech declared his intention of voting against Mr. Monk's amendment to my resolution.

The member for Jacques Cartier advanced reasons which led him to make amendment, and he uttered sentiments which not only can I not endorse, but from which I must disassociate myself as clearly, distinctly and firmly as I can. I do not contend that those who feel it their duty to support that amendment necessarily associate themselves and necessarily affirm the principles and sentiments uttered by the hon. member for Jacques Cartier, but so utterly diverse were they from those which I conceive on subjects that to me are of more than ordinary consequence that I cannot divorce myself too far from, or too strongly state, and too clearly indicate to my constituency, and to this country, that I disaffirm his position utterly.

Mr. Monk's amendment to the amendment was defeated by 175 to 18; my amendment was defeated by 129 to 74.

The following day (March 10) Mr. Northrup moved an amendment to the motion that the Bill be now read a second time, proposing that the second reading be deferred for a period of six months. In proposing this motion he made a lengthy speech in which he contended that the Navy Bill was unconstitutional as it infringed upon the King's admitted prerogative of control. Mr. Northrup's motion was defeated, after considerable debate, by 119 to 78 and the motion for second reading was agreed to.

On April 20, the Prime Minister moved the third reading of the Bill. Speaking in the debate, I summarized the attitude of the Conservative Party in the following terms:

As far as our position is concerned in seeking the mandate of the people at a general election with regard to a basis of permanent co-operation for the defence of the Empire, we have nothing to retract. We stand, as we have always stood in that respect, on two considerations—first, that the emergent condi-

tions of the Empire to demand immediate and effective aid, and, in the second place, that before a basis of permanent co-operation in the naval defence of the Empire is entered upon, the people of this country have a right to be consulted and to give their mandate.

Upholding the principle previously emphasized that "in time of war there should be one united naval force for the whole Empire and that naval force should be available to meet any enemy that might assail the integrity of the Empire," I quoted the Prime Minister's remarks, in committee, in reply to my question:

Suppose a Canadian ship meets a ship of similar armament and power belonging to an enemy, meets her on the high seas, what is she to do? I do not ask what she will do if attacked, but will she attack, will she fight?

Sir Wilfrid Laurier:

I do not know that she would fight. I do not know that she should fight either. She would not fight until the Government by which she is commissioned have determined whether she should go into the war. That is the position we take.

I maintained that:

The proposals of the Government seem to me in one aspect to be absurd and unworkable, but in another aspect they are dangerous and revolutionary. . . . It is absolutely inconceivable that if Great Britain were engaged in a naval war and the Canadian naval force acted as if it belonged not to the Empire or to Canada but to some neutral country, such a condition would not lead or at least conduce to the early separation of this country from the British Empire.

Mr. Fielding, in a lengthy speech, maintained that the Government policy was entirely in accord with the wishes and suggestions of the Admiralty. The Canadian naval service was primarily for the defence of Canada. Under the proposed Bill, he declared that the service would become Imperial whenever the help of Canada was needed for Empire defence.

The measure was passed by a majority of 41.

15: *1910-1911*

On October 18, 1909, Mr. W. B. Northrup, one of the three gentlemen engaged in secret intrigue against my leadership, sent out to members of our party a long letter in which he attacked my position upon the naval question and declared himself ready to fight against me as his leader. It is quite probable that he considered that I was mistakenly sacrificing Canada and the Empire. I have no doubt that this letter was the result of a conference between the three conspirators and was designed to arouse public opinion against my leadership on the ground that my support of the amended resolution respecting naval defence was contrary to the traditions of the Liberal-Conservative Party and was detrimental to the best interests of the Empire. The letter called for a reply but I am not aware to what extent the Conservative members responded.

During the session 1909-10, my leadership was under more or less constant attack from at least four quarters. In the House of Commons there was a cabal chiefly composed of the three gentlemen, already mentioned, who lost no opportunity of discrediting my leadership and who were said to have a singularly grotesque idea as to their course in case I should resign. One of them, a fluent but not particularly impressive speaker, had no such position in the country as would justify his ambitions for the leadership. It was proposed that upon my retirement this gentleman should be selected as temporary leader and that in due course the succession should go to Mr. McBride, the Conservative Leader in British Columbia.

Another group, under the direction of a rather abler man, who eventually became one of my colleagues in 1911, was believed to seek the selection of that gentleman as leader.

Then in Quebec, Mr. Monk was supported by the French-speaking members from Quebec and probably by one English-speaking member. Their repudiation of my leadership naturally weakened my position and was an indication of their desire for the selection of another leader.

In addition to these three groups, I am confident that Mr. W. F. MacLean had an ambition to succeed me, as on many an occasion he took opportunity either to belittle or to attack me through his newspaper, the Toronto *World*, which was ably conducted and which had a considerable circulation. In 1905, he had made a fierce attack upon me which was based upon

my support of the Government's proposal for increased indemnity to members, pensions to ex-Cabinet ministers, and a special
indemnity to the Leader of the Opposition. However, on a
subsequent occasion he spoke with me in the County of
Norfolk. . . .

Thus, among important elements of my nominal supporters
I encountered cabal and intrigue instead of loyalty and co-
operation. Becoming thoroughly exasperated, I finally addressed
a letter to the Chief Whip as follows:

Ottawa, April 6, 1910.

Dear Mr. Taylor:

*It is my intention to retire from the leadership of the party
at the close of the present session. Conditions which have
developed more particularly in the parliamentary representation
of the party during recent months have in my opinion almost
completely destroyed my usefulness. It is desirable that a public
announcement should be made at an early date; but before
this is done it is my duty to communicate my decision to
caucus. You are authorized to show this letter to Mr. Crothers,
Chairman of the General Committee, and to Mr. Perley,
Permanent Chairman of the Caucus. I would be glad to have
the opinion of these gentlemen and yourself as to the best
method of so arranging matters that my retirement may be
accomplished in the manner which is most in accord with the
best interests of the party.*

Yours faithfully,
(Sgd.) R. L. BORDEN

George Taylor, Esq., M.P.
Chief Conservative Whip,
House of Commons

As I kept no diary I cannot accurately recall the incidents
that led to the withdrawal of this letter. Obviously it was
withdrawn as the original is now in my possession. My recollection is that several of our most prominent members, to whom
this letter was shown by the Chief Whip, came to me in great
alarm and with great earnestness entreated me to withdraw the
letter. The situation was discussed at some length and finally,
under pressure, I receded from my attitude.

~ During the summer Borden made an automobile tour of
Ontario and the Maritimes. His reception was "not only cordial
but enthusiastic."

At his meetings he criticized government extravagance, the

increased cost of the transcontinental railway, and immigration policies. In Toronto he characterized the government's naval policy as "untenable from a constitutional point of view and unworkable from a political standpoint."

The campaign for the Drummond-Arthabaska by-election was intensive. Thirty-five Liberal M.P.s took part as did Monk, Bourassa, and some Conservatives. Borden entirely disapproved of the anti-British propaganda used during the campaign and refused to express any preference before the voting. He censured the Conservative Whip for congratulating Mr. Gilbert on his defeat of the official Liberal candidate. ~

From July 10 to September 7, 1910, Sir Wilfrid Laurier made a great tour of the Western Provinces. In one aspect it seemed a triumphal procession as his impressive personality, the charm of his eloquence and courtesy, and his wonderful tact, as well as his prestige, assured him of a warm welcome. He was embarrassed however by the very direct and insistent demands of the western farmers and other organizations who confronted him with his former denunciation of protection and laudation of Free Trade. . . .

Many years before, Sir Wilfred had declared that Canada would never again resort to Washington for the purpose of securing mutual trade arrangements. His unequivocal pledges to abolish Protection had been most imperfectly fulfilled in the British preference of 1897; and the astute Prime Minister perhaps foresaw a further measure of fulfilment in a trade arrangement with the United States. His western tour may have convinced him that such a policy would be warmly welcomed in the West, and accepted by the whole country.

The session of 1910-11 was fraught with great events. At its inception, a powerful Government, perhaps the most powerful in the history of Canada, prepared to place before the people a measure which it was thought would rally to the support of the administration a greater majority than had ever been accorded in the history of our country. Within ten months that same measure resulted in the Government's downfall.

The session was opened on November 17, 1910, by a long Speech from the Throne. The most important reference was to the negotiations then pending for a trade arrangement with the United States; and anticipation was expressed that, without any sacrifice of Canada's interests, there would ensue an arrangement which would admit many Canadian products to the United States on satisfactory terms.

~ In the Throne Speech debate, Borden dealt with the trade talks and spoke on Monk's amendment which censured the government for not consulting the people on its naval policy. He declared that if he were in power he would ascertain the true state of Empire defence from the Admiralty, and if instant and effective action were warranted he would ask parliament for it. On a permanent policy the people had a right to be consulted. He moved a sub-amendment similar to Monk's but one which declared Canada's attachment to the Crown and intention to fulfil all joint responsibilities as one of the nations of the Empire. Both the amendment and the sub-amendment were defeated by large majorities.

An immense delegation of western farmers reinforced by delegations from the five eastern provinces came to Ottawa to urge free trade between Canada and the United States in agricultural products and machinery. They also wanted free trade with Britain within ten years. ~

The Opposition made serious charges against the Minister of the Interior (Mr. Oliver) in connection with the selection by the Canadian Northern Railway of land in the Province of Saskatchewan for which, it was alleged, the Minister had received large sums of money. Sir Wilfrid appointed a Royal Commission to investigate the charges; no report of the Commission's finding was forthcoming and on July 25, when Government members moved adjournment until August 1, Mr. Meighen asked for a guarantee that Parliament would be sitting at the adjourned date. This pledge was given and broken. Parliament was dissolved on July 29.

16: Reciprocity

On January 26, 1911, Mr. Fielding presented to Parliament the Reciprocity proposals which became the subject of a prolonged debate. . . .

The view of the western farmers that Reciprocity should be carried out by concurrent legislation rather than by treaty had been accepted by the Government. Thereupon, Mr. Fielding proceeded to set forth the terms of the proposals which need not be recalled as they have passed into history. . . .

I spoke briefly in reply to Mr. Fielding and did not attempt any detailed examination of the proposals. Their effect upon certain industries in Canada might be serious. I agreed that we must have regard to the fiscal policy of the United States but also an earnest and serious regard for the three hundred millions of people under the British flag. I pointed out the tremendous dislocation of Canadian business interests that had ensued from the repeal of the Treaty of 1854; and emphasized the fact that when Canada was under the necessity of finding new markets she found them for the most part within the limits of the British Empire. What was the duration of this arrangement? Mr. Fielding had stated that it was expected to continue for a considerable time. This, I declared, was extremely unsatisfactory. The arrangement was itself indefinite and unsatisfactory, its duration was uncertain and the dislocation which would undoubtedly ensue upon its termination might be disastrous. I alluded to the timidity shown by the Government during the previous year under the United States' threat that their maximum tariff would be imposed, and I declared that they should have stood firm then. Finally, I declared that the policy of the Liberal-Conservative Party in respect of trade was a policy of Reciprocity within the Empire and that no entangling treaties or alliances should be entered into that might prevent this greatest consideration.

The proposals were presented on Thursday, and on the following day I called a caucus. The atmosphere that confronted me was not invigorating; there was the deepest dejection in our party, and many of our members were confident that the Government's proposals would appeal to the country and would give it another term of office. Foster was greatly impressed by the proposals and said that when they were presented his heart had gone down into his boots. The western members were emphatic in their statements that not one of them would be elected in opposition to Reciprocity. One of them declared that he dare not vote against the Government's proposals.[1]

I stemmed the tide as best I could, although I was under great discouragement. Frank Lalor of Haldimand told me afterwards that the Party owed me a great debt of gratitude for the stand I had made and the influence I had exerted at that caucus. But I had the support of many of our members, although the difference of opinion which had developed seemed in itself to be a forerunner of disaster.

Among the Ontario members a remarkable reaction soon made itself apparent. Many of them were in the habit of going to their homes over the week-end. Those who left Ottawa dejected and wavering came back confident and strong in their opposition to the Government's proposals. In this notable instance, the rank and file of the Party, holding strong opinions, expressed their views with emphasis and gave leadership and direction to their parliamentary representatives. Within a few days I was surrounded by a party practically united in firm determination to fight the reciprocity proposals to the bitter end.

The debate was resumed on February 9 by Mr. Monk who entered a vigorous protest against the unseemly haste with which so important an agreement was being pressed upon Parliament; he concluded by moving a resolution expressing regret that the necessary time and occasion to ascertain the opinion of the people of Canada with regard to the proposed new fiscal regime had not been given. He was answered by Mr. Fielding and the motion was defeated by a majority of twenty-five.

The House then went into Committee of Ways and Means and I immediately took the floor. The proposals seemed to me of too grave and serious a character to be considered from a purely partisan standpoint and, obviously, they involved tremendous consequences. They embodied a new tariff for our country, in so far as United States was concerned. After the repeal, in 1866, of the Reciprocity Treaty of 1854, Canada had sought for markets, had created a national spirit, had provided, at immense cost, transportation by rail and water from east to west, and had rendered herself practically independent of the United States. I emphasized the unwisdom of creating trade conditions in which all this expenditure would count for little

---

[1] Less than a month afterwards he declared in caucus that he would rather cut off his right arm than vote for these proposals.

and lines of trade would run north and south instead of east and west.

The proposals involved a dangerous uncertainty. The Minister of Finance had said that we must take them as a whole, yet he agreed that we were at liberty to impose duties upon any articles on the free list. If we had to accept the Agreement as a whole, our right to do this was illusory:

A treaty stating a definite period during which a certain condition shall continue, is one thing; it must be interpreted according to the usage of nations. But this arrangement which will leave it entirely open to either side to make any alteration, but which penalizes the slightest alteration by a complete abrogation of the arrangement creates a much more delicate and difficult situation.

During the past six years we had sold to Great Britain $300,000,000 in excess of our imports from that country; in the same period we had purchased from the United States $500,000,000 in excess of our exports to that country. British importations were paying higher duties than those from the United States. The British preference had ceased to be a preference. The policy of the Government pointed toward absolute Free Trade and commercial union with the United States. After lines of trade had been diverted, after we had become absolutely dependent upon the newly-established trade relations with the United States, Congress could, and in a moment of pique might, abrogate the agreement in a day and dislocate the conditions of trade. This dislocation would mean little to the United States but might be ruinous to Canada.

After suggesting that the Government would do well to withdraw their proposals, I concluded as follows:

We have begun a great work in this country. Two great races whose mother tongues are spoken in this parliament came into the inheritance of this great country under the providence of God. Our fathers endured many hardships and made wonderful sacrifices in planting their homes in this then wilderness. In times of peril both races have poured out their blood without stint in defence of their common country. In the work of upbuilding a strong nation and a great civilization under the British flag, on the northern half of this continent, they have laboured side by side with mutual sympathy and with high purpose. The heaviest burdens have been lifted, the greatest obstacles have been overcome, the most difficult part of the

*task has been accomplished. I trust that the Canadian people
will not lightly relinquish the task to which their energies and
the energies of their fathers have been consecrated for so many
years. I trust that the standard will not be thrown aside and the
retreat sounded when the battle is more than half won. The
self-denials, the sacrifices, the patriotism, demanded of us today
in order that this nation may maintain and carry out the ideals
and the purposes for which it was called into existence are as
nothing to those which were required of our fathers who
founded this confederation. Loyalty to their memory and to
the ideals which they consecrated demands that we should
continue with firm heart and unabated hope upon the path
which we entered nearly fifty years ago.*

Mr. Patterson (Minister of Customs) followed, emphatically
stating that the proposals would in no way affect the British
preference. He emphasized the advantages to the Canadian
farmer in the reduction of freight rates, should Canadian grain be
carried over United States' transportation routes; and he saw no
reason why Canada should conserve wheat, ores, and fish: "If
the Americans want our wheat and ores and fish and lumber,
why, in the name of good business, should they not have
them?"...

On February 16, at a Board of Trade protest meeting in
Toronto, Sir Edmund Walker, J. D. Allan, and R. S. Gourlay
expressed themselves as actively opposed to Reciprocity.
Sir Edmund, in a keen analysis of the whole measure, was
particularly emphatic in his opposition:

*Although I am a Liberal, I am a Canadian first of all, and
I can see that this is much more than a trade question. Our
alliance with the mother country must not be threatened. We
must assimilate our immigrants and make out of them good
Canadians, and this Reciprocity Agreement is the most deadly
danger as tending to make this problem more difficult. The
question is between British connection and what has been well
called "Continentalism."*

The speeches of the gentlemen alluded to gave evidence of
strong opposition within Liberal ranks; and on February 20,
a manifesto, expressing objection to the Government's proposals
and signed by eighteen Liberals was published. This statement
concluded as follows:

*Believing as we do that Canadian nationality is now threat-
ened with a more serious blow than any it has heretofore met*

*with and that all Canadians who place the interests of Canada
before those of any party or section or individuals therein
should at this crisis state their views openly and fearlessly, we,
who have hitherto supported the Liberal Party in Canada
subscribe to this statement.*

This pronouncement materially strengthened the Conservative cause, both in Parliament and throughout the country.

Shortly after its publication, Mr. Clifford Sifton, on February 28, made a notable speech in the House. After expressing his reluctance to break party ties, he made a most destructive analysis of the Government's proposals and declared himself as unqualified in opposition to their policy in this respect.

Soon I was in touch with men on the other side of the House, and especially with Mr. Sifton and Lloyd Harris, both of whom were willing to co-operate in the struggle against the Government. In these conferences Mr. (afterwards Sir) J. S. Willison joined from time to time; and methods by which the proposals might be controverted were discussed at great length. On one occasion Mr. Sifton sought an interview at which he wished to discuss the future policy of the Conservative Party in certain aspects. He desired greater firmness in our dealings with United States, although he fully realized the importance of most cordial relations with that country. These relations, he believed, would not be less friendly if our attitude should be somewhat firmer. He mentioned also relations between the English-speaking and French-speaking elements of our population. He was impressed with the feeling that too much influence was exercised from Quebec along racial lines. Thoroughly agreeing that the fullest and most generous considerations should be given to the French element of our population in the administration of public affairs, he urged that their demands were sometimes excessive and might, with advantage, be courteously denied. . . .

My negotiations with Sifton, Lloyd Harris, and other Liberals necessarily became known to members on our side of the House; and one of the cabals, seeking to destroy my leadership, thought it opportune to exploit the incident for that purpose. To me it seemed madness that we should refuse the effective aid of powerful elements within the Liberal Party; but then, as afterwards in 1917, the cry went up that my negotiations meant the destruction of the Liberal-Conservative Party and the ascendency of Liberal elements in its councils. To such lengths did this feeling advance that the Party's future was the subject of a caucus at which the minority did not fail to make their voices heard. I became intensely discouraged and began to loathe the situation. Finally on March 25, I sent the following message to Mr. McBride:

Last year's trouble revived. Am convinced that interests of party imperatively demand my retirement. Believe party would unanimously accept you as leader. National emergency absolutely demands your immediate affirmative response to such call. Earnestly hope for favourable answer. Situation urgent. Reply necessary before Tuesday morning.

That evening I told my wife that my political career was finished and that I was glad of it. Late at night a delegation, headed by the late David Henderson, came to my house and besought me, almost with tears, to reconsider my decision which I had communicated to two or three intimate friends. Finally I told them that I would reconsider and eventually, on March 28, a round-robin was presented to me for which I owe much to George H. Perley. It was in the following form and signed by the following members:

March 28, 1911.
We, the undersigned Conservative members of the House of Commons, hereby earnestly request you to continue the leadership of the party in the House, and we pledge to you our loyal and undivided support in the great work which you are carrying on in the interest of the party, of Canada, and the Empire.

~ Then followed the signatures of 65 members. ~

Some of those whose signatures were not appended were absent and otherwise would have gladly joined in expressing their confidence. Among them I would place the following: Samuel Barker, Andrew Broder, George Gordon, and Arthur Meighen.

Those whom I would not expect to sign were: G. H. Barnard, P. E. Blondin, J. A. Lortie, F. D. Monk, R. Forget, W. B. Nantel, W. B. Northrup, Wm. Price, J. D. Reid, W. F. MacLean, and J. Girard.

The members from Quebec were under the influence of Mr. Monk and had been alienated by my naval policy; Barnard was a keen advocate of Mr. McBride; Northrup, Price, and Reid formed the cabal already alluded to; and W. F. MacLean retained his attitude of antagonistic detachment.

The remainder of my nominal supporters who did not sign were Glen Campbell, O. S. Crockett, E. N. Rhodes, W. D. Staples, and A. N. Worthington. Mr. Crockett was perennially dissatisfied; and I am unable to analyze the motives of the others.

If I had carried out my intentions to retire from the leadership and had set forth, as I intended to do, the cabals against my leadership and the dissensions within our party, it is extremely probable that Sir Wilfrid Laurier would have seized the opportunity to make an immediate appeal to the country which, undoubtedly, would have been successful. In 1896, public expression of disloyalty among the Conservative Ministers had very seriously affected the election of that year. I am convinced that there would have been a vehement outburst if I had been forced to resign. It was recognized throughout the country, which I had very thoroughly canvassed for nearly ten years, that I had laboured hard and faithfully. Cabals and disloyalty are bitterly resented by the rank and file of the party. It is possible that public opinion might have forced me to return, but in any event, irreparable mischief, the prelude to certain disaster, would have ensued. It would have been possible for the Government to bring on an election in time to permit the Prime Minister to attend the then approaching Imperial Conference which was to open on May 23. However, I continued in the leadership and directed a fight which went on unceasingly against the passage of the resolution upon which the Reciprocity Agreement was to be founded.

Eventually it became apparent to the Government that we were obstructing the passage of the resolution and that we intended to fight the measure until the country became thoroughly seized of its dangers and disadvantages. But at this time the forces arrayed against the proposals had not gained cohesion and would have been unable to wage a successful battle if the Government, in the face of our obstruction, had made an immediate appeal to the country.

On the other hand, such an appeal would have aroused strong indignation and led to serious losses in the English-speaking provinces in the East, for it would have prevented the Prime Minister from attending the then-approaching Imperial Conference. In the Press there was much discussion of the rumour that Sir Wilfrid did not intend to be present but chose rather to remain in Ottawa while the Reciprocity debate was proceeding.

Taking advantage of this strong trend of public opinion, I

arose in my place on April 28, and, after adverting to the development of the Imperial Conference and the remarkable scope of its importance and activities, I strongly urged that the Prime Minister should not fail to attend; and I offered to co-operate for the purpose of enabling him to do so:

~ Borden suggested three alternatives:

1. *Laurier could go to the Conference leaving his colleagues in charge of House business;*
2. *Prorogation, leaving unfinished items until the next session; or*
3. *adjournment for two or three months.*

The Opposition would readily co-operate in granting interim supply. He reiterated the opposition's uncompromising attitude to the reciprocity proposals." ~

Naturally, Sir Wilfrid did not receive my suggestion with any indication of gratitude. He enlarged upon the obstruction which we undoubtedly had undertaken. . . .

If such be the temper of the opposition, I think it will probably make it necessary for me to resign my determination to go to England, and stay in Canada.

As I had moved the adjournment of the House, I had the right of reply and availed myself of it. In the first place, I pointed out that the debate had proceeded regularly on both sides of the House and that more time had been taken up by Government than by Opposition members. I expressed regret that the Prime Minister had not received in a more gracious spirit a fair and generous offer on my part. . . .

We had been told by Ministers of the Crown that the honour of our country had been pledged to the President and Government of the United States. I did not know when the people of Canada had given any mandate to the Prime Minister or the Government thus to pledge their honour. And if our honour was pledged to the United States, it was still more strongly pledged to the Empire in respect of matters which I enumerated; and again I urged him to reconsider his determination and to attend the approaching Imperial Conference.

The debate continued at great length; and finally at a Liberal caucus, held May 5, it was decided to adjourn Parliament for two months until July 18.

On the same evening (May 5) I entertained at dinner the Liberal-Conservative members of Parliament and several provincial leaders. The Prime Minister's recession from his first intention was regarded as a triumph for my tactics, as it gave to the Liberal-Conservative Party and those co-operating with us an opportunity to consolidate our forces and to arouse the country. At this dinner, which was a remarkably enthusiastic and confident gathering, I referred to the active and antagonistic intervention of the Grand Trunk Railway against our party in 1908, and emphasized strongly that we desired no quarrel with any great corporation in Canada; but that if such corporation desired to attack and persist in attacking our party we were prepared to meet them and to press the quarrel to the bitter end. My audience enthusiastically cheered this utterance. . . .

Mr. McBride and Mr. Hazen and others spoke at this banquet. The impressions derived by the members on this occasion did much to abate the intrigue from which I had suffered for nearly two years. My secretary was told by many members of the House of Commons that this dinner had settled the question of leadership.

~ During the "tedious debate" on Reciprocity, Conservative speakers usually "occupied about three hours." Borden was amused at one member's reference to the Canadian negotiators as having brought back from Washington Pandora's box out of which pranced the Trojan horse! ~

Parliament adjourned on May 19; and I at once started on my tour of Western Canada. I felt confident that if Parliament should be dissolved I would have no other opportunity and I desired to face the issue in the Grain Growers' stronghold. So, as Sir Wilfrid Laurier was reaching the shores of England, I was entering the western country. . . .

The tour occupied twenty-one days and on eighteen of those I spoke—one hundred and twenty-four times in all. I remember that on one day I spoke for an hour in the morning, an hour in the afternoon, and an hour in the evening; and in addition made eight other short speeches.

The first meeting which was at Winnipeg was a complete success. The arguments which I employed need not be repeated. They certainly appealed to the vast majority of the audience.

The next meeting was more dramatic and in the result it exercised an immense influence in Eastern Canada. It was held at Brandon and was preceded by my reception of a great delegation of Grain Growers who presented to me a lengthy memorial in which they demanded, with much earnestness, my support of the Reciprocity proposals. I regarded such a demand as savouring of impertinence and it thoroughly aroused me. After alluding to other items of their programme, I stepped out in front of the table and raising my hand, I said:

Of your powerful influence in this western country, I am fully persuaded; but if it were ten times what it is and if you were able and were prepared to make me Prime Minister tomorrow on condition that I would support this pact, I would not do it.

The hall in which I met the Grain Growers was packed but I recollect one voice from the back ringing out like a trumpet with the words "That's the answer to give."

Throughout this western tour, the Grain Growers pressed upon me similar proposals and demands and in every case they received the same clear-cut answer. They had intended to embarrass if not to lecture me, and in the result I lectured them on every occasion that afforded me opportunity. . . .

Although I encountered everywhere the unbending opposition of the Grain Growers, so far as Reciprocity was concerned, I produced a certain effect by my utterances with regard to provincial autonomy. In the final analysis, the tour probably effected no considerable change of opinion in the West but it exercised a remarkable influence in the provinces east of the Great Lakes.

Parliament re-assembled on July 18; and Mr. Fielding promptly moved consideration of the Reciprocity Agreement. One of our members (W. S. Middleboro) met this with an amendment suggesting consideration for Canadian veterans of the Fenian Raids. There was some discussion of the subject and the subject was defeated.

Several other topics were introduced but the main issue continued to be the Reciprocity Agreement.

Early in the session I had urged that the question of redistribution and representation be dealt with by means of an adequate measure, but no action had been taken. At this juncture I again urged that the question receive the attention of the Government. However, On April 24, the Prime Minister had announced that it was "Reciprocity or nothing this Session."

Mr. Fielding followed and in reference to the Reciprocity proposals he concluded with the following:

But, if perchance the manufacturers in their great power should unite in opposing, and possibly condemning or even defeating this measure, then there will rise up in that western country a storm cloud bigger than a man's hand, and the end will be a change in the fiscal policy of the country, which the manufacturers will find much greater than anything they conceived of.

This veiled threat failed to have the effect which Mr. Fielding anticipated.

~ Parliament was dissolved on July 28 with an election set for September 21. ~

On the day following dissolution, I issued a statement which may be summarized as follows: The Liberal-Conservative Party welcomed an opportunity for appeal to the people on the great issue of Reciprocity. The Government had dissolved Parliament without prorogation, without supply, and without redistribution. Constitutional authorities abounded to prove that dissolution ought not to be granted without provision of the necessary supplies for the public service.

In connection with the inquiry into charges made against the Minister of the Interior, the Government had given its guarantee that Parliament would be sitting on August 1, when a meeting of the Royal Commission of inquiry was to take place; this pledge had been deliberately violated by their action in dissolving Parliament on July 29. It was the duty of the Government to clear up the charges against one of the Ministers of the Crown before appealing to the country; their failure to do so was an "outrageous abuse of their power, and manifested in a most striking manner their utter contempt of decent public opinion."

In this campaign much use was made of the public utterances of President Taft who fought vigorously to obtain Congressional support of the Reciprocity Agreement. . . . President Taft's indiscreet reference to Canada as being "at the parting of the ways" was also useful to us during the campaign. Mr. Champ Clark was even more indiscreet in his declaration that he favoured Reciprocity because:

I hope to see the day when the American flag will float over every square foot of the British North American possession, clear to the North Pole. . . .

On the other hand, the outlook of certain leading British statesmen seemed remarkably restricted; their vision was confined to the effect of the Reciprocity proposals upon the fortunes of political parties within the United Kingdom. It seemed remarkable that outstanding figures such as Mr. Asquith and Mr. Lloyd George had so little conception of the basis upon which the protection of Canadian industries was established and lacked the imagination to realize that Canada, having once become the commercial and industrial vassal of the United States, would inevitably become the political vassal of that country and ultimately would be absorbed.

Neither of these statesmen, nor indeed any statesman in the United Kingdom, seemed to realize the power of sentiment in arraying against the Reciprocity proposals the forces that were determined to preserve the political and economic independence of Canada and to maintain her membership of the British Commonwealth. . . .

On July 29, the Prime Minister issued a manifesto which may be summarized as follows: ￼

For the past forty years all political parties in Canada had been united in a desire to arrange for the free exchange of their natural resources between Canada and the United States.

Within the last twelve months, through negotiations between the United States Government and the Canadian Government, such an arrangement had been agreed to. In the United States there had been strenuous resistance on the part of various interests on the ground that the agreement was more advan-been united in a desire to arrange for the free exchange of their tageous to Canada. However, the view that it was mutually advantageous to both countries had prevailed in Congress.

The Liberal-Conservative Party were not content to debate this question upon its merits in the House of Commons but had organized a system of obstruction to prevent a vote being taken on the measure. To overcome this obstruction would mean a much prolonged session, and in order to avoid this the Liberal Party were appealing to the country on this great issue. The contention that such a trade arrangement would tend to sever or imperil British connection was disregarded as being unworthy of attention, and the opinion was advanced that such an arrangement would tend rather to strengthen the ties between Canada and the mother country on the one hand and those existing between Canada and the United States on the other hand; and would, it was hoped, eventuate into a general treaty of arbitration the effect of which would be to remove forever the possibilities of war between the British Empire and the United States. Further it emphatically emphasized that Canada's fiscal policy was in no way impaired.

Later, on August 14, I set forth in detail the attitude of the

Liberal-Conservative Party upon the great issue before the people, and our policy with regard to other minor issues. The portion of this manifesto, relating to Reciprocity, is detailed in the following paragraphs, and the pledges of the Liberal-Conservative Party are set forth.

My position was that Parliament, just dissolved, had received no mandate to surrender to the United States our fiscal autonomy. The people and not a temporary parliamentary majority must determine that issue. Nearly fifty years ago Canada began her work of nation-building in face of difficulties which seemed insurmountable but which did not daunt her spirit. She had flung her boundaries to the far Pacific in the West and beyond the Arctic circle in the North, thus undertaking the wardenship and development of a territory greater in area than the continent of Europe. Her faith and her courage were unsurpassed but not greater than the success that had crowned her endeavours. In the midst of this success the Government had seriously undertaken to commit our country to a treaty which completely altered the conditions and the policy under which Canada had grown so rapidly, and so surely to her present splendid stature.

Then I emphasized the objections, profound and abiding, to that pact.

In the first place Reciprocity would interlock our finance system with that of the United States and fetter the power of Parliament to alter our tariff according to the just requirements

Then I emphasized the objections, profound and abiding, of our people. Its duration was nominally within the control of either country, but actually within that of the United States. Its tendency and aim were complete commercial union between the two countries, to the exclusion of the rest of the Empire. It opened to the United States our home market which consumes eighty per cent of our animal and agricultural product. In had the effect of opening that same market to twelve foreign countries and to all the British possessions, for which we obtain no reciprocal or compensating advantage. Sir Wilfrid Laurier was sending to these foreign countries a polite invitation to forego and renounce this right to enter our markets. The suggestion that they are likely to be thus considerate and unselfish is so foolish that it requires no answer.

The agreement abandoned the policy of improved trade relations with the British people, and centred our hopes on the American people—our strongest competitors in the markets of the world.

It made a pretence of bringing relief to the farmer; in reality it would expose him to the competition of the world in every thing he would sell while continuing the burden of taxation on everything he might buy.

It threatened the existence of our fishing bounties. It would tend to destroy the distinctive character of our staple products which would be merged in those of United States.

It would expose our natural resources to the depredations of gigantic trusts and would assist those trusts to bring pressure to bear upon provincial governments to abandon the wise policy of conserving our natural resources and converting them into finished commodities by the labour of our own people.

It would give to American trusts a power, influence, and control equal to those exercised in United States.

It would encourage the export of our raw materials and unfinished products for manufacture abroad instead of at home.

The higher and more progressive methods of agriculture would not be encouraged.

The Liberal-Conservative Party viewed it as a rash and perilous experiment, undertaken at a time when Canada had long since outgrown the conditions under which such a policy was once thought desirable.

I then set forth the pledges of the Liberal-Conservative Party as follows:

1. *A thorough reorganization of the method by which public expenditure is supervised. The increase in what is known as ordinary controllable expenditure from $21,500,000 in 1896 to nearly $74,000,000 in 1911 is proof of extravagance beyond any possible denial.*
2. *The granting of their natural resources to the Prairie Provinces.*
3. *The construction of the Hudson Bay Railway and its operation by independent commission.*
4. *The control and operation by the State of the terminal elevators.*
5. *The necessary encouragement for establishing and carrying on the chilled meat industry.*
6. *The establishment of a permanent tariff commission.*
7. *The granting of substantial assistance towards the improvement of our public highways.*
8. *The extension of free rural mail delivery.*
9. *The extension of civil service reform.*
10. *The granting of liberal assistance to the provinces for the purpose of supplementing and extending the work*

of agricultural education and for the improvement of agriculture.

And lastly, we pledge ourselves to a course of policy and administration which will maintain independent and unimpaired the control of our own affairs by the Parliament of Canada; a policy which, while affording no just cause of complaint to any foreign nation will find its highest ideal in the autonomous development of Canada as a nation within the British Empire.

In the past we have made a great sacrifice to further our national ideals; we are now face to face with a misguided attempt to throw away the result of these sacrifices.

The true issue is this. Shall we continue in the course which has led us to our present enviable position of prosperity and national development, or shall we, at the moment of greatest success and achievement, lose heart and abandon the fight for national existence?

Upon this momentous issue I appeal to the people with the utmost confidence and in the firm belief that their verdict will be for the unity and not for the disintegration of Canada; for the strengthening and not the loosening of the ties which bind this Dominion to the British Empire.

My campaign began at London, Ontario, on August 16, and I spoke at many Ontario points and at the principal centres in all the Eastern provinces. Everywhere my reception was all that I could desire. . . .

At St. Andrews, New Brunswick, Sir William Van Horne spoke with me in the afternoon and at St. Stephens in the evening. Sir William's speech was widely quoted. Speaking of the American desire for the acquisition of our natural resources, he said:

It was a saying long ago, "Beware of the Greeks when they bring gifts." We here in Canada may well say beware of the Americans when they bring tariff concessions.

I may sum up the whole situation in this: Our trade is about $97 per capita, and theirs $33 per capita. In other words the water in our mill-pond stands at 97 and theirs at 33; and they want us to take away our dam. Shall we not say "Not by a dam sight!". . .

After a series of meetings in Nova Scotia, I returned to Halifax where, on September 19, I sent forth a final message to the Canadian people. As this was perhaps my best appeal, I venture to quote some of the passages therefrom.

After declaring that the Reciprocity Compact was but a step in a greater process, that in its final outcome it meant the commercial and fiscal union of Canada and United States, the message continued:

> And let us never forget that Canada cannot become fiscally and commercially a part of the United States and remain politically a part—and an important part—of the British Empire. . . .

> Less than two years ago, by the Treaty of Prohibitory Duties, they forced our Government to alter our tariff; do not imagine that the spirit which compelled this unwarranted concession to our powerful neighbour will die on the morrow of its first great success. . . .

> Above all, do not forget that the momentous choice which you must make is for all time. . . .

> I believe that we are, in truth, standing today at the parting of the ways. This compact made in secret and without mandate points, indeed, to a new path. We must decide whether the spirit of Canadianism or of Continentalism shall prevail on the northern half of this continent. . . . With Canada's youthful vitality, her rapidly increasing population, her marvellous material resources, her spirit of hopefulness and energy, she can place herself within a comparatively brief period in the highest position within this mighty Empire. This is the path upon which we have proceeded—this is the path from which we are asked to depart. . . . This question is above all parties and all individuals. I appeal to Liberals as to Conservatives, and I speak to them not as a party leader, but as a Canadian citizen whose hopes are bound up with the hopes of his country.

> To all who are proud of her past, to all who hope for her future, I make an earnest and sincere appeal to rise above all party ties, to take heed of the higher considerations and to determine their course with a sense of the enduring results of their decision. I entreat them not to swerve from the straight path that leads to the making of a great nation. I beg them to cast a soberly considered and seriously considered vote for the preservation of our heritage, for the maintenance of our commercial and political freedom, for the permanence of Canada as an autonomous nation with in the British Empire.

Throughout the whole campaign, in support of our attack upon the Government's Reciprocity proposals there was a great galaxy of powerful speakers, including Mr. Foster, Mr. Sifton, and Mr. W. T. White. In the West our cause was upheld, not only by our candidates, but as well by Mr. Robert Rogers, who very efficiently organized the campaign in the Province of Manitoba, Mr. Roblin, and Mr. McBride. In Ontario, Sir James Whitney was a powerful ally and spared no effort to further our cause. Mr. Frank Cochrane was the organizer for the entire Province of Ontario and had built up a most effective organization in that Province. About a week before the election I had a telegram from him which forecast the victory which came on September 21. . . .

The result of the election was a matter of amazement throughout the country. Seven Ministers of the Crown were defeated – Mr. Fielding and Mr. Patterson, the negotiators of the Reciprocity Agreement, were both defeated. Mr. Charles Murphy was the only Minister re-elected in Ontario. In Ontario the Liberal-Conservative Party scored the greatest majority in the history of that province. In Quebec 27 Conservatives and Nationalists were returned against 38 Liberals. The Maritime Provinces returned 16 Conservatives to 19 Liberals, and British Columbia went solidly Conservative. The total result was 133 Conservatives to 88 Liberals – practically the same majority for the Conservative Party of the Liberal Party had obtained in 1908.

The formation of a Cabinet is a difficult task at any time but it was particularly difficult on this occasion as we had been out of power for fifteen years. For many days my house was beseiged and there were excursions and alarums from all parts of the country. Difficulties arose with regard to four persons. . . .

~ Foster was most anxious to have the Finance portfolio again, but had to settle for Trade and Commerce.

Sam Hughes "had earned promotion" but Borden hesitated because of his erratic temperament. Borden discussed his past vagaries with him, and was promised more discretion in the future. Rogers, Minister of Public Works in Manitoba and a key organizer of victory, desired Public Works, but was given Interior.

Reid, after being lectured for past disloyalty, was given a post. Premier McBride of British Columbia was offered a post but did not accept in time.

W. T. White, an anti-reciprocity Liberal, was given Finance over the protests of some Toronto Conservatives. Monk was included, of course, and was consulted on the other Quebec appointments. ~

The Cabinet as finally determined was as follows:

Prime Minister and President of the Privy Council	Robert L. Borden
Minister of Trade and Commerce	George Eulas Foster
Minister of the Interior	Robert Rogers
Minister of Public Works	Frederick Debartsch Monk
Minister of Railways and Canals	Francis Cochrane
Minister of Finance	William Thomas White
Postmaster General	Louis Philippe Pelletier
Minister of Marine, Fisheries and Naval Service	John Douglas Hazen
Minister of Justice	Charles Joseph Doherty
Minister of Militia and Defence	Sam Hughes
Minister of Agriculture	Martin Burrell
Secretary of State	William James Roche
Minister of Labour	Thomas Wilson Crothers
Minister of Inland Revenue & Mines	Wilfrid Bruno Nantel
Minister of Customs	John Dowsley Reid
Ministers Without Portfolio	George Halsey Perley
	Albert Edward Kemp
	James Alexander Lougheed

Sir Wilfrid Laurier[2] tendered his resignation on October 6; and on the following day I attended the Governor-General for the purpose of submitting to him the personnel of the new Cabinet. We were sworn into office on October 10, and entered upon our duties without realizing that within three years Canada would be involved in such a tempest of war as the world had never known. . . .

[2] After my accession to office, Sir Wilfrid, who had made no provision for his private secretary, E. J. Lemaire, called upon me and requested that I should give Mr. Lemaire a suitable appointment. This, I gladly consented to do; and during the Conservative regime, Mr. Lemaire held an important position in the Post Office Department wherein he rendered excellent service. Later, after the death of Mr. Boudreau, he became Clerk of the Privy Council.

I was rather attracted by a French-Canadian elevator operator on duty in the East Block and I had always given him a kindly greeting. He and I were born in the same year. The cry of political partisanship soon pervaded Ottawa after the election and one morning I found that Rioux had not donned his uniform and was sitting near the elevator looking most disconsolate. He informed me that he was under suspension for political partisanship. Immediately I telephoned the Public Works Department; and upon receiving an explanation, I asked them to cancel the suspension at once. Rioux returned to duty and thereafter he was a most devoted friend.

~ Borden recounts his difficulties in seeking unity and harmony among Quebec Conservatives. Monk was "extremely difficult to work with." Others who were given responsibility for organization were no more successful. ~

On November 15, the opening day of the session (1911-12), I moved the election of Dr. T. S. Sproule as Speaker of the House. Emphasizing the necessity for qualities of intellect and temperament in the incumbent of that position as well as for experience in the rules and procedure of the House, I recalled that Dr. Sproule had been a member since 1878; and I expressed the opinion that he possessed in an eminent degree the ability and qualities necessary for the position.[1]

Replying, Sir Wilfrid Laurier took no exception to Dr. Sproule personally but expressed surprise that the British precedent of regarding the position of Speaker of the House as

[1] It is a well-established custom in the Commons that the prayers shall be read in English and French on alternate days. The two languages are on an equal footing in the Debates and Records of Parliament. Dr. Sproule, in common with many of the Ontario members, was by no means enthusiastic as to the use of the French language; but he was very conscientious and upon his selection as Speaker he felt himself constrained to study this language, of which he was absolutely ignorant, in order that he might be able to read the prayers in French. Accordingly, he came to Ottawa before the opening of the session and engaged the services of a French teacher. For about three weeks the prayers were read in French by the Assistant Clerk but after that the Speaker considered that he was sufficiently fluent to undertake the duty himself. The equivalent or semi-equivalent of the French words was carefully marked on the card containing the French version of the prayers. At the first attempt Dr. Sproule did reasonably well. However, Sir Thomas White told me that on conclusion of the Speaker's effort, he (White) leaned over and made inquiry of his deskmate, Monk. Monk's countenance frequently was of a rather melancholy cast. He was sitting with his cheek on his arm and the following dialogue took place:

WHITE: "That was very good, was it not, Monk? I thought the old man did fairly well, did he not?"

MONK: (in a very deep and rather sepulchral voice) "I have no doubt that Almighty God would understand it."

After a time the Speaker became confused between the French diphthongs "au," "eau," and "eu" and he read the Lord's Prayer with a pronunciation which greatly astonished the French-speaking members, as his pronunciation of the French word for "heaven," sounded to them like the French word for "bucket."

permanent had not been observed. No such practice had ever been followed and it would have been very difficult to establish it in Canada. An unwritten convention, usually observed, requires that in the selection of a Speaker, regard should be had to the alternation of the two languages so that an English-speaking Speaker shall be followed at the next election by the selection of a French-speaking member. Conversely it is usual to arrange that when an English-speaking Speaker presides in the Commons, a French Speaker shall preside in the Senate and *vice-versa*.

The Speech from the Throne alluded to satisfactory trade conditions with both Great Britain and foreign countries, the abundant harvest, the increased revenue, negotiations for improved trade arrangements with the British West Indies and British Guiana, co-operation with the provinces for better highways and for aid to agriculture, revision and consolidation of the grain Acts, the establishment of a Tariff Commission, and other subjects. . . .

The Address was moved by Mr. R. B. Bennett and Mr. Albert Sévigny, both of whom made notable and eloquent speeches. The former, speaking of the proposal of the Government to establish a Tariff Commission, defined a scientific tariff in the following terms:

That is a scientific tariff which will insure to the people of Canada the ordered use and regulated employment of our great resources of river and lake, sea and land, that will insure the manufacture within Canada of all those articles that can be economically produced in Canada, giving employment to Canadian workmen at wages at least equal to those paid to workmen in competing countries, to the end that Canadian farmers may produce the food products necessary to feed the Canadian workmen.

After extending a cordial welcome to Canada's new Governor-General, the Duke of Connaught [and his wife], Mr. Sévigny reviewed the Government's policy. Regarding the naval issue he said:

French-Canadians, like the Canadians of other provinces, are opposed to this unfortunate law voted by the Liberal Government, providing for the construction of a war navy which will be ruinous to Canada and useless to our country and to the Empire.

Sir Wilfrid Laurier followed and paid great tribute to the

"eminent ability" of Mr. Bennett and Mr. Sévigny. Dealing with the Reciprocity issue which he declared was taken up because of the West, he expressed the opinion that it had been defeated by appeals to prejudice and passion. As to the dangers of annexation had the proposal been accepted he said "I have simply to say to the people in Canada who feared annexation and to the people in the United States who hoped for it, that they alike fail to take into consideration the manhood of a proud people who would equally disdain to be cajoled or to be coerced into a course inconsistent with their dignity."

~ Laurier moved an amendment which referred to a flagrant conflict of opinion in the Cabinet on naval policy and declared that the inclusion of members holding diametrically opposite views on a question of highest importance was contrary to the well understood principles of responsible government.

Borden accused Laurier of having dissolved Parliament without taking the "ordinary and constitutional steps" for the provision of Supplies. This was a grave violation of the government's duty. He said that the Laurier government's naval policy had not been debated before the people.

In the long Throne Speech debate, personalities were indulged in and Quebec Nationalism was fiercely denounced. Many Liberals echoed Laurier's taunt, "Is it the Imperial lion which has swallowed the National lamb, or is it the National lamb that has swallowed the Imperial lion?"

The motion to appoint P. E. Blondin as Deputy Speaker brought a bitter attack from a Liberal M.P. who accused Blondin of having made disloyal and anti-Imperial statements during the campaign. Blondin's denial was followed by the withdrawal of the accusation.

The session which had adjourned on December 7 resumed on January 10. Borden had received an Imperial Privy Councillorship in the New Year's honours list.

The Government accepted a resolution moved by the former Minister of Railways urging that the scope of the Intercolonial Railway be extended by having it take over branch and feeder lines. Borden announced the government's intention to proceed with civil service reform. Later a measure was passed providing for the appointment of a third member of the Civil Service Commission. ~

On January 16, I moved the following resolution:

Resolved that it is expedient: (a) to authorize the transfer of

*public records, documents, and other historical material from
the various Government departments to the Public Archives,
which material shall be placed in the custody of an officer to be
called the Dominion Archivist, who shall have the rank and
salary of a deputy head; (b) to provide for the purchase, under
the authority of the Minister named for that purpose, of records,
documents, and material, and for expenses in connection therewith; and (c) to provide for the appointment of such officers
and clerks as are required for the proper care, custody, and
control of the Public Archives.*

I explained that the Archives had not been constituted under
any particular Act. They were attached to the Department of
Agriculture in common with a great many other subjects which
had no particular relation to that department. It was therefore
proposed to introduce a Bill known as the Archives Act which
would provide for the administration of the Archives under
the President of the Privy Council; the Bill passed without
discussion on January 23.

On February 7 the Tariff Commission Bill received its
second reading. Mr. White explained that the Government's
intention in proposing this measure was to establish a Board
whose duties would be to obtain and collate information of
which the Government might avail itself in making tariff laws.
The powers and functions with regard to the making of tariffs
and the responsibility therefor would remain precisely the same
as before. The Commission would not in the least minimize
ministerial or Government responsibility for the tariff. The
proposed Commission was to consist of three members, appointed by the Governor-in-Council for a period of five years
from the date of appointment. The duties and responsibilities of
these officials were then detailed by the Minister.

~ The Liberals vigorously opposed the Tariff Commission
Bill. After failing to give it the "six-months' hoist," they sought
to include a clause which would have the Commissioners
"selected without any regard to the views of any political party
upon tariff or other political questions." Borden declared that
Laurier had laid down principles "to which he had never paid
the slightest attention during the whole fifteen years of his
administration."

The Bill was so greatly amended in the Senate that the
government dropped it.

The Senate also defeated Cochrane's bill for the Improvement of Highways and a bill to provide assistance to the Temis-

kaming and Northern Ontario Railway. Foster accused Laurier of using the Senate for "slaughtering" government measures. ~

Among the unfortunate legacies which came to us from the previous Administration was the question of allotting additional territory to the provinces of Quebec, Ontario, and Manitoba. A severe controversy arose between the Governments of Ontario and Manitoba, as the latter province was insistent upon an outlet to Hudson Bay. The contention of each province was vehemently supported by its representative. There were some stormy scenes and eventually the difficulty was solved by granting to Ontario, for the purpose of a railway line to Hudson Bay, a strip of land five miles in width to be selected under the conditions set forth in the enactment.

The Bill which we introduced for this purpose encountered less opposition than I had anticipated. Mr. A. K. Maclean propounded a rather awkward question in the following terms:

What considerations induced the Government to establish the width of five miles for this right of way?

As a matter of fact there was no principle that could be invoked except expediency and the necessity of abating our unfortunate controversy. Upon the spur of the moment I replied:

We gave consideration to it and concluded that five miles would be a convenient strip.

That rather elusive reply seemed to be regarded as satisfactory; and the question was not further pressed.[2]

During the Easter season I was in New York and after spending a few days in that city I sojourned at Hot Springs, Virginia, for a brief rest. While at the latter place, I accepted an invitation to join President Taft in addressing (over the long-distance telephone) the members of the American Associated Press who were holding a banquet at the Waldorf-Astoria Hotel in New York on the evening of April 25. Among the distinguished guests at the dinner were Alexander Graham Bell and Thomas Edison. The voices of the speakers were conveyed with great clearness to each guest by means of a personal receiver. I stressed the wonderful triumph over time and space which had been achieved by human ingenuity and skill during the preceding quarter of a century. . . .

[2] Sir Thomas White has often reminded me that he was wholly at a loss to imagine what reply I would make and he was much amused that it put an end to any further discussion.

18: Visit to England *1912*

Immediately after the session, I had begun to make arrangements for my proposed visit to Great Britain. The necessity of reaching a decision with respect to naval co-operation with Great Britain made the visit not only desirable but necessary. There was serious discussion as to the personnel of my party. I was anxious that Mr. Monk should accompany me but he showed marked disinclination which arose, probably, from his well-known reluctance to be concerned in any measure of that character. Mr. Hazen (as Minister of Marine and Fisheries and Naval Service) was necessarily a member of the party. It was important to name a French Canadian and, next to Mr. Monk, Mr. Pelletier was obviously the best choice. Mr. Doherty's calm judgment, his knowledge of conditions in the Province of Quebec, his ability, and his outstanding position led me to select him as the fourth. Admiral Kingsmill, Sir Joseph Pope, and my secretary, A. E. Blount, were also members of the party.

So far as I remember there was no advance discussion on policy, as that was postponed until after my colleagues had been made acquainted with the results of our visit.

My last Council meeting before departure was held on June 25, and we sailed from Montreal on June 26 (my birthday) on *The Royal George*, leaving at 4:30 a.m. and arriving at Quebec at 2 p.m.

During the voyage I had an opportunity of reading some works on constitutional government, and I arranged every day a conference with Hazen, Doherty, and Pelletier at which our mission was discussed. The subject chiefly dealt with was naval defence but we also discussed copyright, naturalization, and several other matters. . . .

Details of this memorable visit are set forth in my diary. The strain of official duties, as well as the more tremendous strain of social functions, was greater than I had hitherto experienced. Our responsibilities with regard to co-operation in Empire defence weighed heavily upon us. Then, I was determined to make clear to Mr. Asquith and to the members of his Government my attitude with respect to the direction of foreign policy. . . .

My first day in London was rather overwhelming; there were numerous callers, including Bonar Law and Lord Lansdowne; I called on Mr. Asquith, as well as on the First Lord of the Admiralty (Mr. Winston Churchill) with whom I discussed the naval situation for an hour. He expressed great apprehension that Germany intended to strike at the first favourable opportunity. . . .

An extended description of the weeks we spent in England would be tedious. I shall merely allude to the official discussions and incidents and certain of the social functions.

On July 9, we went to Spithead to see the Fleet. During the day I met many members of Parliament on the *Armadale Castle*, as well as Sir George Reid of Australia; on board the cruiser *Enchantress* I had a conversation with Mr. Asquith and Mr. Churchill.

Pursuant to an invitation from the Royal Colonial Institute, I addressed the members on the evening of July 10. Any detailed description of my speech is unnecessary. I was determined to give my audience an impressive description of Canada's immense area. My remarks in this connection may be summarized as follows:

When I resided in Halifax, Nova Scotia, I was one thousand miles nearer to London than to Vancouver on our western coast. If you could pivot Canada upon its eastern seaboard it would cover the northern part of the Atlantic Ocean, the British Islands, Norway, Sweden, Denmark, Holland, Belgium, the northern part of France, the entire German Empire, and a considerable portion of European Russia.

I am convinced that many persons in the audience regarded this description as an indication of my lineal descent from Ananias and as a convincing proof that I had inherited the great qualities of my distinguished ancestor. However, a London journal came to my rescue by producing a map in which it was clearly shown that I was entirely accurate.

On the following day, July 11, there was a meeting of the Defence Committee which we attended. Mr. Asquith presided and spoke, after which Sir Edward Grey gave an interesting description of the foreign relations of the Empire. He did not enlighten us as to a certain agreement between Great Britain and France which was to come into effect in case of attack by Germany; this arrangement, however, seems to have been disclosed only to the Prime Minister. Afterwards, Mr. Churchill spoke and emphasized the German menace. I made very brief remarks at this meeting, suggesting only that we might be afforded an opportunity to discuss the matter with the First

Lord of the Admiralty and such of his officials as he might think proper to bring in touch with us, and arrangements were made for such a conference. . . .

Again on July 13, we had a conference at the Admiralty at which Churchill, Bridgeman, Trowbridge, and other officials were present. The discussion covered rather a large field including docks, merchant cruisers, and so on. At this meeting a conference with Mr. Churchill was arranged for the following Tuesday (July 16). Following the conference we attended a luncheon at Buckingham Palace which was arranged for us in lieu of presentation at Court in order that we might receive invitations to the State Ball.

On July 16, I had a conference with Mr. Churchill and our conversation was very frank and intimate. Mr. Churchill was fair and reasonable and was entirely disposed to give us assurance in writing as to the peril which seemed everywhere to be apprehended in Great Britain and as to the necessity for strong co-operation in naval defence by the Dominions. He spoke of coming to Canada with the Prime Minister.

That evening (July 16) I spoke at a dinner given by the Empire Parliamentary Association. My remarks were well received and my statement, concerning the critical period for the Empire, was particularly featured by the Press; I said:

The next ten or twenty years will be critical in the history of this Empire; they may be even decisive of its future. God grant that whether we be of these Mother Islands or of Dominions beyond the Seas we may so bear ourselves that the future shall not hold to our lips the chalice of vain regret for opportunity neglected and dead. . . . It has been said that the British Empire of today is a very modern organization. This observation carries weight when we consider the modification of constitutional relations within the Empire during the past half century. At one time this Mother of Parliaments was in truth and in fact an Imperial Parliament in the highest sense. If I understand correctly the conditions of today, that status has ceased to exist. A Parliament elected upon issues chiefly, if not altogether, local and domestic, a Parliament which expends so large a portion of its time and energy in discussing and determining questions of purely domestic concern, can hardly be regarded as an Imperial Parliament in the highest or truest sense. The complete autonomy which has been granted to the great Dominions of the Empire has given them practically full control of their own affairs. As a result the Crown has become the strongest, if not the chief tie, which unites the Dominions with the Motherland, and preserves the integrity and cohesion of the Empire.

On July 19 I went to Buckingham Palace at eleven to be sworn in as Privy Councillor; Lord Morley, Mr. Harcourt, and Sir Charles Fitzpatrick were present. . . .

In the afternoon (July 19) I conferred with Churchill as to the character of the speech which he proposed to deliver on the following Monday. In the evening we attended the State Ball. It was most brilliant in every way; I particularly remember the wonderful display of gold plate. . . .

The following afternoon we left for Hatfield where we were to be guests that evening and the following day; there we were greeted by Lord Salisbury with whom we had conversation. In the evening there was a distinguished gathering at dinner, including Lord Kitchener and Lord Robert Cecil. One of the guests questioned Kitchener as to his opinion of the German Ambassador about whom we had heard much. Kitchener dismissed him with the reply: "Oh, just a lawyer fellow."

On July 22, I attended the House of Commons and listened to a debate which is historical. It interested me particularly because of the Prime Minister's virtual withdrawal from his position at the Imperial Conference of 1911, when he had declared, in reply to Sir Joseph Ward, that with respect to foreign policy, the conclusion of treaties, the declaration of war, indeed all relations with foreign powers, the authority of the Imperial Government could not be shared, and must be exercised by that Government, subject only to its responsibility to the Imperial Parliament. His withdrawal from that decision was wholehearted, and was expressed in the following words:

Side by side with this growing participation in the active burdens of the Empire on the part of our Dominions, there rests with us undoubtedly the duty of making such response as we can to their obviously reasonable appeal that they should be entitled to be heard in the determination of the policy and the direction of Imperial affairs.[1]

For the next two days I was very busily occupied in various discussions with Mr. Asquith, Sir Edward Grey, Mr. Harcourt, and Walter Long on a variety of subjects including the best methods of giving the Dominions a voice in the determination of Foreign Policy; our difficulties occasioned by adverse ma-

[1] This subject is dealt with in *Canadian Constitutional Studies*, pp. 89-93.

jority in the Senate; and especially the proper method of effective co-operation in naval defence.

On July 27 I left for Paris. . . .

At a dinner given by the Société France-Amérique at which Hanotaux presided, and at which M. Poincaré was a guest, I responded to the toast in French. Both Hanotaux and Poincaré complimented me upon my French and said that they understood me much better than they understood Mr. Pelletier; I never dared communicate this to Mr. Pelletier.

We returned to London on July 31, and another meeting of the Defence Committee took place on August 1, at which Kitchener was present. I spoke my mind on various subjects and the debate on the whole was interesting and instructive; Doherty made a particularly good speech. . . .

On August 2, Lloyd George entertained us at his official residence; many members of the Cabinet were present. I found Lloyd George a wonderful personality with a keen sense of humour. . . .

That evening (August 2) we were the guests at a great dinner given by the Carlton Club. A large and impressive gathering had been invited; it was the first time in the history of the club that a dinner of this kind had been given. . . . At this dinner the menu would have delighted the heart of any epicure but I would have none of it, dining merely on tea and dry toast; in periods of great strain and exhaustion I found that comparative fasting was my surest safeguard against collapse.

Following the dinner I addressed the "1900" Conservative Club which had established itself in a house once occupied by Nelson; next door or near at hand was the house said to have been occupied by Wellington. In speaking on co-operation in Imperial Defence I said:

> The people of Canada are not the type that will permit themselves to become merely silent partners in such a great Empire. If there is to be Imperial co-operation, the people of Canada propose to have a reasonable and fair voice in that co-operation. I do not doubt but that it is the wish of all the statesmen in the British Isles to accord them that voice.

We spent the week-end in the country and I resumed my official duties on August 6. My correspondence was extremely heavy and occupied most of the day; however, I had time to call on Lloyd George by appointment and was much impressed by his vigorous personality. . . .

On the following day I had a long interview with Churchill

with respect to the method and extent of our co-operation in naval defence; and I told him that everything depended upon the cogency of the statement which he would put forward as to the emergency. He promised to give the subject his closest personal attention. The discussion was renewed on the following day (August 8) with Mr. Asquith to whom I communicated the substance of my conversation with Mr. Churchill. Asquith observed that Mr. Churchill was extremely capable and would be forceful in the preparation of such a statement as we desired.

During the next few days, until August 13 when we left various social functions.

During our visit to Scotland, I received from the Admiralty a memorandum, respecting co-operation in naval defence, which was so entirely inadequate as to justify belief that it had not received reasonable attention from Mr. Churchill. In returning it, I wrote to him that if this contribution was the best we could expect it would be idle for him to anticipate any results whatever from the Government or the people of Canada. Mr. Churchill promptly asked me to join him on the *Enchantress* at Harwich but engagements made it impossible for me to do so. Later (August 26) I received from him a confidential memorandum respecting the naval situation which had been prepared with great care and illustrated his wonderful ability. I returned it with some suggestions and informed him that there must be not only a confidential or secret memorandum but also a memorandum which could be submitted to Parliament and thus made public.

On August 28, I received a delegation of suffragettes. . . . Explaining the Canadian position, I informed them that we would be guided by reason and our best judgment; and that they must not imagine that any coercive measures, which seemed to be suggested in their speeches, would have the slightest influence upon us. Further, I explained that in each of the Canadian provinces the matter would be determined not by Federal but by the Provincial Governments. Apparently they were unable to understand or realize this constitutional practice; and later they sent out to Canadian suffragettes a most amusing misinterpretation of my remarks.

Immediately after the suffragette delegation, I received a delegation of anti-suffragettes who said nothing of importance except to express surprise that they did not find the windows broken and the furniture smashed up.

~ Borden and party had many social engagements to meet.

One of the most interesting was a visit to Arundel Castle where the Duke of Norfolk told Doherty that at some future time the castle would probably be utilized as a public building, "an asylum or something of that character." Among the highlights were dinner with Balfour, a weekend with the Astors at Cliveden, visits to country homes of Harcourt and Asquith. Borden went to Headcorn, the ancestral seat of the Borden family. After an uneventful crossing they were greeted with receptions at Quebec, Three Rivers, and Sorel and given a rousing welcome at Montreal. ~

We arrived in Ottawa on September 8, and demonstrations of welcome were renewed on the following day when there was a civic reception and procession. I was presented with an address at the City Hall and was greeted by great crowds. Then I proceeded to the Exhibition Grounds for luncheon where Sir Wilfrid gave me a kindly welcome when he spoke. Returning to my office, I held an informal reception and met many old friends.

During the voyage home, I had suffered considerable pain from an abscess. About six o'clock, after the busy day described above, I called in my physician who strongly advised an operation which I did not desire, as I had to speak at a banquet that evening. Nevertheless, the operation took place and the doctor said it was most fortunate that it had not been delayed. . . .

19: *1912-1913*

Apart from the preparation of the Navy Bill and the discussions and conferences in connection therewith, which are dealt with in a separate chapter, many and varying matters claimed my attention before the opening of the session on November 21, 1912.

Mr. Cochrane, whose strong antagonism to the Grand Trunk Railway was quite manifest, precipitated some heated discussions and rather violent scenes in connection with the affairs of that railway and of the Grand Trunk Pacific Railway. White and I were agreed and determined that nothing should be done to injure the credit of the two railways.

On September 20, I left for Montreal to fulfil my engagement to speak on the following evening at a banquet to celebrate the first anniversary of the Conservative victory given by the Liberal-Conservative Club of Montreal. My friend, L. T. Marechal, one of the most eloquent of a race of orators, presided, and Guy Drummond (who three years afterwards gave his life for his country) was secretary of the committee. It was an immense gathering and there were many speakers, including my colleagues Monk, White, and Rogers. When I arose to speak I received a tremendous ovation. Speaking briefly in French, I emphasized the importance of co-operation between the great pioneer races and expressed grateful recognition of my reception throughout the provinces upon my return. The interests of each province were interlocked with those of Canada as a whole; upon that basis our policy would be framed. After adding a tribute to Sir Charles Tupper and speaking of the warmth of my reception in Great Britain and in France, I said that the mother country vividly realized Canada's importance. I had gone over in pursuit of a pledge to the people upon the question of naval co-operation; one question was concerned with our action in case of a sudden emergency; the other and more difficult question related to permanent co-operation in defence. I told the people of the motherland that Canada did not propose to be a mere adjunct even of the British Empire and that with co-operation in defence there must come a certain voice by Canada in the interests of peace and war. Any proposals that we would make would be presented in no spirit of partisanship.

I spoke of our success in carrying on the Administration

during the preceding twelve months and alluded to the feeling which pervaded the mind of a party long in power, that the country would go to ruin in case they should be relegated to the Opposition benches. Men accustomed to power for many years had the habit of imagining that they entered into an offensive and defensive alliance with Providence; and the late Administration had suffered from this feeling.

Speaking of Canada's immense heritage and the birth of a consciousness of nationhood and of the national spirit with which the youth of Canada was inspired, I expressed the hope and the confident belief that in the developing of this great heritage and in the shaping of our mighty destiny none of those upon whom so great a task had been imposed would fail either in endeavour or in fulfilment.

Leaving Montreal by the night train on September 22, we arrived at Toronto early the next morning.

During the forenoon I received a deputation of suffragettes to whom I explained that while federal elections were conducted according to the Dominion Franchise Act and while provincial lists of voters were being used, they would have to place their appeal before Provincial Legislatures. They were mildness itself compared to their English sisters.

The banquet that evening was entirely non-partisan and was the largest I had ever attended; indeed, in point of numbers it was the largest ever held in Canada. There were 1,500 guests and 10,000 persons in the audience. To make myself audible to so vast a gathering was a tremendous effort and I was not at all satisfied with my speech.

Sir James Whitney proposed my health in graceful and eloquent terms, paying me a very generous tribute.

I said that Canada had a great heritage and a great future but we should never forget the greater heritage and future of the Empire. In Great Britain we had borne ourselves as representatives not of a party but of the whole people. The visit of Canadian Ministers had attracted on the continent of Europe almost as much attention as in Great Britain. British people were as much concerned as the people of Canada in maintaining Empire unity; and they were equally determined that the path across the seas should be kept safe. I could not announce our proposals for co-operation in naval defence as they must be reserved for Parliament. Canada had grown from a mere fringe of communities on the Atlantic seaboard until her Dominion extended to the Pacific:

We speak of East and West in sentiment and ideals. Let there be no East or West, but one Canada.

After speaking of many domestic problems, I touched upon the essential consideration of the Empire's unity; and I expressed the certain conviction that if the need should come the people of Canada as one man would come to the aid of the Empire's defence: "Although the Dominions of this Empire may be sundered by oceans, for the preservation of its unity, for the preservation of its power and influence, for the maintenance of its work, the Motherland and the Dominions are one and are indivisible."

I was surprised at the enthusiasm with which my remarks were received. This was perhaps due to my emphasis in setting forth the probable need of an emergency contribution toward naval defence.

Hon. N. W. Rowell (then Ontario's Liberal Leader) made a strong Imperial speech declaring that:

As Canadians, as a self-respecting, liberty-loving, virile people, shall we not say the time has come when we must bear our share and take up our burden with you?

During October, a variety of matters engaged our attention. Discussions as to the propriety of Doherty's attendance at a proposed reception to John Redmond in Montreal (eventually I decided he should go); intriguing activities of Father Burke who claimed to have had an interview with President Taft respecting the release of Dillon, a prisoner in Kingston Penitentiary; an interview with the Editor of *Leipzig Illustrierte Zeitung*, Herr Horst Weber, who was desirous of issuing a Canadian edition and of obtaining a subsidy from the Government therefor; *inter alia,* he hoped and indeed urged that the Government would defray, wholly or partly, the expenses of a party of German leaders in finance and industry whom he proposed to bring on a tour through Canada;[1] all these and other matters were sources of annoyance and took up time.

Then, after Mr. Monk's resignation there were of course numerous conferences as to the selection of his successor. L. T. Marechal was strongly urged to enter the Government, but he seemed to lack decision and to be uncertain as to his course; finally, the conclusion was reached that he should defer his

---

[1] I happened to mention this request to the Duchess of Connaught at a dinner at Government House. "Don't give them one penny," was her advice.

entry into public life and that Louis Coderre should enter the Government as Secretary of State. Mr. Rogers took over the Department of Public Works, and Dr. Roche the Department of the Interior.

Shortly after the formation of the new Administration, I had made enquiries as to the availability of an experienced and competent person who would be prepared to undertake an investigation of the Civil Service of Canada, and Rt. Hon. Sir George Herbert Murray, G.C.B., was recommended.

He arrived in Canada during the summer of 1912; and after my return from England I met him on many occasions. . . .

John Graham Haggart died on March 13, 1913; he was many years my senior and had been Minister of Railways from 1888 to 1896 in the Conservative Governments. He was a man of fine ability, a vigorous but not a finished speaker, and he possessed a very wide range of useful information as well as an excellent knowledge of English literature. He had favoured Sir George Foster for the leadership, but he was extremely considerate to me and highly sympathetic with my efforts. On many occasions he spoke to me of Sir John A. Macdonald and he told me of these two maxims by which Sir John had been guided. A political leader should never be influenced by personal likes or dislikes in the selection of his colleagues, and he should never quarrel so vehemently with a political opponent as to prevent his receiving that opponent as a colleague in case occasion should arise therefor. In later years I bore these maxims in mind and I added to them a third. A political leader should use discretion in attack and should not always hit with all the strength at his command. . . .

After the close of the session, I left for Halifax where I arrived on June 14. After a sleepless night I was obliged to spend the following day in bed owing to myalgia of the muscle of my neck. I was under medical treatment and in the care of a trained nurse. However, I received numerous visitors that day and the next. Sometimes the nurse gave me massage during the interviews.

I paid a brief visit to my home at Grand Pré where I found my dear mother bright and cheerful, and I left for Ottawa on June 19.

During the next two weeks I was under medical treatment and underwent various tests as to my physical condition. There were many important interviews on a variety of subjects. I was on the verge of exhaustion arising from the intense and prolonged strain and from the continued recurrence of carbuncles.

I quote from my diary for June 25, 1913: "Countless interviews with people who have been hovering like vultures eager to have various matters dealt with before my departure for St. Andrews."[2]. . .

On August 31, I had conferences first with Sir Charles Fitzpatrick and then with Lord Haldane, who was to be the principal speaker at the meeting of the American Bar Association in Montreal. With the latter I discussed the naval question, and the possibility of making appointments to the Senate under Section 26 of the British North America Act.[3] This had previously been the subject of a conference with Mr. Asquith while we were in London. . . .

On September 2, I spoke at the laying of the cornerstone of the memorial to Sir George Etienne Cartier. In part, I said:

No one can fail to be impressed by the wide vision and the far-reaching foresight of this great statesman. He divined the need of unity for the scattered and disunited provinces of Canada. He foresaw that understanding, co-operation and mutual endeavour were all-important if the two peoples of the two great races were to accomplish all that their opportunities, their traditions and their past achievements should properly demand.

But more than this he realized that the great purpose that he had in mind could only be accomplished by the maintenance of provincial autonomy, and by the establishment of a union upon a federal basis.

During this month (September) I again visited Nova Scotia, returning to Ottawa on the twenty-first. In my diary for September 15 and 16, I note that the greater part of these days was occupied with interviews with applicants for office (they were as thick as "autumnal leaves in Vallombrosa!") and in listening to the complaints of the County Executive and Ward Chairman with respect to the distribution of patronage. My engagements were incessant in connection with these and other matters.

[2] I quote from my diary of June 24, 1913: "Rev. Mr. MacKay, my pastor, came for a very delightful visit. He told me that having called on a parishioner in Lower Town (a district in Ottawa) who discussed St. Jean Baptiste celebration, he asked her what she thought it was and she expressed the opinion that it was the celebration of the sixtieth anniversary of the saint's wedding"!

[3] 26. If at any Time on the Recommendation of the Governor General the Queen thinks fit to direct that Three or Six Members be added to the Senate, the Governor General may by Summons to Three or Six qualified Persons (as the case may be), representing equally the Three Divisions of Canada, add to the Senate accordingly.

During the remainder of the month my time was occupied with various matters including conferences with Mr. Smithers concerning the Grand Trunk Pacific Railway. At my interview with him on September 25, I told him that the Government had no desire to force the hand of the railway and that we desired them to carry out their contract to operate the line from Winnipeg to Moncton but that we would be obliged to take over the entire line to the coast if they did not fulfil that contract. He expressed hope that we would give them better terms. . . .

20: Sessional Activities *1912-1913*

Parliament opened on November 21, 1912.[1] The Speech from the Throne had been prepared with a great deal of care and touched on the prosperous conditions of the country, the increase in trade, the continued expansion of Dominion revenues, the large and welcome stream of immigration, and the abundant harvest.

The most important legislation proposed was a Bill for the purpose of strengthening without delay the naval forces of the Empire. In addition to this, other important measures included Bills to ratify the West Indies Treaty; to co-operate with the provinces for improving the highways; to aid the agricultural industry along the lines of agricultural instruction; to revise and extend the charters to the banks.

On the following day I discussed with the mover (Rainville) and the seconder (Nickle) of the Address the character of their speeches. By curious coincidence they happened to sit for seats which, in the old days, had returned Cartier and Macdonald. . . .

The Highways Bill, rejected by the Senate during the previous session, was again introduced by Mr. Cochrane (Minister of Railways) on December 11, 1912. The Bill empowered the Minister of Railways, with the authority of the Governor-in-Council, to enter into an agreement with each province for the expenditure of a certain sum appropriated to that province by the estimates in each year. The sums so appropriated were to be expended by the Provincial Governments, but only for the purpose of constructing new highways or improving existing highways, and proper safeguards were provided by appropriate agreement. One clause in the Bill contained a provision that with the consent of the Provincial Government, and with the authority of the Provincial Legislature, any portion of the money so appropriated might be expended by the Federal Government. Not one dollar could be expended without the consent of the Provincial Government and the authority of the Provincial Legislature. The expenditure proposed was one

[1] That evening there was a State Dinner at Government House. The Lieutenant-Governor of New Brunswick (Hon. Josiah Wood) was a man of the most punctilious propriety. His predecessor's A.D.C., whom he had retained, was of a bibulous habit and celebrated the occasion by indulging too freely in stimulating potations. He offered to fight one of the Aides who endeavoured to keep him quiet. Eventually he had to be removed.

million dollars for 1911-12 and one million and a half for 1912-13. The sums were allocated to each province in exact proportion to its population.

The Bill came up for second reading on April 21. Speaking on the measure Sir Wilfrid declared that there was no point of difference between the Opposition and the Government as to the merits of the Bill and its usefulness to the general community, but he objected, as he had done in the previous session, to the distribution of the money which he declared was to be kept within the discretion of the Minister. Mr. Cochrane definitely stated that the money would be divided *pro rata* between the different provinces and that it would be voted separately in the estimates for the provinces. The Leader of the Opposition contended that, while the Government might have no intention of discriminating between province and province, the measure should definitely provide for the appropriation to be allotted according to population. In conclusion he moved the following amendment:

> *That the Bill be not now read the second time, but that it be resolved—That this House, whilst recognizing the importance of assisting out of the Federal Treasury in the matter of highways, is of opinion that all appropriations for that object should be allotted and paid to the Governments of the respective provinces in proportion to the population of said provinces respectively, as determined by the latest decennial census.*

Following Sir Wilfrid, I questioned the sincerity of his desire to promote the passage of the measure in view of his action in moving an amendment on second reading instead of waiting until the Bill was in Committee. The Leader of the Opposition had proposed an amendment which, if carried, would necessitate that the Bill be reinstated on the order paper. He had pursued the same course in the previous session; this year he had given as his reason the example of the Agricultural Aid Bill; the distinction between the two measures was obvious. The Agricultural Aid Bill proposed a specific sum and, therefore, it was necessary that it should provide how it was to be distributed among the provinces. In the Highways Bill there was no provision whatever for the spending of any sum of money except what might be voted by Parliament. We had pledged ourselves that the money to be voted would be apportioned to the different provinces exactly upon the same basis as the provincial subsidies, and so it had turned out. The Bill was not a money bill but merely an enabling measure; when the necessary appropriations were submitted the Opposition would have full power and right to maintain their principles by their present arguments which, in the meantime, were idle and premature.

After much debate the Bill passed, but once more Sir Wilfrid, by his control of the Senate, insisted on the amendments which had been defeated in the Commons. We declined to accept the amendments, the Bill did not pass, and our proposals for aiding highways were dropped.

On December 18 I laid on the table the report of Sir George Murray who had been commissioned under Order-in-Council to investigate and report on all matters pertaining to the Canadian Civil Service; this report was very elaborate and far-reaching and went somewhat beyond the scope of the proposed inquiry. Several reasons contributed to the delay in taking definite and immediate action thereon. In the first place, the naval controversy was absorbing the whole attention of the Government for several months, and the imminence of war, followed by its actual outbreak, diverted attention from even so important a reform. Another reason why no action was immediately taken was the very sweeping character of the report, and its mixture of practical and impractical suggestions. It dealt not merely with civil service matters in the stricter sense, but with more general questions of administration as, for example, the importance of relieving the Cabinet of many administrative details with which it was burdened and of devolving more responsibility upon Ministers and Deputy Ministers, the abolition of the Treasury Board, and the control of estimates and appropriations by the Department of Finance, corresponding to the Treasury in Great Britain. This was so formidable and far-reaching a programme that it would have been out of the question to carry it into full effect. Further, as regards the strictly Civil Service recommendations, there was strong opposition in various quarters to depriving the Commission of power over promotions, to a non-contributary system of pensions, and to the stricter distinction between the First, Second, and Third Divisions. In fact, Sir George Murray had probably an imperfect conception of the difficulties that would confront any administration in the attempt to put in force some of his recommendations, however valuable they appeared to him; *inter alia* he probably did not fully appreciate the considerations that had induced Sir John A. Macdonald in the early days of Confederation to bring many matters of administration, and especially of expenditure within the ambit of the Governor-in-Council's control. In conversations with him he seemed unduly to minimize the importance of some branches of our public service, and I was especially struck with his failure to realize the value of the work then and since being performed in the Public Archives.

The House adjourned on December 18 until January 14.

Before Parliament re-assembled I had a discussion with White respecting estimates and tariff, and I told him that he and I would settle tariff matters and thus avoid protracted discussion in Council.

An important measure, designed to grant aid for the advancement of agricultural instruction, was introduced by Mr. Burrell (Minister of Agriculture) on January 24, 1913. It was proposed that the sum of $10,000,000 should be voted for this purpose and that its distribution should be spread over a period of ten years, beginning with the year ending March 31, 1914. Speaking on this measure Mr. Burrell said:

It is not necessary in this day or hour to defend or justify generous assistance to agriculture. We all recognize the soundness of such a doctrine. To increase the farmers' output; to improve the conditions of rural life, to swell the numbers of those who till the fields . . . to do these things . . . we are doing something to solve the greatest problems and avert many of the manifest evils that face us in modern life. Two problems especially confront us today, as they confront other nations; the ever-increasing cost of living, with its heavy burdens, and the increase of urban as against rural population.

He further emphasized the importance of freely and generously assisting the cause of agricultural education and thus encouraging our citizens to resume the healthy activity of agricultural life.

A lengthy debate ensued in which the Opposition approved the principle but took exception to the method and details of distribution. The Bill received third reading and was passed on April 29.

During this session a curious incident occurred in the Public Accounts Committee. In an investigation of payments to the Diamond Light and Heating Company of Montreal it appeared in the evidence that the sum of $41,026 had been paid for the purpose of securing contracts from the Dominion Government amounting to about $117,000. Mr. R. C. Miller, who had been President of the Company, had been examined before the Committee and had refused to divulge to whom the money had been paid. Thereupon the Chairman of the Public Accounts Committee (Mr. Middlebro), on February 17, brought the matter to the attention of the House, and upon his motion, Mr. Miller attended at the Bar of the House on the following day. He was accompanied by counsel who declared that Miller declined to answer the question put for the reason that it would incriminate him. This answer was insufficient as under the law any answer that a witness might give to such a question was privileged. It was therefore ordered that Miller should be taken into custody and the Speaker's warrant was issued accordingly. On February 20, Miller, in custody of the Sergeant-at-Arms, was brought to the Bar of the House and the question was again put to him. He proceeded to make a long statement and a lively debate ensued in which several members of the legal profession participated.

Mr. Pugsley and Mr. Carvell, supported by other members of the Committee, raised questions chiefly of a technical character and spoke at great length and for the purpose of inducing the House to take no such action as was proposed by motion of Mr. Middlebro, that the witness should be adjudged as "guilty" of contempt in refusing to answer. Their arguments were effectively controverted by Mr. Meighen in an exhaustive speech. Finally Mr. Doherty defined the powers and duties of the House in a moderate, reasonable, and lucid speech in which he declared that it was the imperative duty of the House to take the action proposed by Mr. Middlebro.

Sir Wilfrid Laurier, always mindful of the dignity of the House and determined to uphold its powers, brushed aside the contentions of Mr. Pugsley and Mr. Carvell by his concurrence in the opinion expressed by Mr. Doherty, to whom he offered warm congratulations. At the end he suggested that it was a serious thing to send a respectable citizen to jail or to keep him within the precincts of the House, and he thought I would be well advised to take the matter into further consideration.

The motion declaring Miller to be guilty of contempt was carried upon division, and on my motion Miller was brought to the Bar to hear the judgment of the House.

Miller remained in jail until prorogation, still persisting in his refusal to answer.

On March 17, Mr. L. J. Gauthier asked for an inquiry into certain charges against Mr. Coderre in connection with the then recent election in Hochelaga. He read various documents and four affidavits, indicating personation with the knowledge of Mr. Coderre, promises of money, positions, and patronage by other Ministers. Mr. Coderre, after giving the charges absolute denial, withdrew while the matter was being discussed. The

Minister of Justice at once took the floor. He analyzed the affidavits of the four deponents and produced an affidavit of one of them who denied the truth of the allegations and swore he had signed without reading upon the assurance of another deponent that it would enable them to obtain money from Ministers at Ottawa. Another deponent had made a like recantation and a third had fled the country to avoid arrest for other causes.

Speaking after Sir Wilfrid Laurier, I pointed out and emphasized the fact that every one of the charges related to matters which, under the terms of the Contraverted Elections Act, had been relegated to the courts for investigation. If Mr. Gauthier's motion should succeed, then any member, rising in his place and making an accusation that the offence of bribery or other corrupt practices had been committed by any other member, would have the right to have such charges tried in the Committee on Privileges and Elections although the power and procedure of the courts had never been invoked. If we were to try allegations in respect of the Hochelaga elections, why not try allegations in respect of the general election of 1911? In at least one case we had been asked to bring up the matter respecting the election of a member of the Opposition and, "Our answer was that given by the Minister of Justice this afternoon; your proper remedy and your proper tribunal is to be found in the courts of this country."

Sir Wilfrid had charged that one of the deponents had been rewarded by appointment to office. In reply I emphatically stated that he had not been appointed to any public office and that so long as I should be connected with the Government of Canada he never would be so appointed. Mr. Gauthier's motion for an inquiry was defeated.

On March 27, 1913, I introduced a resolution and a Bill founded thereon for the adhesion of Canada to a treaty between Great Britain and Japan. The new treaty was entered into on April 3, 1911, and Canada had the right, until May 5, 1913, to adhere to it.

The only difference of any consequence between the new and the old treaty was that the former reserved to Canada the right to control Japanese immigration; in other words, Canada was placed in the same position as United States in this respect.

To ascertain the exact position of our country, so far as Japanese immigration is concerned, it is necessary to go back to 1894, when Japan made treaties with Great Britain and United States. The treaty with Great Britain was signed on July

16, 1894, and in the same year a treaty was signed with United States. Great Britain was not interested in Japanese immigration which explains why a clause, appearing in the United States' but not in the British treaty, declared that it did not in any way affect the laws, ordinances, and regulations respecting "immigration" and trade.

On August 6, 1895, the Canadian Government passed an Order-in-Council with the following recommendation:

The Canadian Government in adhering to this treaty would desire a stipulation with respect to Japanese immigration similar to that inserted in the treaty between Japan and the United States.

This Order-in-Council was transmitted to the Japanese Government by the British Minister at Tokyo on October 18, 1895.

On July 29, 1896, the Laurier Government passed an Order-in-Council recommending that Canada should not adhere to the treaty, but in 1907 the same Government negotiated a supplementary treaty or convention under which Canada adhered to the treaty of 1894 without reserving the power to control immigration.

Following this, there was a rush of Japanese immigrants to Canada. Mr. Lemieux was sent to Japan and an understanding was reached to restrict such immigration.

The Treaty passed during this session (1913) contained the following clause which is not to be found in the previous Treaty:

Nothing in the said treaty or in this Act shall be deemed to repeal or affect any of the provisions of the said Immigration Act.

Thus, Canada retained the same control over Japanese immigration into this country as had all along been insisted upon by United States. In this connection, it should be pointed out that, notwithstanding Canada's proper assumption of the right to control immigration, Japan agreed to continue the restriction of such immigration which it had practised during the past few years. In this way Canada retained the advantages of the Lemieux arrangement, and in addition reserved full control over immigration.

Canada might at any time issue an order closing the country to settlers from all foreign Asiatic countries or to people of particular races. The only sure guarantee of protection from Japanese immigration was the retention of the power—which the previous Government had failed to accomplish—to legislate and regulate whenever it might become necessary. As there was no conflict of policy between the two countries, there was no need for action, but should a difference arise, the Government was safeguarded in the same way as United States against allowing control to slip out of its hands.

The Opposition initiated and carried on a rather lengthy debate in which they strenuously contended that by corre-spondence which had been exchanged between myself and Mr. Nakamura (Consul-General for Japan), Canada's control over emigration from Japan was diminished. In concluding the debate on third reading, I went rather fully into this question. I quote the following:

I desire to add that the provisions of the Immigration Act, whether this treaty shall go into force or not can be exercised and may still be exercised, without any offence to the great and friendly nation with whom the treaty has been negotiated. As I have pointed out over and over again, although hon. gentlemen on the other side of the House have continued to ignore that consideration, the question is not, at the bottom, one of race or of discrimination against a nationality, but the question is one of economic concern. Therefore, it would be perfectly possible, whether this treaty did come into force or not, for the Govern-ment of Canada to pass regulations under the Immigration Act which would prevent the immigration of persons of a certain occupation whose competition would not be fair to the labouring men of Canada. The situation in that regard will be precisely in the future what it has been in the past, since the treaty of 1894 ceased to have effect. . . .

21: Naval Aid Bill *1912-1913*

Soon after my return from England in September of 1912, I began to take up again ordinary routine matters. Many rumours as to the coming session were current; among them was a report that the Opposition intended to obstruct Supply in the Senate and thus force us to the country. To this gossip I paid little heed, but of much more serious concern was the persistent rumour that my friend and colleague, F. D. Monk, was hostile to us on the question of naval aid.

I had numerous discussions with Monk during September, and I particularly recall a most earnest appeal, that I made to him in the presence of Pelletier, in which I implored him to remain if possible as his retirement would be most unfortunate and even disastrous at that juncture. He seemed anxious to comply but apparently he lacked courage to face the fierce criticism with which, undoubtedly, he would have been assailed had he remained.

Late in September the two documents, secret and publishable, arrived from the Admiralty and immediately after their arrival I read them to my colleagues in Council. The secret memorandum was most impressive but the publishable document had not been so well prepared, and it omitted the important statement that capital ships were required. Following perusal of the documents, discussion arose as to the advisability of consulting the people by plebiscite. Monk admitted that the situation was grave and emergent but was very strong in his opinion that this course should be followed and Nantel was his echo. The Ontario Ministers, as well as Hazen, Rogers, Burrell, and Roche, were strongly opposed to an appeal to the people.

On October 14, I presented to Council a draft of the Naval Aid Bill which I had previously submitted to White and to Perley. There was about an hour's discussion which resulted in unanimous approval. Monk, however, did not utter a word.

During the next few days much pressure was brought to bear, especially in Montreal, upon Monk in a last endeavour to induce him to stand to his guns, but it was all in vain.[1]

I had hoped that he would first submit to me his letter of

---

[1] Lord Shaughnessy came to discuss the situation with me; and lengthily denounced Monk, characterizing him as lacking in "backbone."

resignation but he did not do so, and it was received on October 18,[2] in the following terms:

My dear Premier,

I regret to find that I cannot concur in the decision arrived at by the Cabinet yesterday to place, on behalf of Canada, an emergency contribution of $35,000,000 at the disposal of the British Government for naval purposes, with the sanction of Parliament about to assemble, but without giving the Canadian people an opportunity of expressing its approval of this important step before it is taken.

Such a concurrence would be at variance with my pledges and the act proposed is of sufficient gravity to justify my insistence; it goes beyond the scope of the Constitutional Act of 1867.

Holding this view, as a member of your Cabinet, I feel it my duty to place my resignation in your hands.

Permit me to add that my decision has been reached with regret, on account of my agreeable relations at all times with yourself.

Early next morning, I called him into conference and explained how I thought this letter should be modified. We held council on October 21 but Monk was not present. That morning he forwarded to me his amended letter of resignation but not in the terms I had suggested.

On October 22, I arranged with the Duke of Connaught to receive me at noon and Monk at 12:30. I explained the cause of Monk's resignation and the Duke agreed that there could be no plebiscite.

On account of failing health and disinclination to participate further in public affairs, he resigned his seat on March 3, 1914. He told me once that he had entered public life simply for the reason that he desired appointment to the judicial bench and had been assured that it would be advantageous, and indeed essential, to enter the House of Commons. His temperament absolutely unfitted him for such a life; and I fear that he obtained very little satisfaction or enjoyment therein. His death occurred in Montreal about two months after his retirement. . . .

In the meantime, early in September, Sir Wilfrid had commenced at Marieville, Quebec, a series of speeches on naval

[2] It had been rumoured that Monk was looking for the position of Representative at Washington. This, however, he said he would not accept; that he intended to travel, and that he would not oppose us except on the naval issue.

affairs. It was his first appearance in rural Quebec since his defeat of the previous year. The general trend of his remarks was that he was prepared to discuss with "calmness and dignity" any naval proposals put forward by the Government. He was reported as having said:

May my tongue wither in my mouth before I inaugurate a war of races in this country so blessed of Heaven.

He particularly stressed the opinion that if actual danger to England arose he and other French Canadians would assist in every possible way but he was against a contribution for any "pretended emergency."

Early in November I had a conference with several prominent members of the Press to whom I communicated our proposals regarding naval co-operation and to whom I explained the conditions of emergency as disclosed in the Admiralty's secret memorandum. The general opinion was that, on the whole, the proposals would be well received.

On November 7, I submitted to Premier McBride of British Columbia, the confidential and secret communications from the Admiralty. This had been arranged with the Admiralty from whom I had permission also to show the documents to any member of our Privy Council. On the following day I resumed discussion with McBride to whom I explained our policy more fully and described the position I had taken in England. He suggested the appointment of a commission to consider a permanent policy but otherwise he was heartily in accord with the proposals.

The discussions and conferences continued at great length, especially with members of the Press. On November 16, I gave Sir Wilfrid Laurier a copy of the secret memorandum. On the 18th, J. S. Willison, with whom I had an interview, expressed satisfaction with the proposed measures. On November 20, in council I read my speech introducing the Navy Bill. Some unimportant changes were suggested and made, and I decided to omit any reference to our permanent policy.

Shortly after the opening of Parliament (November 21), I learned that some of the Quebec members were restless with regard to the naval question and would probably bolt.[3] Thus, on Wednesday, November 27, I had a meeting of the French members and explained to them that we proposed to repeal the Laurier Navy Bill; and I gave them an outline of our permanent

[3] Mondou was said to be particularly unreliable.

policy. Several of them (Boulay, Barrette, Bellemare, Achim, and Guilbault) agreed that the proposals were wise but declared that they were bound by promises to vote against them. Paquet, Lavallée, Gauthier, Rainville, Blondin, and Sévigny promised to support us.

Mondou had prepared an amendment, which he insisted on moving on December 3, to the effect that so long as the people of the United Kingdom, alone, reserved to themselves the exclusive management and control of Imperial and international questions, the Canadian Parliament had no right to impose upon its people responsibilities in regard to defence of the Empire. The amendment was defeated by a majority of 179, only three other members voting with Mondou.

I had arranged to introduce the Bill on December 5, and to postpone its second reading until the following week. Apparently there was great interest in the matter as many people from all parts of the country arrived to hear the proposals.

The Speaker had an obsession with regard to the necessity of putting the motion before the speech was commenced or proceeded with. This was entirely unnecessary on this occasion and it caused me a good deal of inconvenience. When about to make an important speech I had the habit of pushing my chair out into the aisle so as to allow myself more freedom of movement. When the Speaker interrupted me to put the motion, I sat down on nothing and, in the resulting tumble, broke my glasses.[4] Fortunately just before the House opened something had prompted me to send for another pair of glasses—otherwise I should have been in a quandary as my notes were quite elaborate.

Before outlining the course the Government proposed to take, I emphasized that I would speak in no controversial spirit but would give frankly to the House the reasons which had led the Government to introduce the measure about to be explained. Proceeding, I said:

In this constitutional development (Empire) we are necessarily confronted with the problem of combining co-operation with autonomy. It seems essential that there should be such co-operation in defence and in trade as will give to the whole Empire an effective organization in these matters of vital concern. On the other hand each Dominion must preserve in all important respects the autonomous government which it now possesses. Responsibility for the Empire's defence upon the

---

[4] At the moment I would gladly have broken, also, the Speaker's head.

high seas, in which is to be found the only effective guarantee of its existence, and which has hitherto been assumed by the United Kingdom, has necessarily carried with it responsibility for and control of foreign policy. With the enormous increase of naval power which has been undertaken by all great nations in recent years, this tremendous responsibility has cast an almost impossible burden upon the British Islands. . . . That burden is so great that the day has come when either the existence of this Empire will be imperilled or the young and mighty Dominions must join with the Motherland to make secure the common safety and the common heritage of all. When Great Britain no longer assumes sole responsibility for defence upon the high seas, she can no longer undertake to assume sole responsibility for and sole control of foreign policy which is closely, vitally and constantly associated in that defence in which the Dominions participate.

During my recent visit to England I had, on many occasions, ventured to propound the principle just enunciated, and no declaration that I made was more enthusiastically and heartily received. Indeed, leaders of both political parties in Great Britain had apparently accepted this principle.

~ Borden recalled his pledge to ascertain from Britain whether conditions of emergency had arisen and, if so, to ask Parliament for immediate aid. This he had done. As to a permanent policy, any proposals would be submitted to the Canadian people. He spoke of the vast armies of continental Europe and noted that the Empire was not a great military power but based its security almost entirely on naval strength. The Admiralty had been compelled to withdraw forces from far-flung areas so that the navy was now predominant only in the North Sea.

He was not proposing a system of regular contributions, but a $35,000,000 vote for three battleships to be controlled and maintained as part of the Royal Navy. They could be recalled as part of a Canadian unit if that should eventually become Canadian policy. Canadians would be given special opportunities to serve on these ships. They would be built in Britain but the Admiralty had agreed to place orders for smaller craft with Canadian ship building firms.

The proposal was moderate and reasonable. Canada for years had enjoyed the protection of the British Navy without the cost of a dollar. The protection of the flag and the prestige of Empire had meant much to Canadian citizens. ~

And I concluded as follows:

The next ten or twenty years will be pregnant with great results for this Empire; and it is of infinite importance that questions of purely domestic concern, however urgent, shall not prevent any of us from rising "to the height of this great argument." But today, while the clouds are heavy and we hear the booming of the distant thunder and see the lightning flashes above the horizon, we cannot and we will not wait and deliberate until any impending storm shall have burst upon us in fury and with disaster. Almost unaided, the Motherland not for herself alone, but for us as well, is sustaining the burden of a vital Imperial duty, and confronting an overmastering necessity of national existence. Bringing the best assistance that we may in the urgency of the moment, we come thus to her aid, in token of our determination to protect and ensure the safety and integrity of this Empire, and of our resolve to defend on sea as well as on land our flag, our honour and our heritage.

My speech was splendidly received and throughout there was tremendous applause; at the end, not only the House but the galleries sang the national anthem. "Rule Britannia" was also started but was overcome by "God Save The King." Messages of congratulation, by wire and telephone, began to pour in from all parts of the country. The House was adjourned at six o'clock, as the members were much too excited to work that evening. On the following day the congratulations continued to arrive in great numbers; and I especially appreciated a very fine message from Field-Marshal Earl Roberts. . . .

[On December 12] Sir Wilfrid Laurier proceeded to set forth the policy of the Opposition. His speech did not appeal to me as impressive, and he seemed nervous and anxious. It was evident that he was aiming at dissolution, depending on his prestige in Quebec and on his proposals in the other provinces. In conclusion he moved for two fleet units, to be stationed on the Atlantic and Pacific coasts of Canada respectively, rather than to assist by a contribution of money or ships direct to Great Britain. The galleries were crowded and at the end of his speech the national anthem was again sung.

Hazen replied in an excellent speech which, however, was too long. Graham, who followed, was witty and sarcastic and indulged greatly in quotation; in his efforts at humour he sometimes degenerated into "near-vaudeville." Then came Pelletier in a speech which read much better than it sounded.

The debate was resumed on December 16 and 17, when a lengthy discussion took place. On the following day Foster's speech was a magnificent effort; he took up point after point put forward by Laurier, Graham, and others and he fairly smashed each one.

Mr. Guthrie began his speech in reply by challenging us to dissolve. . . .

On New Year's Day I attended the Governor-General's Levée. The Duke of Connaught gave me a very cordial welcome and told me that the King had written to him a very appreciative letter respecting our policy and my speech.

On January 14, 1913, debate on the Naval Aid Bill was resumed. Mr. Guthrie made a long and rather critical speech in which he ridiculed the idea that a condition of emergency existed or that there was any immediate danger of war with Germany. However, his keen sense of loyalty to the Empire made itself felt; and toward the close of his speech he urged that a spirit of compromise should prevail and that the two parties might agree on a reasonable compromise of their respective policies. It was quite evident from his speech that if he were convinced of actual danger he would have been prepared to endorse any policy that could reasonably be regarded as necessary to ensure the safety of the Empire. The debate continued until February 13, when the vote was taken upon the various amendments which had been proposed to the resolution. The chief amendment was that proposed by Sir Wilfrid Laurier regarding the establishment of two fleet units. This was defeated by a majority of 47 – all the Quebec Conservatives voting with the Government.

~ In the vote on the resolution some Quebec Conservatives voted against the Government. The House went into Committee of the Whole and the real fight began. ~

The debate dragged on until February 27, when a motion that the Bill be not proceeded with until after Redistribution and a general election was defeated by a majority of 36; and second reading of the Bill carried by a majority of 30.

I spoke in reply to Sir Wilfrid and I had no trouble in exposing the extremely inconsistent position which the Opposition occupied by reason of the confusion arising from several amendments and sub-amendments. Towards the conclusion of my speech I alluded to:

Certain threats . . . thrown out both in the Liberal Press and sometimes on the floor of this House, as to what hon. gentlemen opposite propose to do in connection with this measure. We are not in the habit of making threats. We do not propose to make any. If any unexpected difficulties should arise, we shall endeavour to deal with them firmly, reasonably and adequately, and we have every belief that we shall be able to meet them.

On March 2, I discussed with Arthur Meighen, R. B. Bennett, and J. A. Currie, the probable necessity of introducing closure.

The Bill was now in Committee, and the debate was resumed on Clause 2 (which was supposed to be non-contentious) on March 3. However, a long and obstructive debate ensued and at midnight Sir Wilfrid asked for adjournment and I asked for progress. At one a.m. I again asked progress and he asked adjournment. At two a.m. he moved a dilatory amendment. At 3:45 a.m., I went home leaving the opposing forces in line of battle; and I returned at 9:45 a.m.

We then entered upon a discussion which involved practically continuous sitting for two weeks. The debate went on, night and day, until Saturday, March 8, at two o'clock in the morning. Members on each side were divided into three relays or shifts and were on duty for eight hours at a time. We had to adopt unusual precautions because we did not know at what hour the Opposition might spring division and have a majority concealed and available. Naturally, a very warm feeling arose.

On Monday, March 10, I held caucus. All the members seemed enthusiastic and determined. They left the question of closure for the decision of the Government.

On this day (March 10) the debate was resumed and it continued at great length throughout the week. Having received the necessary permission, I placed before Sir Wilfrid certain correspondence with Mr. Churchill dealing with the cost of a fleet unit. The Opposition attacked Mr. Churchill and protracted the discussion throughout the week. On Friday, March 14, and again on the following day the debate became so violent as to occasion apprehension of personal conflict. After two hours' sleep, I had returned to the House on Friday afternoon. As midnight approached, the Speaker twice had to take the Chair amid scenes of great disorder.

The excitement continued on Saturday. During the absence of the Deputy Speaker, who had been compelled to retire through exhaustion and whose place had been taken by an English-speaking member, objection was made by two French-speaking Liberals. They were perfectly right in their contention;

but after I had spoken briefly in French and explained the situation, they withdrew their objection and the debate continued.[5] As the evening progressed the scene became more and more tumultuous. At one period the whole Opposition were on their feet, shouting and gesticulating. Dr. Clark was named by the Speaker. I prepared a resolution suspending Clark; but before proposing it I suggested that he should make amends for his conduct by a complete apology to the Chair, which he immediately gave; he then came over to my seat and thanked me. Our men were intensely angry and disappointed, as they thought I should have moved for Clark's suspension; within forty-eight hours they were satisfied that I had taken the better course.

Considering in retrospect these weeks, the most strenuous and remarkable that had ever occurred in Canadian Parliamentary history, I am satisfied that it was a mistake to carry out our tactics during the second week. We were determined to make it manifest to the country that there was systematic and organized obstruction for the purpose of preventing the passage of the Bill. I am convinced that the second week added little, if anything, to our case in that regard. During that week the nerves of members on both sides were so frayed by excitement, strain, and exhaustion that they lost in great measure their usual self-control. The proceedings of the first week must have made it abundantly clear to any reasonable person that we could not carry our Bill through the Commons except by means of closure. And it was to closure that we next resorted.

Parliament adjourned for the Easter recess on March 19, until March 25.

On Thursday, April 3, I had an interesting conference with Sir Wilfrid who frankly admitted that they were obstructing and in that respect were following our example in 1908 and 1911. Finally, I asked him to fix a date for the third reading of the Bill and declared that he could have all the time for debate that he desired. On leaving, he stated that he would consider and would give me an answer on Saturday (April 5).

On that day he called and said that he was not prepared to make any arrangement. This decision I announced to Council and told them we must proceed with closure.

For many weeks during this debate I had suffered from carbuncles on my neck, and twice I was obliged to leave my bed and proceed to the House of Commons, upon the call of

[5] At six o'clock in the morning one of them came across the floor of the House and offered his congratulations upon my French speech.

my colleagues, with my neck swathed in bandages. I became greatly exhausted by the intense strain of the long debate, the night hours, and the tumultuous scenes.

On April 7, I was called to the House and spent three hours in the Chamber during which I asked Sir Wilfrid to agree upon a date for the conclusion of the committee stage and for third reading. He replied in a lengthy and evasive speech to which I made answer.

The rules for enforcing closure had been prepared and we decided to put them to the House without referring them to Committee as, in the latter case, there would be the same opportunity for obstruction as that which had arisen upon the Bill.

On April 9, my physician was at my house and dressed my neck preparatory to my attendance at the House. We held caucus at noon and I enjoined our members not to raise points of order and not to interrupt.

Althought we did not intend to refer the proposed rules to Committee, we realized that it would be possible for the Opposition to offer at least fifty amendments and to debate each amendment at such length as to make it practically impossible to bring the rules into force within any reasonable time. It was imperatively necessary, therefore, to prevent motions for amendment; and to do this it was equally imperative that the previous question which would prevent amendment should be moved and carried. Accordingly, we arranged that when Sir Wilfrid arose Hazen would also arise and that W. B. Northrup should then move that Hazen "be now heard."

The Rules of the House which authorized our proposed procedure were as follows:

17. When two or more Members rise to speak, Mr. Speaker calls upon the Member who first rose in his place; but a motion may be made that any Member who has risen "be now heard," or "do now speak," which motion shall be forthwith put without debate.

44. The previous question, until it is decided, shall preclude all amendment of the main question, and shall be in the following words, "That this question be now put." If the previous question be resolved in the affirmative, the original question is to be put forthwith without any amendment or debate.

In introducing the motion for closure I went very fully into the reasons why closure had become necessary and explained the proposed rules. The programme already arranged was then

carried out and the House voted that Hazen "be now heard."
He thereupon moved the previous question which was carried.

We did not disclose to our members the proposed procedure
and, as they had been cautioned not to raise points of order or
to interrupt, they were much disturbed when Mr. Northrup
arose, apparently in disregard of this warning, and there were
some mutterings that "Northrup never opened his mouth without putting his foot in it." However, our strategy soon became
apparent and Northrup's prestige was speedily restored.

I was very reluctant to adopt this procedure as it involved
not a real but seeming discourtesy to the Leader of the Opposition whose long public service and high position both in the
House and in the country entitled him to most respectful
consideration. But, either this method, which was fully authorized by the Rules of the House, had to be adopted or we had to
acknowledge defeat of our attempt to proceed further with the
Naval Aid Bill. While I fully realized that Sir Wilfrid Laurier
and his followers would be extremely resentful, I trusted that
upon consideration of the circumstances they must acknowledge
that my action was justified. It was singular that the rule which
prevented discussion on the motion that Hazen "be now heard"
had been introduced at the instance of Sir Wilfrid Laurier in
1906.

As was anticipated, Sir Wilfrid became violently enraged
and his rage was shared by all his followers who made loud
demonstrations.

The debate on the closure resolutions continued for some
days but became more and more lifeless. Finally the vote was
taken at midnight on April 23; and our rules were carried by
a majority of thirty-five. There was very little demonstration
by the Opposition who seemed to have lost their fighting spirit
as they realized that their confident anticipation of preventing
the passage of the Naval Aid Bill in the Commons could not be
realized.

On April 27, Senator Lougheed (Conservative Leader in
the Senate) informed me that he had had an important interview
with Sir George Ross (Liberal Leader in the Senate) who
suggested a compromise on the naval question. . . .

~ While not objecting to a contribution *per se*, Ross thought
that it if were combined with a substantial vote for a Canadian
navy, it could command the support of the Senate.

He advised a comprehensive bill including both types of aid
or a supplementary vote of $20,000,000 for a Canadian navy. ~

In discussing the various proposals made by Sir George, I explicitly explained to Lougheed that, while we were prepared to discuss the subject, it was essential that Sir George should make sure that any proposal which he put forward would receive the sanction of Sir Wilfrid Laurier. Eventually, I learned that Sir Wilfrid refused to entertain any of the proposals offered as a compromise by Sir George. Sir George had been very confident that he would be able to induce members of his party in the Senate to approve the Bill if amended in accordance with his suggestions. However, at a conference of Liberal Senators his views were not endorsed, and the Liberal Senators, under the influence of Sir Wilfrid Laurier, expressed their approval of the course pursued by the Opposition in the Commons and determined to reject the Bill.

The debate continued on May 6; and fireworks again commenced to explode. It was apparent that the Opposition intended to make us apply closure and we were quite prepared to do so.

The form of the closure rules was somewhat technical, and probably a simpler method would have been more effective. We were obliged to take up each clause in Committee and postpone consideration in each instance. Thereupon, I gave the necessary notice that there would be no further postponement. It seemed apparent that the Opposition, realizing our determination to pass the Bill, were quite as anxious as we were to have done with it. All day Friday, May 9, the discussion continued, and the Bill finally went through Committee at 3:15 a.m. on Saturday. Throughout the day, the Opposition had been very quiet, but at the end they made a disturbance when they sought to move an additional clause in order to prolong the agony.

On Thursday, May 15, the Bill passed on third reading without closure by a majority of thirty-three, five of our Quebec supporters voting against us. Sir Wilfrid and Mr. Guilbault contended for the honour of moving the six-months' hoist.

On May 19, accompanied by Pelletier and Hazen, I arrived at Toronto and received a magnificent reception. The streets which had been decorated and later illuminated were thronged with people. We attended a luncheon at the York Club; and that evening were guests at an immense banquet. Then we proceeded to the Arena where the crowd was enormous. Practically every person in attendance had a small Union Jack, and as they cheered I looked across a sea of flags. A wonderful ovation was accorded me when I rose to speak. I reviewed our naval policy, our reasons for the emergency measure, and the gravity of the situation as explained to us during our recent visit to England.

On May 23, definite and reliable news reached me that the Senate would certainly reject the Bill, and this was confirmed on May 30 when it was sent back to the Commons with the following message: "This House is not justified in giving its assent to this Bill until it is submitted to the judgment of the country."

It had been anticipated that the Bill might pass the Senate with certain amendments which we were disposed to accept. Allusion has already been made to confidential proposals from leading Liberals in the Senate; and the measure as proposed to be amended would have fulfilled an important purpose, as at least two battleships or battle-cruisers would have been provided for the common defence of the Empire, while the balance of the appropriation would have been devoted to harbour and coast defences and auxiliary ships. In the end, however, Sir Wilfrid insisted upon the rejection of the Bill, giving to his friends in the Senate the choice between that course and his resignation. Several Liberal Senators who voted against the measure did so with reluctance and against their better judgment.

The action of the Senate naturally involved much disappointment throughout the country, and the situation was under careful consideration by the Government for some days after the rejection of the Bill.

On the day of prorogation (June 6), Sir Wilfrid came to the House with a carefully prepared speech, and he asked this question:

I think we are entitled to know what action the Government proposes to take as a consequence of the action of the Senate in this regard.

His question gave me the opportunity which I desired of making an announcement that eventually we expected to take over and pay for the three ships which Great Britain proposed to lay down in substitution for those which Canada would have provided under our Bill. The announcement, which was received with much acceptance and approval throughout Canada, seemed to surprise Sir Wilfrid and it obviously disconcerted and nettled him.

During the autumn there were further interviews and negotiations between Sir James Lougheed and Sir George Ross with respect to such modification of our naval proposals as would ensure their acceptance in the Senate. I was willing to go at least half-way in the endeavour to meet his views, and if Sir George Ross could have carried his own views there would have been no difficulty. . . .

However, at every stage Sir George Ross met the inflexible opposition of Sir Wilfrid Laurier to any proposed compromise. So, we were obliged to drop our proposals; and Sir Wilfrid at the beginning of the next session was enabled triumphantly to announce, six months before the most terrible conflict the world had ever known, that there was no emergency, no danger of war; that my declaration to the contrary was a mere sham and pretence.

The secret memorandum, which I had given to Sir Wilfrid on November 16, 1912, and which I had authorized him to exhibit to any of his colleagues who were members of the Privy Council of Canada, set forth most significant reasons for anticipating war with Germany within a measurable period. It was to this I had alluded in the closing words of my speech in introducing the Naval Aid Bill:

But today, while the clouds are heavy and we hear the the booming of the distant thunder and see the lightning flashes above the horizon, we cannot and we will not wait and delibe-rate until any impending storm shall have burst upon us in fury and with disaster.

This elicited mirthful and sarcastic comments from members of the Opposition. Even Mr. A. K. Maclean was unwise enough to speak as follows:

We are told that the clouds were low and heavy; we were asked to listen to the booming of the thunder and to look at the lightning's flash upon the horizon; and, with this vast amount of éclat and unnecessary theatrical display, this measure was presented to the House. . . . There is no emergency or threaten-ing danger to justify the settlement of the question of naval defence upon other than principle and permanent policy. . . . No greater danger confronts the British Empire today than did in 1909. There is not the same amount of alarm and concern in the minds of the British public today as there was then, and present English public opinion endorses that idea. . . . Hon. gentlemen opposite have no right to make this so-called German scare an issue in this country when the English people refuse and have refused for four years to do so in their own country. . . .

22: *1914*

Parliament opened on January 15, 1914. . . .

Sir Wilfrid criticized the Government for failing to summon Parliament in November; later he discovered that his opinion in this respect was not unanimously accepted by his followers, as it was warmly criticized by Dr. Michael Clark and other members from distant constituencies who found a November opening extremely inconvenient. . . .

Defending the action of the Senate (taken under his direction) in the previous session in rejecting the Naval Aid Bill, Sir Wilfrid expressed himself as follows:

The Bill which was brought in last session was not even a measure of emergency, although it was so called. It was simply a measure of expediency involving a policy of contribution, a policy which had been denounced by the very men themselves who introduced the Bill, a policy which was not justified by anything which then existed. They introduced it upon the shallow pretence of emergency. Emergency? Who speaks today of emergency? Twelve months have elapsed since my right hon. friend the Prime Minister introduced his measure. Twelve months and more have passed since that time when he saw the German peril. He saw Germany almost ready to jump at the throat of Great Britain. He saw clouds on the horizon; he saw these clouds rent by lightning; he heard the murmurs and rumbling of the distant thunder. But my right hon. friend today may live in peace. The atmosphere is pure, the sky is clear. . . . The light has been let in on that question, and we know now how much the country and Empire and the civilized world has been deceived upon that question of so-called emergency.

Six months later, Sir Wilfrid realized that his knowledge of international relations had been extremely limited.

Continuing his address, Sir Wilfrid dealt with minor matters and then undertook to defend the action of the Senate in so amending the Highways Bill as to make it unworkable. He criticized the increase of unemployment and the advance in the cost of living; and he declared that the Government was recreant to their trust in failing to remove the duty from wheat so that our wheat might be admitted to the American market. He concluded by moving that the following clause should be added to the Address:

We regret to have to represent to Your Royal Highness that in the gracious Speech with which you have met Parliament, whilst it is admitted that business is in a depressed condition, yet there is no indication of any intention on the part of your advisers to take any steps towards relieving such a situation.

After the usual compliments to the mover and seconder of the Address, I countered Sir Wilfrid by admitting that there were many pebbles on the Conservative Beach, i.e., many men capable of filling the office of Solicitor-General with ability, and I expressed great satisfaction that I had not been in the position of Sir Wilfrid who on five different occasions could find no pebble on his own beach, because he went outside the House to select a Minister of Justice, a Minister of Railways and Canals, a Minister of Labour, a Minister of Public Works, and, last but not least, a Secretary of State. So I congratulated the Conservative Party that it was not afflicted with that unfortunate poverty of parliamentary talent which was indicated by Sir Wilfrid's course. I defended the appointment of the Minister of Trade and Commerce to a position on an important Commission which had its origin in the resolution of the Imperial Conference in 1911.

Then I attacked the Leader of the Opposition upon his apparent determination to use his majority in the Senate, not in the public interest but in the supposed interest of his party and in disregard of the purpose for which the Senate had been created.

Coming to the Naval Aid Bill, I said that in at least one foreign country the Senate's unfortunate action had been welcomed with rejoicing as a clear indication that in providing for the common defence of the Empire the mother country must stand alone so far as Canada was concerned. I quoted from a great German newspaper, the *Hamburger Nachrichten* of June 5, 1913:

Whatever may be decided upon later, the actual decision of the Canadian Senate means at any rate a heavy moral and material loss for the defence of the Empire, for Mr. Borden's promise had been foolishly enough counted on. His offer made an enormous impression in the whole world.

And I quoted also from the London *Morning Post* which declared that the Senate's decision would be eagerly welcomed by rivals and enemies and regarded as ominous by friends, and that the impression would inevitably be created that the solidarity of the Empire was a myth.

Recognizing the determination of Sir Wilfrid Laurier and his followers again to defeat the Naval Aid Bill if introduced, I declared that we would deny to the Senate another opportunity of bringing discredit to our Dominion and detriment to the Empire; and I quoted the determination I had expressed in my remarks on the last day of the session of 1913.

Then I summed up our position in the following words:

When we are in a position to press the Naval Aid Bill to a final and satisfactory conclusion in the Senate, it will be our duty to consult with the Imperial Government respecting these grave and important considerations. If it should then appear that, by any naval arrangement entered into or about to be entered into by the great powers, a restriction or diminution of the present lamentable rivalry in armaments could be brought about, we should always be ready, until our ships have actually been begun, to review the situation so far as these proposals are concerned; and if a general cessation or temporary suspension in the building of great ships of war were at any time to be seriously entertained, Canada would gladly participate in such a desirable result. Otherwise, we should proceed in due course with the construction of the three ships, holding it to be our duty, under the conditions disclosed last year, and for reasons then elaborated with great fullness, to bring this assistance as speedily as possible to the great purpose of our common defence and security.

With regard to Sir Wilfrid's defence of the Senate's action in rejecting the measure, I said:

My right hon. friend spoke of the good relations between the British Empire and the German Empire. I am glad to know that they are good relations. It is my fervent hope and wish that those relations may always continue to be as satisfactory as they are at the present; but, as I pointed out last year, the destinies of the world are sometimes influenced by the mere fact that predominant naval power does exist and can be utilized in one quarter or another. . . . If the right hon. gentleman will look at the observations made by the First Lord of the Admiralty in the British House of Commons on the 5th day of June, 1913, and on the 17th day of July, 1913, he will find that his view as to the necessity of maintaining and even increasing the strength of the naval forces of this Empire is not borne out by the view of the British Admiralty.

After considerable debate Sir Wilfrid's motion was defeated by the usual party majority; and on January 29 the Address was passed.

~ A private member's bill to abolish titles of honour in Canada was defeated on second reading. Foster opposed it and Laurier stated that the subject should be dealt with not by a bill but by a recommendation or address to His Majesty.

A bill to amend the Criminal Code by abolishing capital punishment was talked out. ~

The following is an extract from my diary for February 6, 1914:

House yesterday disposed of Bill to abolish honours and a Bill to abolish capital punishment. No one seems to have noticed the humour of dealing with the two subjects in immediate sequence. . . .

~ On the usually controversial question of redistribution it was Borden's determination to accord "fair and even generous treatment to the Opposition." He followed the Liberal precedent of 1903 and on February 10 introduced a bill with blank schedules which was to be referred to a special committee. He accepted Laurier's suggestion that the committee consist of nine rather than seven members.

The committee reported the bill to the House of June 10 and there was less debate than Borden had anticipated. The government accepted an amendment regarding the representation of Prince Edward Island and the bill was passed unanimously on third reading.

The redistribution committee had also recommended changes respecting the Senate. ~

On June 11, 1914, I moved an Address to His Majesty praying for the passage of an Act by the Imperial Parliament providing that:

1. The number of senators should be increased from 72 to 96;

2. That Ontario should be represented by 24, Quebec by 24, Maritime Provinces by 24 (Nova Scotia 10, New Brunswick 10 and Prince Edward Island 4), Western Provinces by 24 (six being allotted to each province);

3. That the number of additional senators under Section 26 of the British North America Act should be increased from 3 or

6 to 4 or 8; and that the total number of senators should not at any time exceed 104;

4. That in case Newfoundland should enter the Confederation its representation in the Senate should be 6 instead of 4 members in which case the normal number should be 102 and the maximum number 110.

5. That a province should always be entitled to a number of members in the House of Commons not less than the number of senators representing such province.

The subject of this resolution had been under discussion several times during the session. In presenting the resolution I explained that so far as Alberta, Saskatchewan, and Manitoba were concerned, the Parliament of Canada had power to increase representation in the Senate but with respect to British Columbia an amendment of the British North America Act would be necessary. Sir Wilfrid Laurier, during the session, had suggested a fourth division, comprising the Western Provinces, which should be represented by twenty-four members and I concurred in that view. The provision with regard to Section 26 and with respect to Newfoundland would follow as a matter of course. Then I set forth the considerations upon which I based my proposal that no province should be represented in the Commons by a smaller number than in the Senate; and I explained that at present it would have no application except in Prince Edward Island.

Sir Wilfrid, in a moderate and reasonable speech, was disposed to agree with the measure which, as he explained, was based upon the unanimous recommendation of the Committee on Redistribution. Then followed a discussion respecting Senate reform and general principles of representative government. But eventually, the resolution, in the terms in which I had proposed it, received unanimous approval.

Notwithstanding this unanimous approval of the House, and although the Address had been based upon the unanimous report of the Committee on Redistribution, the Liberal majority in the Senate, true to its partisan instincts, amended the resolution by adding thereto the following proviso:

This Act shall not take effect until the termination of the now-existing Canadian Parliament.

Thereupon, I moved that the amendment should not be concurred in for reasons which I set forth. The Senate insisted upon its amendment, and the Bill was defeated. . . .

On February 24, Mr. W. A. Buchanan brought up the subject of transferring to the three Prairie Provinces their natural resources. He quoted my speeches both in Parliament and on the hustings while I was Leader of the Opposition and declared that in fulfilment of the pledges thus given to the people it was my duty to carry out these promises. Then he read the following letter which had been addressed to me by the Premiers of Manitoba, Saskatchewan, and Alberta—the former being a Conservative:

December 22, 1913.

Dear Sir,
After having an interview with you in regard to the questions in respect of which the Prairie Provinces received different treatment from the other provinces of Canada, and, at your suggestion, a meeting of the Premiers of Manitoba, Saskatchewan and Alberta was held, and it has been agreed between us to make to you on behalf of said provinces the proposal that the financial terms already arranged between the provinces and the Dominion as compensation for lands should stand as compensation for lands already alienated for the general benefit of Canada, and, that all the lands remaining within the boundaries of the respective provinces with all natural resources included, be transferred to the said provinces, the provinces accepting responsibility of administering the same.
Yours very truly,
(Sgd.) R. P. ROBLIN
WALTER SCOTT
ARTHUR L. SIFTON

In replying I commented upon Mr. Buchanan's change of heart, as in 1905 he had vehemently opposed the proposal which he now urged. Then I quoted the pronouncements of Liberal leaders, both in the House of Commons and in the Legislatures of Alberta, Saskatchewan, and Manitoba; especially the language of Premier Scott of Saskatchewan who had suggested a doubt as to the sanity of any Saskatchewan man who desired what Mr. Buchanan urged. . . .

Coming to the letter of December 22, 1913, from the three Prairie Premiers I had expressed my desire that the subject should be discussed at the Provincial Conference during the previous autumn. The reason why it was not then discussed was the well-known opposition of the Maritime Provinces to any such proposal, except upon compensation to other provinces. Under the circumstances, I declared my inability to regard the proposal of the Prairie Premiers as reasonable or as setting forth any such terms as I had asked them to place before me at my conference with them.

Further, I had transmitted to each of the Maritime Premiers a copy of the letter from the three Prairie Premiers and had asked for their impressions. In each case the reply was distinctly opposed to the claim set forth in the Prairie Premiers' letter. Finally I stated that the views put forward by the Prairie Premiers ought to be considered and dealt with at one and the same time.

Concluding, I said:

We are desirous of dealing with this question in a reasonable way, but it did not seem to me that the proposal put forward to us in December last by the three Prime Ministers of the prairie provinces was one that they really expected us to entertain. I assumed that they put it forward more especially as a basis for further negotiation. At all events, at the moment I have only this to say, that up to the present time those negotiations have had no further results. . . .

~ Borden regarded the Act respecting British Nationality, Naturalization, and Aliens as "perhaps the most important legislative enactment of the session." Under existing legislation a person naturalized in Canada was not a British subject outside Canada. A person naturalized in Britain would in Canada probably possess that status.

Under the new legislation a certificate of naturalization granted by Britain would be effective in any Dominion which would adopt the provisions of the proposed British statute. "Conversely the Secretary of State of such Dominion could grant a certificate which would confer the status of a British subject not only within such Dominion, but within the United Kingdom and within every other Dominion or Colony adopting the provisions of the proposed British enactment." A five-year period of residence was to be a necessary prerequisite with the last year to be in the jurisdiction granting naturalization. Laurier objected to the discretionary power being granted the Canadian Secretary of State. Justice Minister Doherty said that "if such powers might with propriety be vested in the British Secretary of State it would be unfortunate, and indeed humiliating, to conclude that they would not be fairly and honourably exercised by the same officer in this country." The bill finally passed unaminously.

The government proposed a measure to provide up to

$1,200,000 to compensate creditors of the Farmers' Bank which had failed. A Royal Commission appointed by the Borden government had found that the Treasury Board had given its certificate on the basis of false and fraudulent representation on the part of W. T. Travers, the bank's General Manager. The debate on the bill produced much criticism of former Finance Minister Fielding for his failure to heed warnings or investigate the bank's affairs more fully before authorizing its certification. After many lively debates the measure passed the Commons. ~

The Senate defeated the Bill; and, on reflection, I am disposed to admit that on this occasion they took the proper course, although there was no truth whatever in the suggestion that we had connived in any way at the defeat of the measure. While in certain aspects the proposals of the Government could be supported upon reasonable, or at least plausible grounds, yet, on the whole, the passage of the Bill would have created an unfortunate precedent. The Bill was not introduced in the following session. Probably there might have been pressure upon us to do so if war had not broken out in the meantime. Travers was prosecuted in the Criminal Courts and sentenced to imprisonment for a term of years. . . .

~ It was necessary to provide assistance to the Canadian Northern Railway system and also to the Grand Trunk Pacific Company. R. B. Bennett* and W. F. Nickle strongly opposed the Government's action in reference to the Canadian Northern, but fourteen Liberal senators supported it.

The Liberals 'treated the Grand Trunk proposals with great kindness, due no doubt to the fact that it was their own proposal and their own action which had created a serious situation involving the country in a further commitment." ~

Parliament was prorogued on June 12. We held council on the following morning with everyone very tired and all denouncing the Opposition for failing to observe their agreement for increased representation in the Senate.

There had ben much discussion and rather intense excitement respecting the carrying of arms by the sixty-fifth Regiment at the *Fête-Dieu* procession in Montreal. The Minister of Militia was technically right in refusing permission, but it was an old

---

* On May 14 the debate was enlivened by cross-fire between two future Conservative leaders, Bennett, and Meighen. Bennett called the Solicitor General "the gramophone of Mackenzie and Mann" and said he would not be diverted by his "impertinent interruptions."

custom to which the people were sincerely attached and they regarded Hughes' refusal as an insult. Doherty at times was almost in tears and talked of resigning. On the other hand, Hughes was pressed and perhaps oppressed by the Orangemen. Eventually a solution was arranged.

On June 17, I had a letter from the Governor-General stating that the King had cabled his desire that I should accept the honour of [Knight Grand Cross of the Order of St. Michael and St. George], which I had hitherto declined. At the Cabinet meeting next day, I invited the opinion of my colleagues and they all thought I should accept the honour although we agreed that from the party point of view it would be rather a detriment. The following day the announcement of my G.C.M.G. appeared in the Press.

During this period our time was very fully occupied with administrative questions. White began to weary of the strain and confided to me his wish to retire; in reply, I assured him that I was equally anxious to be relieved of the burden I was carrying.

On June 24, I attended with the Governor-General the military manoeuvres at Petawawa. So far as I could judge, they were efficiently carried out, the Duke seemed pleased and Colonel Hughes was in his element.

Returning from Petawawa on June 25, I found that the question of admitting Hindus, which had been troublesome for some time, had become disturbing. A Japanese vessel, the *Komagata Maru*, had sailed from Shanghai with five thousand Hindus for Vancouver. Except for an unfortunate delay in communicating to me a telegram from the Shanghai authorities, the vessel would have been detained and not permitted to clear for Vancouver. A Press rumour stated that the leader of the Hindus, Gurdit Singh, had chartered the steamer from the Japanese owners for the purpose of testing the validity of Canadian laws and regulations. It was found that a small number of immigrants had been domiciled in Canada; and, after inquiry, these were admitted, the others were not permitted to land and the validity of the Orders-in-Council was tested in the courts and upheld.

It was reported that the Japanese Consul at Vancouver was endeavouring to embarrass the Government. I sent for the Japanese Consul-General but he was absent. On July 18, we received a report that the Hindus were endeavouring to procure arms from the United States and on the nineteenth I learned that they had resisted with great violence the attempt of our officers to board the ship. The situation was so serious that I sent for Meighen and Robertson and got into telephonic communication with Doherty. We ordered H.M.C.S. *Rainbow* to the scene and I telegraphed Burrel who was in British Columbia, asking him to proceed immediately to Vancouver. The militia was ordered to co-operate in every way with the commander of the *Rainbow*.

Finally the Hindus abandoned their resistance upon the offer of the Government to provide food and other necessary supplies, which had been offered some time before. On July 23, the ship left the harbour of Vancouver for Hong Kong. After the arrival of the Hindus in India serious disturbances broke out and there was much discussion of the incident not only in Canada and Great Britain, but in India as well.

On June 29, I left for Nova Scotia, arriving at Halifax late the following evening. Here I received various delegations, chiefly respecting patronage.

I visited Grand Pré and found my mother entirely an invalid. She was then in her ninetieth year and it was difficult to understand her when she spoke. However she seemed at times very bright and cheerful. . . .

It had been arranged with Mr. Churchill that Admiral Sir John Jellicoe should come to Canada during 1914, for further discussion of naval aid. At first it was proposed that he should come in August but this was inconvenient as I had in contemplation a political tour of the Western Provinces. On July 23, Mr. Churchill cabled that Admiral Jellicoe could arrive either in August or in October. I postponed my reply until my return; and on that day I left for Muskoka where I arrived that evening.

After the strain of the session and the difficult weeks that had followed, I was greatly fatigued and still suffered from the disorder of carbuncles. Thus, I looked forward with joyful anticipation to four restful weeks at Muskoka. It was my first visit to that delightful district, and I retain a happy memory of my very brief holiday before events compelled my return. Golf and bathing were available, the air was delightful and we were surrounded by friends, all of whom were most kind and hospitable. So my week's holiday passed very quickly and delightfully.

23: The War

Never was a holiday dream followed by a more terrible awakening. During my visit to England in 1912, I had reached the conclusion that war was probably inevitable; but European conditions had seemed peaceful. The assassination of Archduke Franz Ferdinand at Sarajevo on June 28, had been alarming, but on both sides of the Atlantic none, I imagine, believed that the situation would develop, with such startling suddenness, into a war that in its effect upon both belligerent and neutral nations would almost shatter the very framework of modern civilization.

Telegrams from Ottawa began to acquaint me with the possibility that a general European war was impending. On July 28, I learned that Great Britain was endeavouring unsuccessfully to keep peace but that she would almost certainly be involved if France should be attacked. It was reported that Germany and Russia were quietly mobilizing. On July 30, a telegram arrived from my secretary, A. E. Blount, that the situation was serious but that the Ministers thought I need not come if I could be ready to leave on short notice. I decided to go immediately; and, after despatching telegrams, I left early on the thirty-first for Ottawa where I arrived the following morning. The Governor-General was absent in the West;[1] and very few Ministers were in Ottawa. Under my telegraphic instructions Blount had requested the Ministers to return immediately. The King's secretary had cabled to the Duke that, although the situation was most serious, there was a faint hope of peace.

With the approval of such colleagues as were available, I immediately despatched to the British Government on August 1, the following telegram in the name of the Governor-General:

My advisers while expressing their most earnest hope that peaceful solution of existing international difficulties may be achieved and their strong desire to co-operate in every possible way for that purpose wish me to convey to His Majesty's Government the firm assurance that if unhappily war should ensue the Canadian people will be united in a common resolve to put forth every effort and to make every sacrifice necessary to ensure the integrity and maintain the honour of our Empire.

[1] The Governor-General did not return until the morning of August 4.

THE WAR – 211

To this message which was made public immediately, the following reply was received:

With reference to your telegram of August first, His Majesty's Government gratefully welcome the assurance of your Government that in the present crisis they may rely on wholehearted co-operation of the people of Canada.

On the following day I despatched to the British Government in the name of the Governor-General a further telegram which was made public subsequently:

In view of the impending danger of war involving the Empire, my advisers are anxiously considering the most effective means of rendering every possible aid and they will welcome any suggestion and advice which the Imperial naval and military authorities may deem it expedient to offer. They are confident that a considerable force would be available for service abroad. A question has been mooted respecting the status of any Canadian force serving abroad as, under section sixty-nine of Canadian Militia Act, active militia can only be placed on active service beyond Canada for the defence thereof. It has been suggested that regiments might enlist as Imperial troops for a stated period, Canadian Government undertaking to make all necessary provision for their equipment, pay and maintenance. This proposal has not yet been maturely considered here and my advisers would be glad to have views of Imperial Government thereon.

In reply to this message the following cable was received:

With reference to your cypher telegram of August second, please inform your Ministers that their patriotic readiness to render every aid is deeply appreciated by His Majesty's Government but they would prefer postponing detailed observations on the suggestions put forward pending further developments. As soon as situation appears to call for further measures I will telegraph you again.

While in England in 1912 I had felt it my duty to become acquainted with the arrangements effected by the Imperial Defence Committee and its organization for immediate, effective action upon the outbreak of war. Details were procured from Lieutenant-Colonel Sir Maurice Hankey, Secretary of that Committee, and in January, 1914, proceedings were taken to consummate similar arrangements in Canada. A conference of deputy heads of various departments was constituted under the chairmanship of Sir Joseph Pope, then Under Secretary of State for External Affairs. The work went on during the spring of 1914, with results that were embodied in the following report to me on August 17, 1914:

Memorandum relating to a conference of deputy heads of certain departments of the public service, which met in Ottawa in the early part of 1914 to concert measures for the drawing up of a general Defence Scheme or War Book, embodying a record of the action to be taken in time of emergency by every responsible official at the seat of Government.

In 1913 the Secretary of State for the Colonies communicated to this Government certain memoranda of the Oversea Defence Committee outlining the action to be taken by the naval and military authorities when relations with any foreign power became strained, and on the outbreak of war. The suggestion was conveyed that the Governments of the various self-governing Dominions might advantageously prepare a similar record in each case to meet such contingencies. By the direction of the Government these recommendations were considered by the local Interdepartmental Committee (which is composed of the expert officers of the Naval and Militia Departments sitting together). The committee reported that a conference of those deputy Ministers whose departments would primarily be affected by an outbreak of war, should be held to consider how best to give effect to the proposals of the Oversea Committee.

This suggestion was submitted to the Prime Minister and received the approval of the Government. Thereupon, a meeting of the undermentioned deputy heads, together with the Governor-General's Military Secretary, was held under the chairmanship of Sir Joseph Pope, Under Secretary of State for External Affairs, on the 12th January, 1914:

The Deputy Minister of Militia and Defence,
The Deputy Minister of the Naval Service,
The Deputy Minister of Justice,
The Deputy Minister of Customs,
The Deputy Postmaster-General,
The Deputy Minister of Railways and Canals,
The Deputy Minister of Marine and Fisheries,

with Major Gordon Hall, Director of Military Operations (representing the Department of Militia and Defence), and Lieutenant R. M. Stephens, Director of Gunnery (representing the Department of the Naval Service) as joint secretaries.

At this meeting it was decided that the secretaries should

acquaint each member of the conference of the various contin-
gencies which might arise in the event of which the co-operation
of his department would be required; thus enabling him to
decide what steps would be necessary to give effect to the deci-
sions of the conference and to detail an officer of his department
to confer with the secretaries in the actual compilation of the
War Book.

Meetings of subcommittees were subsequently held from
time to time at which the necessary action to be taken by the
various departments in the event of certain contingencies arising
was carefully considered and determined. Each department then
proceeded to develop its own line of action in detail, the whole
being subsequently co-ordinated and incorporated in one
scheme, indicating the course to be followed by the Government
as a whole on an emergency arising. This scheme was then
submitted to and approved by the Prime Minister.

The taking of these precautionary measures proved most
fortunate, as on the receipt of intelligence during the last few
weeks of the serious situation in Europe, this Government found
itself in a position to take, without the slightest delay, such
action as the exigencies of the moment demanded, concurrently
with His Majesty's Government and with the sister dominions
of the Empire.
August 17th, 1914.

As a result of this systematic organization the communications from the Imperial authorities were acted upon promptly
and with an entire absence of confusion. Each detail was worked
out with precision.

On Sunday and Monday (August 2 and 3) we spent practically the whole day in Council. We established censorship,
declared bank notes legal tender, authorized excess issue of
Dominion notes, empowered the proper officers to detain
enemy ships, prohibited the export of articles necessary or
useful for war purposes, and generally took upon ourselves
responsibilities far exceeding our legal powers. All these measures, which were wholly without legal validity until they were
afterwards ratified by Parliament, were accepted throughout
the country as if Council had possessed the necessary authority.

The Canadian banks were extremely apprehensive of a
devastating run upon their funds and it was learned that in
several cities safety-deposit boxes had been secured for the
purpose of hoarding gold. Any such attempt became absolutely
futile as soon as we decreed that bank notes should be legal

tender. The anticipated run on the banks did not take place; and the preparations for hoarding gold to be withdrawn from the banks became entirely useless.

We placed the Canadian naval vessels at the disposal of the King for co-operation with British naval forces; and we purchased at Seattle two submarines which got away just ahead of the United States' order to detain them, and succeeded in evading United States' cruisers which pursued them.

There were many rumours as to German attacks upon our coasts and guns were provided from Quebec for the defence of Vancouver, Glace Bay, Canso, Sydney, and St. John. The *Rainbow* went south, in the face of powerful German cruisers in the Pacific which easily could have sunk her, to bring back two small boats, the *Shearwater* and the *Algerine*, which were in southern waters at the outbreak of war. Some deck hamper thrown overboard in preparation for action drifted to the United States coast and gave rise to a rumour that she had been sunk.

We were in Council on August 4 at eleven and again at four. During the evening, while again in Council, at 8:55 p.m. the momentous telegram arrived announcing that war had been declared. Immediately, an Order-in-Council was passed summoning Parliament to meet on August 18.

Although the events of the past few days had quite prepared us for this result, it came at the last as a shock. None of us, at that time, anticipated the terrible duration of the war agony; but we did realize that the struggle would be intense. White graphically described it as "the suicide of civilization." It was difficult to retain one's balance in the unexpected and bewildering environment that had enveloped us in what seemed but a moment.

A question that arose at once was our attitude towards German and Austrian army reservists resident in Canada. There was pressure from the British Government to arrest or intern them. We had no reason to believe that they were animated by the militarist tendencies which influenced the German and Austrian Governments, or to doubt that they would be loyal to the country of their adoption. Therefore, by Order-in-Council and proclamation, we declared that these persons, as adopted citizens of our country, were entitled to the protection of the law and would receive it; that they should not be molested or interfered with unless they should attempt to aid or abet the enemy or to leave Canada for the purpose of fighting against Great Britain and her Allies, in which case we should be obliged to follow the laws and usages of war but with all possible humanity.

On August 6, upon Perley's[2] suggestion and after discussion in Council, a cable message was despatched offering one million bags of flour as Canada's initial gift to the mother country; this elicited a very grateful response. . . .

Mobilization of the First Canadian Division had been ordered and Colonel Hughes, Minister of Militia, displayed astonishing energy. The camp at Valcartier was organized with remarkable expedition; and on August 10 the Order-in-Council authorizing the Expeditionary Force went into effect. From Atlantic to Pacific there was an outburst of patriotic enthusiasm and offers of assistance poured in.

Throughout the period from the outbreak of War until Parliament met on August 18, I worked to the point of exhaustion in connection with myriad matters touching the conduct of the War and in preparation for the session.

It was known that we proposed introducing a War Measures Act at the session of Parliament summoned for August 18, and from E. M. Macdonald (Liberal member for Pictou, whose devotion to the Empire was very deep and sincere), a suggestion came that it should be a very far-reaching measure which would give the Government immense powers for the conduct of the War.

The principal measures prepared were as follows:

1. The War Appropriations Act *which provided fifty million dollars for expenses incurred by or under the authority of the Governor-in-Council for the following purposes: (a) the defence and security of Canada; (b) the conduct of naval and military operations in or beyond Canada; (c) promoting the continuance of trade, industry and business communications whether by means of insurance or indemnity against war risks or otherwise; and, (d) the carrying out of any measures deemed necessary or advisable by the Governor-in-Council in consequence of the existence of a state of war.*

2. The War Measures Act *which confirmed all acts and things done or omitted to be done after the outbreak of war and prior to the passing of this Act. It conferred on the Governor-in-Council power to do and authorize such acts and things, and*

---

[2] George H. (afterwards Sir George) Perley had gone to London as Acting High Commissioner during June of this year. I had proposed this as a temporary arrangement for a few months. He remained there until March, 1922, during which time, and especially during the War he rendered most valuable service.

to make from time to time such orders and regulations, as he might by reason of the existence of real or apprehended war, deem necessary or advisable for the security, defence, peace, order and welfare of Canada, all of which regulations were to have the force of law.[3]

3. *The Finance Act, 1914 which confirmed Orders already made with respect to Dominion notes and conferred upon the Governor-in-Council wide powers with respect to further advances to chartered banks and extending the powers of the banks with respect to excess circulation.*

4. The Dominion Notes Act *provided for excess issue of Dominion notes.*

5. The Customs Tariff Amendment Act *proposed additional duties on certain articles.*

6. *An Act proposing additional inland revenue duties.*

There was also an amendment of the Naturalization Act, 1914, and an Act Incorporating the Canadian Patriotic Fund.

All these measures were passed without amendment and with a minimum of discussion.

Parliament had a very business-like opening on August 18.[4] The Duke and his staff were in khaki. The Speech from the Throne was taken into consideration next day. Sir Wilfrid[5] was as eloquent as usual. Striking passages from his utterances are the following:

If in what has been done or in what remains to be done there may be anything which in our judgment should not be done or should be differently done, we raise no question, we take no exception, we offer no criticism, and we shall offer no criticism so long as there is danger at the front. . . . It is our duty to let Great Britain know, and to let the friends and foes of Great Britain know, that there is in Canada but one mind and one heart, and that all Canadians stand behind the mother country, conscious and proud that she has engaged in this war, not from any selfish motive, for any purpose of aggrandisement, but to maintain untarnished the honour of her name, to fulfil her obligations to her allies, to maintain her treaty obligations, and

---

[3] This section was very comprehensive and practically conferred upon the Governor-in-Council power to legislate on all matters arising out of or relating to the state of war.

[4] On the day before Parliament opened the Governor-General complained that Hughes had spoken to him disrespectfully. I called Hughes and warned him not to repeat the offence.

[5] In confidence he told me that he was having trouble with some of his followers and would hold caucus on the following day.

to save civilization from the unbridled lust of conquest and domination. . . .

It is an additional source of pride to us that England did not seek this war. It is a matter of history—one of the noblest pages of the history of England—that she never drew the sword until every means had been exhausted to secure and to keep an honourable peace.

If my words can be heard beyond the walls of this House in the province from which I come, among the men whose blood flows in my own veins, I should like them to remember that, in taking their place today in the ranks of the Canadian army to fight for the cause of the allied nations, a double honour rests upon them. The very cause for which they are called upon to fight is to them doubly sacred.

In following Sir Wilfrid I congratulated him upon the patriotic fervour and eloquence which distinguished his speech. After dwelling upon the efforts of the British Government to preserve peace and describing the incidents which led to the outbreak of war, I adverted to the violation of the neutrality of Belgium and the consequent action of the British Government:

We have absolutely no quarrel with the German people. I believe that they are a peaceable people, that they are not naturally a warlike people, although unfortunately they are dominated at the present time by a military autocracy. No one can overestimate what civilization and the world owe to Germany. In literature, in science, art and philosophy, in almost every department of human knowledge and activity, they have stood in the very forefront of the world's advancement. Nearly half a million of the very best citizens of Canada are of German origin, and I am sure that no one would for one moment desire to utter any word or use any expression in debate which would wound the self-respect or hurt the feelings of any of our fellow citizens of German descent. . . . The future is shrouded in uncertainty, but I believe that the people of Canada look forth upon it with steadfast eyes. But, while we are now upborne by the exaltation and enthusiasm which come in the first days of a national crisis, so great that it moves the hearts of all men, we must not forget that days may come when our patience, our endurance and our fortitude will be tried to the utmost. In those days let us see to it that no heart grows faint and that no courage be found wanting.

I then described the precautions taken by the Government

and read the cable messages from the British Government. In conclusion, I spoke as follows:

It is not fitting that I should prolong this debate. In the awful dawn of the greatest war the world has ever known, in the hour when peril confronts us such as this Empire has not faced for a hundred years, every vain or unnecessary word seems a discord. As to our duty, all are agreed, we stand shoulder to shoulder with Britain and the other British Dominions in this quarrel. And that duty we shall not fail to fulfil as the honour of Canada demands. Not for love of battle, not for lust of conquest, not for greed of possessions, but for the cause of honour, to maintain solemn pledges, to uphold principles of liberty, to withstand forces that would convert the world into an armed camp; yea, in the very name of the peace that we sought at any cost save that of dishonour, we have entered into this war; and while gravely conscious of the tremendous issues involved and of all the sacrifices that they may entail, we do not shrink from them, but with firm hearts we abide the event.

In the early days of the War, the Duke of Connaught failed to realize that his status and powers as Commander-in-Chief in Canada, under the British North America Act, were purely nominal. He was Commander-in-Chief of the Canadian forces only in the same sense as the King was Commander-in-Chief of the military forces of the United Kingdom. On August 26, I explained to Colonel Farquhar (the Duke's Military Secretary) that the Duke's impression was wholly false in this respect. . . .

During this period there was pressure both from my colleagues and from prominent Conservatives throughout the country for dissolution of Parliament and the holding of a general election. The more active and aggressive of my colleagues were very earnest in their belief that this course was not only important, but indeed essential in the interests of our party and was thoroughly justified on constitutional grounds; but on the other hand, with the support of, perhaps, a minority of my colleagues and many prominent Conservatives throughout the country, I felt that it would be most unfortunate and perilous to plunge our people into the throes of an election campaign seeing that Sir Wilfrid Laurier and his party had given us their unanimous support during the war session and that the country seemed united in support of our policy. Further, I felt that this course which would bring about intense disunion and fierce controversy was not justified on patriotic grounds. This view I eventually maintained and on October 16 I announced to the

Governor-General that there would be no immediate dissolution of Parliament.

From time to time during the mobilization and training of the first contingent at Valcartier, there were disturbing reports as to the conduct of the Minister of Militia at Valcartier. On September 16, the Governor-General reported to me that Hughes' language to his officers had been violent and insulting.

When I formed my Government in 1911, I was extremely doubtful as to including Hughes; while he was a man of marked ability and sound judgment in many respects, his temperament was so peculiar, and his actions and language so unusual on many important occasions that one was inclined to doubt his usefulness as a Minister. There was much pressure on his behalf from various sources; and my cousin, Sir Frederick Borden, who sought an interview with me on behalf of Hughes, expressed the firm, and I believe the sincere opinion that Hughes, under proper control, would be of great service to the country. I discussed with Hughes when I appointed him his extraordinary eccentricities. On one occasion when I impressed strongly upon him the mischievous and perverse character of his speech and conduct, he broke down, admitted that he often acted impetuously, and assured me that if he were appointed I could rely on his judgment and good sense. This promise was undoubtedly sincere but his temperament was too strong for him. He was under constant illusions that enemies were working against him. I told him on one occasion that I thoroughly agreed that he was beset by two unceasing enemies. Expecting a revelation he was intensely disappointed when I told him that they were his tongue and his pen. In my experience his moods might be divided into three categories; during about half of the time he was an able, reasonable, and useful colleague, working with excellent judgement and indefatigable energy; for a certain other portion of the time he was extremely excitable, impatient of control, and almost impossible to work with; and during the remainder his conduct and speech were so eccentric as to justify the conclusion that his mind was unbalanced.

Throughout the training of the First Division at Valcartier Camp, Hughes could not resist his absurd inclination to fill not only the role of Minister of Militia but that of Military Commander. His intense vanity, and a rather vindictive temper which developed during this period, contributed to the difficulty of the situation. However, notwithstanding all this, his inexhaustible energy and resourcefulness were a great asset to Canada at that time. No other man could have accomplished during a similar period what he did achieve in the training and organization of the First Canadian Expeditionary Force.

All through September there was much outcry from officers and prominent citizens with regard to his language and conduct. His usual dictatorial attitude towards subordinates (except those for whom he had an especial liking) had been accentuated by the strain and anxiety of his work. Quarrels developed between him and officers of the Expeditionary Force but in some cases these were due not entirely to his excitable temperament but to unfortunate provocation.

Considerable pressure was brought to bear to permit Hughes' promotion to the rank of Major-General. Although not particularly impressed with the advisability of such a step, I eventually consented. . . .

It was at first proposed that the Canadian Expeditionary Force should consist of about 20,000 men. More than 30,000 arrived in camp; and there arose the difficult problem of selecting those who should go overseas and those who should remain. The intense disappointment of the latter can be imagined; they had sacrificed every material consideration and surmounted every difficulty in order to reach camp and have an opportunity of enlisting. The duration of the War was, of course, uncertain. Financial experts had loudly proclaimed that it could not last long, as the financial burden would become intolerable. Wagers were laid in August, 1914, that, with the beginning of the coming year, we would see the end of the struggle.

What were we to do with the additional 10,000 or 12,000 men? I had but the faintest appreciation of the inevitable wastage when our men reached the Front, but I felt certain that reinforcements and reserves would be required at no distant date. Accordingly, I proposed to my colleagues that we should send the entire force assembled at Valcartier; and I gave them my reasons for that conclusion in which they instantly concurred. Thereupon I proceeded to Valcartier and at a conference with General Hughes, I announced without preliminary discussion that I had decided to send abroad the entire contingent. He was silent for a moment and then he suddenly broke down and sobbed audibly. He presently explained his emotions as joy and relief; he had been, he told me, agonized by the thought of a selection for which he would be responsible and which he must determine. In reviewing his character and actions, allowance must always be made for his extremely emotional temperament.

When the Expeditionary Force finally sailed from Gaspé on

October 3, its safe passage was assured by strong naval forces protecting the convoy. As to the adequacy of that force, we had had much correspondence with the Admiralty. On October 14 I received the welcome tidings that it had reached Plymouth.

Hughes delivered (and later published) a flamboyant and magniloquent address to the troops, based apparently on Napoleon's famous address to the Army of Italy. It did not enhance his prestige; and indeed excited no little mirth in various quarters. After the departure of the forces, he became obsessed with a desire to visit England. This proposal did not arouse our enthusiasm. Finally we consented, but not before I had given him grave warning that he must control his temperament and have no friction with the authorities on the other side.

In Hughes' absence Hazen was acting as Minister of Militia, and we immediately began consideration of preparation for further contingents, as the news from the Front indicated that the War would not be of short duration. On Ocotber 17, I held conference with Hazen, Gwatkin (Chief of Staff), and Denison (Adjutant-General). They urged a programme of training for 30,000 men. We went over the whole question of defence; and on the following day I sent for the Acting Minister and told him to instruct Gwatkin to get up such a programme—30,000 men continuously in training to go forward by detachments of 10,000.

The need of immense supplies, not only for our own forces but for those of Great Britain and France, created a situation of extreme difficulty and perplexity. The organization of the Department of Militia and Defence was not constituted adequately to deal with such a situation. I bear witness to the devotion to duty of all the officers of that Department with whom I was brought into touch, especially of Colonel Fiset, the Deputy Minister, and H. W. Brown, Director of Contracts. Some of the supplies, however, were not such as could appropriately be dealt with by that department. Moreover, there was among my colleagues a lack of confidence in the administrative methods of General Hughes who would not hesitate, it was believed, to override his officers to the advantage of some favourite friend. Thus, early in the autumn a Committee of Council was formed for the purpose of supervising and dealing with contracts for supplies. Undoubtedly this method was useful for the purpose of preventing possible abuses; but, on the other hand, it was an unwieldy body and delay was occasioned in some cases by its failure to act promptly.

With respect to the provision of supplies ordered for the

British Government, or for any Allied Powers, I prepared and circulated among my colleagues on September 30, 1914, the following memorandum:

MEMORANDUM AS TO FILLING SUPPLIES ORDERED FOR
BRITISH GOVERNMENT OR ANY OF THE ALLIED POWERS.

1. *These orders will come in some cases to the Department of Militia and Defence and in other cases to the Department of Agriculture.*

2. *All orders for arms, equipment and munitions of war should be filled by the Department of Militia and Defence with as little delay as possible.*

3. *All other orders for military supplies, such as clothing, footwear, saddlery, vehicles, binoculars, etc., should be immediately taken into consideration by the Director of Contracts of the Militia Department, assisted, if necessary, by such persons as may be appointed for that purpose, who will forthwith collect and tabulate all possible information as to the capacity of manufacturers and dealers to fill such orders and as to quality, prices, etc., before any order is given. A complete memorandum setting forth the information so tabulated, the order and the proposed method of filling it, should be submitted to the Prime Minister, or to a Committee of Council appointed for the purpose by him.*

4. *All orders for other supplies, such as flour, wheat, hay, oats, fodder and all other food products, whether for men or for horses, should be immediately taken into consideration by an officer of the Department of Agriculture appointed for that purpose, and assisted, if necessary, by such persons as may be selected therefor, who should immediately collect and tabulate all possible information as to the capacity of producers and dealers to fill such orders and as to quality, prices, etc. Before orders are given a complete memorandum setting forth the order, the information so tabulated and the proposed method of filling it should be submitted to the Prime Minister, or to a Committee of Council appointed for the purpose by him.*

5. *The above procedure applies to orders from the British Government, or any of the Allied Governments.*

6. *In each Department a systematic arrangement for dealing with such orders should be established and proper forms of application, contract, etc., should be prepared,*

> *so that the purchases may be made in a systematic man-*
> *ner and by business methods.*

7. *Inspection and supervision of the articles supplied*
   should be made by the officers of the respective depart-
   ments, supplemented by any additional assistance which
   may be found necessary to the end that such inspection
   and supervision shall be efficient and complete.

8. *Cost of collecting information, tabulation, supervision*
   and inspection and other necessary work shall be
   charged to the Government for which the supplies are
   furnished.

9. *Payment for all such supplies should be arranged*
   through the Department of Finance by letter of credit
   issued by that department. Accounts and vouchers for
   all payments must be furnished.

10. *It is essential that there should be no unnecessary delay;*
    and if the staff of any department is found insufficient
    for the purposes above indicated, the Prime Minister
    should be consulted.

About this time disturbing rumours began to arise as to
alleged boasts by Colonel J. Wesley Allison of his wonderful
profits in placing contracts for the British Government in the
United States. He was a prime favourite of Hughes upon whose
request the British War Office had apparently given Allison
authority to arrange such matters.

Further rumours of attempts to defraud the Government
had been brought to my attention, and on October 19 I directed
Hon. Arthur Meighen, Solicitor-General, to make a thorough
investigation of all such attempts, so far as they had been discovered, and I further directed him to obtain such assistance as
might be necessary from Colonel Sherwood, Commissioner of
Dominion Police. I also directed that the Minister of Justice
should be consulted whenever necessary. And I concluded:

> *You have my authority and direction to prosecute to the*
> *utmost limit of the law all persons who appear upon reasonable*
> *information to have been concerned in such attempt.*

Again on October 22 I wrote to Mr. Meighen emphasizing
my directions to spare no expense in making a thorough investigation and to prosecute to the utmost limit any conspiracy or
attempt to defraud the Government.

After a short holiday at Hot Springs, Virginia, where I was
greatly impressed with the strong sympathy of the Americans

for the Allies, I returned to Ottawa on November 16, accompanied by Sir Cecil Spring-Rice, Lady Spring-Rice, and the Secretary of the Embassy at Washington.[6]

One of my first duties on returning to Ottawa was to summon Hughes with regard to the administration of his department and again to warn him against intimacy with undesirable persons such as Allison.

On November 18, I gave to General Hughes the following written direction:

When acting as Minister of Militia during your absence at Valcartier, I instructed Colonel Fiset, Deputy Minister, that the use of outside agents and middlemen should be avoided and that contracts should be made directly with manufacturers so that any unnecessary commissions or increased prices might be avoided. This is undoubtedly the wise policy and is entirely in accordance with principles laid down by our party during years past. If, for any good reason, you may think it desirable in the public interest that a different course should be pursued in any particular instance by reason of conditions arising out of the war, I hope that you will first consult me as I consider the principle to be of prime importance.

On December 15, I addressed to Sir George Foster, who was Chairman of the Committee of Council for the purchase of supplies, the following letter:

In connection with the supply of clothing and equipment, etc., for the Second and Third Expeditionary Forces, I hope that the members of the Committee will bear in mind the importance of efficiency and of promptness. It is most desirable that there should be such an allotment of work as will give a reasonable share to every part of the country and particularly to those communities where unemployment largely obtains. On the other hand it is vitally essential that the articles of equipment, etc., should be of the best quality, should be furnished at a reasonable price and should be delivered with such promptness as would avoid any delay in the despatch of the forces.

I fear that the necessary consideration of the 120 items and the distribution of the work among so large a number of persons

[6] Immediately upon my return from Hot Springs I had an interview with the Governor-General who spoke of the wonderful spy system which the Germans had organized. In the years immediately preceding the War, Prince Henry of Prussia frequently came to London without apparent reason and the Duke was strongly of opinion that his mission was espionage.

*as are listed in respect of every item will produce very serious
and unfortunate delay, unless very prompt and unremitting
attention is given to the subject by members of the Committee.*

*The Director of Contracts explained yesterday that it is
relatively a simple matter to allot among a few persons who
have been known as departmental contractors but an allotment
among a larger number necessarily comprises much more time.
If he could be assisted by a larger staff matters might be expe-
dited and I am to see the Deputy Minister on this subject at
10:45 this morning.*

Upon my return to Ottawa on December 8, from Montreal
and Toronto, where I made many speeches, visited camps, and
reviewed troops, there was tremendous pressure to speak in
different parts of the country. During the next three weeks I
visited Halifax, Winnipeg, and Fort William for the purpose of
reviewing troops and fulfilling speaking engagements.[7]

In the meantime, two of my colleagues, Pelletier and Nantel,
decided to resign. Pelletier was evidently alarmed at the development of hostile public opinion in Quebec and assigned as a
reason for his retirement certain symptoms including a swelling
of the feet. Eventually he became Judge of the Superior Court
in Quebec. Nantel was appointed to the Board of Railway
Commissioners. They were succeeded by T. Chase Casgrain as
Postmaster-General and Pierre E. Blondin as Minister of Inland
Revenue.

Throughout the period–August 1 to December 31–I was
working at very high pressure, sometimes under the care of a
physician; but occasionally I obtained relief from a short holiday. It would be tiresome to enumerate the thousand-and-one
incidents, some of them of a highly disturbing and exciting
character, which pressed upon me during that period and which
are mentioned in my diary. There was constant correspondence
with the British Government and with the Acting High Commissioner respecting our co-operation in the War and touching
upon our capacity to supply food, arms, munitions, and indeed
every description of material necessary for war purposes. Further, there was disturbing unemployment in some of our cities;
and, unfortunately, British officials seemed disposed in some

---

[7] I reached Ottawa at 6 a.m. on January 1, and worked at correspondence until noon when I attended the Governor-General's Levée. It
was very largely attended, and Colonel Stanton (Military Secretary)
who was of mediocre ability and lacked good sense, had great
difficulty in deciphering cards. He called Machado, "MacAdoo" and
he anglicized "Gagnon" and gallicized "Anglin."

instances, to obtain supplies from the United States which could have been procured in Canada and the provision of which would have given employment to some of our people. I made sharp protests against this practice; and on one occasion I learned that a British official had sent a considerable order to a city in the United States under the impression that he had placed it in Canada.

24: *1915*

From the first of the year until the opening of the session on February 4, I was working to the utmost limit of my strength. Not only the imperative necessities arising out of our participation in the War, but matters of grave internal or domestic concern were continually pressing upon us.

The question of proceeding with by-elections arose, and relevant interviews with Sir Wilfrid Laurier took place. He was rather indefinite and it was impossible to bring him to a straight decision. I was disposed to let them go by acclamation, retaining the seats which we already held. Eventually the five vacant seats were filled on February 1, by acclamation.

The eccentricities of General Hughes continued to take up time and to call for great patience. As a curiosity I quote the following extract from my diary for January 8:

Hughes asked me to call at hospital where he still is. Discussed many matters with him. On matters which touch his insane egotism he is quite unbalanced. On all other matters able and sometimes brilliant. . . .

~ During this period there was much negotiation with the Government of Newfoundland on the question of the colony's joining Confederation. Borden felt that the initiative would have to come from the Colony and not from the Dominion. Pressure of other important matters prevented his discussing the matter while in Britain. ~

To add to the difficulties and complexities which surrounded me, both the Canadian Northern and the Grand Trunk Railways were in trouble and the discussion of their unfortunate condition was continuous and wearying. On January 13, Mr. Chamberlin, president of the Grand Trunk, desired us to make an offer for the operation of that line by the Government. In reply I told him that we desired him to carry out his company's contract.

On January 21, I discussed with the Minister of Finance a proposal for income tax which was considered in Council. The objection was raised that direct taxation should be left to the provinces. . . .

On January 30, Casgrain (Postmaster-General) threatened to resign unless the Quebec Terminals were proceeded with at full speed. I informed him politely that we would not do it, but he did not carry out his threat. . . .

My dear mother who was approaching her ninetieth year, had been gradually losing strength throughout the winter. My sister who was with her at Grand Pré kept me constantly informed as to her condition. On March 26, an alarming telegram reached me; and I left immediately by special train for Grand Pré, arriving in twenty-five-and-a-half hours from Ottawa. Just fifteen years before the date of my arrival my father had passed away in his eighty-fifth year. I found my mother unconscious. My brother Hal and I slept on the private car and early in the morning of March 29, we learned that mother had passed away peacefully at 3:10. I quote the following from my diary:

Fifty-seven years this summer since mother came to live in this house, then just built. A long life, nearly 90 years, happier in later years, I believe. A woman of unusual ability and strength of character, passionately fond of her children, sensitive, perhaps too much so, taking a keen interest in life even to the last, just, but passionate, the embodiment of motherhood of the world in her love of children. . . .

The close of the session (Parliament was prorogued on April 15) found me in a condition of serious physical exhaustion. A slight operation on my nose was necessary and intense bleeding ensued on April 17 and 18. However, voluminous correspondence and matters of very serious import had to be dealt with and, although I found it difficult to keep on my feet, I persevered. . . .

~ The appointment by Order-in-Council of a War Purchasing Commission was a most important matter. Borden gave "grave consideration" to the question of personnel for the Commission and he sharply censured Hughes who regarded the move as "an impairment of his dignity."

The Commission, except in "case of urgency," was to call for tenders for all purchases and award contracts at the lowest figure. The Commission was to report to the Prime Minister. All government departments were to afford the Commission all possible information concerning areas under its purview. ~

From* [a report covering the years 1915 and 1916] and from my knowledge of the work of the Commission, I am

---

* [Report by A. E. Kemp, Chairman of the War Purchasing Committee, January 3, 1917.]

satisfied that its service to the country was of the highest advantage. Indeed, I am convinced that an amount of not less than fifty millions was saved to Canada through the efficient methods which the Commission established. . . .

It gives me great satisfaction at this distant date to realize that the course which I took on this occasion was wise and timely and that in selecting the personnel of the Commission I made a wise choice.

It is the ill fortune of every Government in time of war to be assailed by unworthy men with every possible fraudulent device and scheme for the purpose of profiting during national emergency at the expense of the country's resources. I am satisfied that one method of such attack was successfully resisted and overcome by the establishment of the War Purchasing Commission.

Before leaving for England at the end of June there was much discussion as to dissolution of Parliament and the holding of a general election. Fierce controversy took place among my colleagues—those favouring the election being in the majority. The Governor-General, whom I consulted, deprecated such a course but said he would consent if I advised it. Finally, I concluded that it would be undesirable from the standpoint of our party and especially (and this determined me) from the standpoint of the country. Although there had been evidence of partisan attack during the recent session, still I had to consider the attitude of Sir Wilfrid Laurier and his followers at the war session in August, 1914.

Further, there came the news of the tremendous casualties which the Canadian Division had suffered in the Second Battle of Ypres. The story of their gallantry has been told many times and I will not repeat it. All Canada was deeply moved. . . .

The feeling, already manifest, against the holding of a general election was greatly stimulated by the casualties in that famous battle.

During this period there were innumerable reports from General Hughes, among them on May 3 the story of the Battle of Langemarck in which the Canadian casualties amounted to about 6,000. In the letter which accompanied this report Hughes bitterly attacked the strategy of the British command. He expressed the opinion that nothing was accomplished but the loss of some Canadians and concluded "it is more congenial to bury the dead of the enemy than to have the enemy bury ours." Further correspondence from him advised the displacement of Alderson as "unfit" and recommended Turner to replace him.

Many charges were made against General Alderson, and Hughes' communication was sent to England for Alderson's defence which was given at great length. Eventually General Alderson asked for an interview with me during my visit to England and matters were arranged satisfactorily. . . .

I thought it desirable and necessary to establish a commission for the investigation of purchases by the Government during the ten months which had elapsed since the outbreak of War. These purchases had been, to a considerable extent, investigated by the Public Accounts Committee, but it seemed expedient to continue and enlarge the investigation. Accordingly Sir Charles Piers Davidson of Montreal, retired Chief Justice of the Supreme Court of Quebec, was appointed on June 2, to be "a Commissioner to enquire into, investigate and report upon the purchase, by and on behalf of the Government of Canada, through whatever agency the purchases may have been effected, of arms and munitions, implements, materials, horses, supplies and other things for the purpose of the present War and as to the expenditures and payments made or agreed to be made therefor."

There could be no question as to the high character, perfect integrity, and outstanding ability of the Commissioner. He proceeded with the investigation with promptitude and vigour. A summary of his work may be quoted from *The Canadian Annual Review** for 1915:

No one, partisan or otherwise, questioned the thoroughness and efficiency of the succeeding eight months' investigation. From the Atlantic to the Pacific, beginning on June 18th, Sir Charles P. Davidson held sittings, 8,000 pages of evidence were taken, the work of the Public Accounts Committee carried on, and new ground covered such as the purchase of horses and fodder in Western Canada and Ontario and the purchase of submarines in British Columbia. The Garland and deWitt Foster cases were further investigated and the unpleasant details of the horse purchases in Nova Scotia carefully probed. Munitions were not dealt with as coming under a committee dealing directly with the British Government, nor were purchases by or for the Allied Governments touched.

This probe as far as it went was deep, the examination of witnesses close, and few criticisms were heard as to procedure. . . .

* Reprinted by permission of the publishers.

On May 30, the Governor-General wrote to me with regard to a copy of *Le Devoir* which he enclosed. He expressed the opinion that we should censor this newspaper. I quote from my diary of that date:

Bourassa would like nothing better. I would not be so foolish. Besides, Campbell Bannerman, and especially Lloyd George were far worse in South Africa War, and Carson respecting Ulster.

On June 2, I had a complaint from the Governor-General with respect to the conduct of General Hughes. On June 5 and again on June 10, I had to take up with Hughes his extraordinary ebullitions. On the latter date my diary contains the following:

Sharp reproof to Hughes for insolent language to H.R.H. *respecting telegram to Kitchener. He was much cut up and when I spoke to him in afternoon over the telephone he broke down and wept. Most mercurial. . . .*

Besides my sessional activities and the duties involved in preparation for and during my visit to England, as well as the time and work involved in the addresses I was called upon to deliver at various centres throughout Canada, much time was occupied with a tremendous mass of correspondence. This reached me from various sources and covered a wide range of subjects, principally the conduct of the War. Many letters from men serving at the Front reached me; and at one time I was rather embarrassed by the number of reports, official and otherwise, from Eye-Witnesses at the Front.

Disturbing and rather alarming rumours as to the discomforts and hardships endured by Canadian troops at Salisbury Plain were rife. Investigations were made; and on February 22, word was received through the Governor-General from Lord Kitchener that the Canadians were being removed to Shorncliffe: "I am sorry that Salisbury Plain has got such a bad name in Canada, but I am glad to be able to inform Your Royal Highness that not a single complaint was received from either officers or men of the Canadian Contingent." In truth, the Canadians well realized that the fault lay, not with the War Office, but in the extraordinary weather conditions then prevailing. Lord Kitchener remarked also that the Canadians "showed an excellent spirit which I feel sure they will carry with them to France where they are doing so well."

There was a strong feeling throughout the country that another and still another Canadian division should be recruited

at once. Numerous Canadian organizations as well as individuals communicated this suggestion to me. I quote my letter
of May 29, 1915, to a Canadian club in a Western city, as it is
characteristic of the replies made to the suggestions:

> *Will you permit me to observe that it is much easier to
> propose the organization, arming and equipment of a force of
> 250,000 men than to accomplish it.*
>
> *We have been in constant communication and thorough
> co-operation with the British Government on the subject of
> arms, guns and ammunition ever since the outbreak of war.
> Without these vital necessities and without organization and
> training, especially of officers, a so-called army would be a mere
> mob. If your club is aware of any source from which could be
> procured in the immediate future, the rifles, guns and ammuni-
> tion for so large a force as you suggest, I know that the Cana-
> dian Government and I feel sure that the British Government
> would be glad of the information.*
>
> *In a word, the — of — may be assured that the problem of
> organizing, arming and equipping in every branch of the mili-
> tary service the largest available forces for despatch to the front
> has received the most earnest and energetic attention and con-
> sideration of which the Government is capable.*

Much tiresome correspondence and criticism in the Press
was occasioned by reason of what seemed undue detention of
the Second Contingent in Canada. On April 5, I issued a statement showing the standing of the Second Contingent and giving
the explanation for the delay in sending them over:

> *The Second Contingent—that is to say, the 2nd Canadian
> Division with certain additional units required for administra-
> tive purposes—is still in Canada; but as soon as it can be suit-
> ably accommodated on the other side, its embarkation will
> proceed.*
>
> *Some comment has been made on the fact that while men
> are being called for and recruiting vigorously going on in Great
> Britain, the Second Expeditionary Force has not yet sailed from
> Canada. It could have been despatched at the end of last De-
> cember or early in January but for reasons which the War
> Office considered adequate the despatch of the Second Contin-
> gent has been delayed up to the present time. In the interval
> training has proceeded. It must be remembered besides infantry
> it is necessary that there should be the necessary artillery force
> accompanying every division and that guns and ammunition*

are absolutely essential to make the Force effective. Moreover the enormous number of men under training in Great Britain necessarily causes delay in providing accommodation for contingents from the Overseas Dominions. It is not desirable in the public interest that the subject should be further pursued.

There was considerable opposition to my proposal to visit England[1] and a good deal of criticism of my intention to sail from New York on the *Adriatic*. It was thought that I should have taken passage in an American boat for fear of the submarine menace. I felt very strongly that I should sail under my own flag and did so, leaving Ottawa on the afternoon of June 28. . . .

On June 30, I had another conference with the British Ambassador who entrusted me with further messages. On this day Mr. R. B. Bennett who was to accompany me arrived; and we went on board ship where we were the prey of many Press men and photographers. . . .

I spent the week-end of July 10-11 with Sir George Perley at Sunningdale and had a long conference with him as to the status of High Commissioner. He considered that legislation should be passed constituting the High Commissionership a portfolio in the Cabinet; and he was under the impression that his status as a member of the Government without portfolio, but discharging the duties of High Commissioner, was inadequate. In this connection he called my attention to the Orders-in-Council under which he visited Great Britain in the first instance; and they certainly seemed inadequate.

I emphasized the view that as a member of the Canadian Government, he had a much higher status than any of the other High Commissioners who were merely servants of their respective Governments and not members thereof.

Subsequently, I consulted Bonar Law who entirely concurred in my view. Bonar Law thought that the presence of a member of the Canadian Government in London had been a marked advantage during the War; but he would not commit himself as to its advantage in time of peace. He was of opinion that a much more advanced step would be necessary than arranging for the presence of Dominion Ministers in London. He feared that having a voice in foreign affairs might commit the Dominions to a larger naval and military expenditure than they would care to undertake.

---

[1] On June 11 I had received a cable from Sir George Perley expressing Bonar Law's desire that I should visit England that summer.

The note which I made of my conversation with Bonar Law contains the following observations:

Evidently he does not realize that the share of the various Dominions in such expenditure cannot be based merely on population. At least three considerations (perhaps more) must be taken into account: 1st, population; 2nd, wealth; 3, necessary work in development of resources. While we are obliged to spend large amounts on transportation, development and equipment of harbours, etc., and Great Britain is in a position to provide old age pensions, which, certainly, we cannot yet afford, it is impossible not to take into account relative wealth and revenue. . . .

On the same day (July 13) I attended a Parliamentary luncheon given in my honour at which I spoke. Among the many warm congratulations on my address, I especially appreciated those from Balfour and T. P. O'Connor. Following the luncheon I had a conference with Kitchener who was very non-committal as to the probable duration of the War; but, apparently, he believed that it would extend over a long period.

At noon on July 14 I attended a meeting of the Cabinet in pursuance of a formal summons. I sat next to Mr. Asquith who spoke of my presence as a new precedent but said it was a day for making new precedents. He greatly enjoined me as to the tradition which forbids one to make any note of Cabinet proceedings.

The principal subject discussed was the question of making cotton contraband. There was a good deal of difference of opinion; the arguments pro and con were put forward with a great deal of earnestness. Eventually the view of Sir Edward Grey, which carried my judgment, prevailed; namely, that it would be undesirable at the moment to take any such action, but that it might probably be required to be taken in the early future. I expressed the view that while the *Lusitania* outrage was still fresh in the minds of the American people it was undesirable to take immediate action which would divert their attention from that subject. I thought it also very important to ascertain through the Ambassador, who had confidential means of knowledge, whether such a course would be confidentially approved by the Government of United States. . . .

It had been my intention to visit every wounded Canadian in Great Britain and France; but I discovered that this was impossible as it would have involved visiting something like 100 hospitals in the British Isles to which just a few Canadians had been sent for treatment. As it was I visited those hospitals in which the greatest number of Canadians were to be found.

One's impressions from such visits were of a varied character. On the one hand I was inspired by the astonishing courage with which my fellow-countrymen bore their sufferings, inspired also by the warmth of their reception, by a smile of welcome, by the attempt to rise in their beds to greet me. In many cases it was difficult to restrain my tears when I knew that some poor boy, brave to the very last, could not recover. On the other hand, the emotion aroused from these visits had an exhausting effect upon one's nervous strength; and frequently I could not sleep after reflecting upon the scene through which I had passed.

The director of each hospital was most kind and considerate and, unless engagements prevented, he would accompany me throughout my visit. In every instance I found the hospitals well organized, with every comfort provided and excellent attendants.

In each hospital where there were men sufficiently convalescent to be gathered together I was called upon to address them; and never did I fail to have intent audiences and enthusiastic receptions.

In my mind I divided the hospital directors into three classes, forming my estimate by the impression which their conversation and attitude left with me. In the first class were those whose chief interest was in the technical aspects of surgery, in the remarkable success of varied operations, in all that concerned the welfare of their patients from the purely technical standpoint. Then there was a second class consisting of those whose interest was not so much occupied with the surgical aspect as with the orderly arrangement of organization and thoroughness of detail in every aspect. But besides these there was still another class comprising those who, naturally and necessarily, were concerned with technical aspects and thoroughness of organization but whose absorbing interest was in the men themselves, in the human aspect, the touch, men who liked to hear from the patients themselves the story of their lives, their service, and their homes. Of course there were directors in whom all these qualities were more or less observable; but usually one or another of the characteristics I have noted seemed to be predominant.

In the hospital at Cliveden "Nancy" (now Lady) Astor exercised a most benign, on might say magic, influence upon the Canadian wounded, each of whom came to regard her as his special friend and counsellor. Her presence in any of the wards was like a ray of sunshine. The brightness of her charm, the aptness of her cheering words, the intense sympathy which she radiated exercised a remarkable psychological influence upon all the wounded who had the good fortune to be sent to Cliveden.

Altogether I visited in Great Britain and in France fifty-two hospitals which sheltered our wounded. The memory of those visits has never faded and will endure as long as my life.

From July 20 to July 26 I was in France where, in addition to visiting many hospitals, I reviewed various units of Canadian troops and saw our Forces in action. . . .

On Sunday afternoon, August 8, I discussed with Lord Bryce the future constitutional relations within the Empire and he agreed that the Dominions must have a voice in foreign policy. I told him they would either have such a voice or each of them would have a foreign policy of its own. . . .

On August 10, I attended the French Ambassador and received the Grand Cross of the Legion of Honour. On the same day the Belgian Minister called and offered his country's thanks for Canada's effort.

On August 14, I motored to Bexley Heath to visit Sir Charles Tupper. Although in his ninety-fifth year, his mind was wonderfully clear; and he was as keenly interested as ever in the affairs of the Empire. His views were much the same as mine with respect to Canadian representation in London. He thought the High Commissioner should be one of our ablest men, a good speaker, as well as a member of the Government. In discussing Perley, he did less than justice to his ability, resourcefulness and tact. . . .

On the following day (August 21) I had a conference with Bonar Law at Margate. There was a considerable gathering of public men who discussed their colleagues with great frankness. In answer to my inquiry as to when the supply of munitions would be ample, Churchill replied, "the middle of the following year" and Law "about five months." I told them I must have definite information.

I had gone from pillar to post, from one member of the British Government to another, for the purpose of obtaining definite information as to when the British Empire would be in a position to throw its whole strength into the War. I had one idea from one Cabinet Minister and another from another, merely conjectures; so finally, on August 24, I sought and obtained an interview with Mr. Bonar Law to whom I said:

I have come overseas for the purpose of visiting hospitals and going to the front to see the Canadian troops; but I have come very largely for the purpose of obtaining definite and precise information as to matters of extreme importance and urgency.

After defining these, I continued:

I must tell you, as Secretary of State for the Colonies, that unless I get precise information as to these matters, I shall return to Canada with no definite intention of urging my fellow countrymen to continue in the war work they have already begun or with the intensive preparation which I am sure they are ready to undertake if I inform them that the British Government takes the War seriously, realizes the immensity of the task, is making preparation accordingly, and that there is no more cry of "Business as usual."

Mr. Lloyd George was ill in the country, but Mr. Bonar Law got him to come to London, and we sat down for two hours in the Carlton Hotel, where he detailed to me, with great particularity, the character of the preparation that had been made, the neglect there had been in the past, his hope for the future. Mr. Lloyd George was very graphic, as usual, in some of his statements. Speaking of a highly placed official in an important department he said, "I don't say that that man is a traitor, but I do say that if he had been a traitor he would not have acted otherwise than as he did."

After this conference I made up my mind then, and so reported, on my return, to my colleagues, as well as to Sir Wilfrid Laurier, that at least eighteen months from that time would elapse before the British Empire would be able to throw its whole force and power into the War. . . .

Immediately after my return from England on September 4, I reported to my colleagues in Council the impressions derived from my conferences with British Ministers, especially from my interview with Lloyd George and Bonar Law on August 24. Then I sought an interview with Sir Wilfrid Laurier to whom I gave the same information, emphasizing the fact that Great Britain could not attempt to throw her full strength into the War for at least a year, perhaps eighteen months. He seemed much impressed, looked very thoughtful and finally said: "I am afraid this wil be a very long war."

During my absence there had been a tremendous volume of correspondence, and for some weeks I was busily engaged with that, as well as with numerous conferences on many important and urgent subjects. I had a long conference with Lougheed who acted as Minister of Militia in Hughes' absence and who expressed the strong opinion that "Hughes has no executive ability and is really incapable of administering a department."

On September 10, the reorganization of my Ministry was suggested by Casgrain (Postmaster-General) who told me that Coderre (Secretary of State) was "absolutely useless." Dr. Reid (Minister of Railways) was inspired to confide in me Robert Rogers' (Minister of Public Works) desire to represent Canada at Washington. To add to all these difficulties and complexities there arose trouble and controversy as to the grain situation, due to Foster's (Sir George Foster – Minister of Trade and Commerce) lack of business sense and inexperience and his keen desire to undertake tasks of a practical nature for which he was entirely unfitted.

From September 13 to the end of the month the demands upon my energies were very insistent and exhausting; innumerable delegations, callers, conferences, in Council and out, on matters of first importance, the difficulties of the railway situation, dissatisfaction with and criticism of some of my Quebec colleagues, and many other matters of a wearying nature.

The need of Cabinet reconstruction was being stressed. Incessant applications for senatorships had to be dealt with and the sensibilities of disappointed ambitions had to be soothed. There were rumours of dissatisfactions among our followers in the House. All there difficulties together with the depressing influence of bad news from the Front were most trying and exhausting; and by the end of September my nervous energy was very much below par. . . .

On October 5, E. L. Patenaude was sworn in as Minister of Inland Revenue and P. E. Blondin as Secretary of State. My diary notes the following day as "a tremendously hard day, with the 'Old Man of the Sea' (Sir Wm. Mackenzie) on my back with regard to the Canadian Northern payment due next Saturday." There were delegations and conferences all day until I left that evening to review troops at Valcartier Camp "tired and discouraged."

As various complaints had come to the Government regarding the treatment of individual cases amongst returned soldiers, a commission was established in July under the chairmanship of Senator Lougheed to look after returned men. This Commission was known as the Military Hospitals

Commission. In October Senator Lougheed reported that eleven
convalescent homes were under organization throughout Canada and 600 invalided soldiers already taken under care. The
question of vocational training was gone into, and a Disablement
Fund was organized to supplement the pension granted by the
Government in cases where this was insufficient for the support
of dependents.

Another important Commission established during this
month was the Natural Resources Commission of which Senator
Lougheed was also Chairman. Sir William Van Horne had
consented to act in that capacity—a condition which his death
prevented. A large deputation of Canadian mayors had waited
on me in May and presented a memorial describing unemployment conditions throughout Canada, the need for more men,
and the general difficulty, arising out of war conditions, in
fitting the work to the workers. Before my departure for
England I had recommended to Council the advisability of
appointing a Commission to inquire into such subjects as
immigration, agriculture, transportation, the borrowing of
capital, the marketing of food products, and other related
matters.

Delay in establishing the Commission had been occasioned
by the death of Sir William Van Horne, but on October 19,
the personnel was announced and the objects stated.

On October 29 I prepared an Order-in-Council increasing
the Force to 250,000; and I gave a statement to the Press as well
as the following message to *The Times*:

*The war brought with it the necessity of organizing great
armies upon a scale unexampled in our history and of arming
and equipping them. During the past twelve months the response
in all parts of the King's Dominions has been most encouraging
but the need is still great and a supreme effort is now necessary.
If that effort is made there can be no doubt as to the issue of the
present struggle for the allied nations are notably superior in
numbers and in resources to the enemy nations. To be worthy of
the heritage for which so many sacrifices have been made by
those who have gone before and which we hold as trustees for
those who are yet to be born, we must make that supreme effort.
Considering the history and the traditions of our race and
believing that those of this generation are inspired by the same
courage, patriotism and devotion which animated their ancestors, I do not doubt that such effort will be made. Be assured
that Canada will not fail to do her part until victory is achieved.*

Early in October I had heard that Sir Wilfrid would probably agree to extend the parliamentary term and on October 14 he had called on me to discuss this subject, which he seemed to favour. On November 2, I had a long interview with him respecting this matter and arrangements regarding by-elections in vacant constituencies. He said that he was practically in favour of extension of the parliamentary term but he suggested that my proposal should be put in writing and extension should be suggested for one year. Accordingly I put my proposal in writing.

On November 8, Sir Wilfrid's reply to this communication was received. It was rather evasive as he introduced irrelevant considerations respecting our legislative programme. I replied on November 9; and on November 13 a letter arrived from Sir Sir Wilfrid in which he practically withdrew from the proposed arrangement as to the parliamentary term. The correspondence which passed between us was as follows:

Ottawa, Ont.,
November 3, 1915.

Dear Sir Wilfrid Laurier,
I beg to put in writing as requested by you at our interview of the 2nd inst., the proposals which I made at our interview on the 14th October last. They are as follows:

1. *That the term of the present Parliament of Canada, which expires on the 7th of October, 1916, shall be extended until one year after the conclusion of peace.*
2. *That there shall be no general election during the war; and that after the conclusion of peace a reasonable period shall be allowed in order that the Canadian forces now serving overseas may have the opportunity of first returning to their homes.*
3. *That during the interval by-elections shall not be contested and that each party shall retain the seats which it now holds.*
4. *That in Parliament and as far as possible in the public press, party warfare shall be suspended and the united efforts of both parties directed toward the best means of assisting to bring the war to a successful conclusion.*

At our interview on the 14th October you appeared to have some hesitation about extending the life of Parliament until after the conclusion of the war as the period thus fixed would be indefinite. If you regard that consideration as a serious one I am prepared in lieu of proposal number one to agree that the life of the present Parliament shall be extended for the period of one year leaving for future consideration and discussion the necessity, if any, of further extension in order to avoid an election during the war.

Yours faithfully,
(Sgd.) R. L. BORDEN

The Right Honourable,
Sir Wilfrid Laurier, P.C., G.C.M.G., *& etc.*
House of Commons,
Ottawa, Ont.

Ottawa,
November 8, 1915.

CONFIDENTIAL.
My dear Borden,
In answer to yours of the 3rd I beg to observe:
I persist in the opinion verbally expressed to you that the proposal to extend the term of the present Parliament until one year after the conclusion of peace would be absolutely objectionable for want of definiteness. I add that your subsidiary proposal that the life of the existing Parliament be extended for the period of one year as set forth in the last paragraph of your letter, is a fair basis for consideration and acceptance.
I must, however, further observe that before any undertaking can be reached I should be informed of the extent and nature of your legislative programme. I would expect to know if you intended to confine such programme exclusively to war measures, or if you propose to introduce measures of general policy. In particular I would like to be exactly informed as to your railway policy.
In our recent conversations, I understood that owing to the present financial situation, the Grand Trunk Pacific and the Canadian Northern might require some legislation. Full information, both as to the character of the legislation required and as to the proposed action of the Government is rendered necessary by the very importance of the matter involved.
I also call your attention to the fact that according to persistent press reports the Minister of Railways lately visited and inspected a line of railway on the Lower St. Lawrence with the view of either purchasing or assisting it. It would be equally imperative to be informed of the exact policy of the government as to this concern.

With regard to the other matters mentioned in your letter, they can be reserved for adjustment when those above set forth have been disposed of.

I can, however, at once declare in respect of the by-elections, that for such vacancies as were caused by death your suggestion is entirely acceptable, but as to those which were caused by resignations, I could not now make any agreement.

I desire to add that whilst it is quite proper that the correspondence which is now going on between us should be confidential, yet when completed it may at the proper time be made public.

Yours very sincerely,
(Sgd.) WILFRID LAURIER

The Right Honourable,
Sir Robert Borden, P.C., G.C.M.G.,
Prime Minister's Office,
Ottawa.

Ottawa, Ont.,
November 9, 1915.

My dear Sir Wilfrid Laurier,

Your letter of the 8th instant reached me last evening and I hasten to reply.

During the continuance of the war we intend to confine our programme to measures relating to or arising out of the war, following in that regard the course which we pursued in the special session of 1914 and in the session of 1915. We have not in contemplation or under consideration at present any measure of general policy.

Neither of the Railway Companies to which you allude has made any application to the Government for assistance. In case any such application should be made, it must of course receive consideration; but I should be glad to discuss it with you before coming to any conclusion.

With respect to the Railway on the Lower St. Lawrence upon which a large amount of money has been expended and which is almost completed, it appears to me that the application for aid has considerable merit, having regard to the interests of the population concerned. However, I would not allow it, if opposed, to stand in the way of an agreement upon the momentous question which we have now to decide.

Having regard therefore, to the above facts, that we propose no general programme outside of war measures, and that I shall be willing to consult with you regarding policy to be fol-

lowed with respect to the several railway matters referred to, I again repeat my proposition.

That the term of the present Parliament be extended for one year from its legal expiration.

That the holding of a general election shall be deferred until a reasonable period, say six months, after the conclusion of peace.

If peace be not declared when the said term expires, the subject of holding an election or further extending the life of Parliament to be considered de novo.

By-elections not to be contested. Each side to hold the seats it now holds or held before the vacancy occurred. As the arrangement is being made to further a political truce I see no difference between cases of vacancy by death or resignation.

That in the meantime in Parliament and in the Press so far as the leaders on both sides can effect it, party warfare shall be suspended.

In view of the extreme gravity of the war situation and the fact that His Majesty the King has appealed to the nation for the largest possible number of troops, which appeal we are endeavouring now to answer by enlisting and equipping 100,000 additional men to be probably followed by further enlistments, I strongly urge upon you the desirability of acceding to my proposition in order that we may all have our hands free to promote what for the present must be regarded as the supreme object.

> *Yours faithfully,*
> *(Sgd.)* R. L. BORDEN

The Right Honourable,
Sir Wilfrid Laurier, G.C.M.G.,
Ottawa, Ont.

> *Ottawa,*
> *November 13, 1915.*

My dear Borden,

While I have been unable to concur in your proposal of an extension of the Canadian parliamentary term until a year after the conclusion of peace, I have intimated and I repeat that your later suggestion to extend the life of the present Parliament for one year offers a basis for consideration and acceptance.

I am obliged, however, to attach more importance than you seem to do, to the question of the measures to be considered by Parliament at its next session. With reference to the railways mentioned by me, I understand you to say that no application for assistance has yet been made by any of them. That I need hardly point out to you, is no indication that there will be no such application. In affairs of this kind projects may be in the air and widely discussed before formal applications are filed. The railway situation may be such as to require legislation, even if no assistance out of the Treasury were involved. Any such legislation would be of importance, and in the absence of knowledge of what may come, all members will naturally desire to maintain freedom of action.

The very fact that whilst some measures relating to these railways are widely foreshadowed in the Press, you are not in a position to make any statement concerning them, serves to confirm me in the opinion that, although at a later stage arrangements for some extension of the Parliamentary term may become expedient, the time has not arrived, when any of us should be asked to come to a settled agreement on the subject. Our Parliament has yet nearly a full year to run. Why should we, at a time when great events are happening, which may change the situation, come to a conclusion today as to what may be done some months hence?

I may here observe that the term of the British Parliament is to expire only a few weeks hence, and no steps have yet been taken towards its prolongation.

I certainly agree with you that the war situation is of extreme gravity, and I will in the future as from the first, to the fullest extent of my ability facilitate all necessary war measures.

In my judgment the business of Parliament should proceed as usual. It is possible that events may so shape themselves as to give us new light as to what would be the best course to take. But if when the session is approaching its end, the war is still on, we may then consider the advisability of extending the life of Parliament on the lines above set down.

With reference to the by-elections, it seems to me that there is a material difference between the vacancies caused by death and those that have been caused by resignation. In the case of vacancies caused by death, I would count on my friends consenting that contests be avoided by allowing each party to hold that which it has had. The other seats are in a notably different position, because the vacancies have arisen under circumstances which have naturally aroused much strong feeling. In some of the electoral districts, it may not be easy to avoid contests. At all events I do not feel as free to make an agreement in these cases as I do in the case of vacancies caused by death.

As to what should be the attitude of members of Parliament and the press on party matters, my desire all along has been that the field of party controversy be narrowed and the field of common action broadened. It would have been most agreeable to me if an understanding could have been reached some months ago, that there would be no elections this year. I will be prepared, as far as my influence goes, to advise that party conflict be minimized, and that the most cordial support be given to the Government in the prosecution of Canada's part in the war.

Neither in Parliament nor in the Press can we expect nor should we desire the suppression of all discussion. Even in the Mother Country where there is a degree of unity between party leaders that is most gratifying, there is still much freedom of discussion. The Canadian Parliament cannot be expected to abdicate its functions.

There will naturally be enquiry into matters of public interest, that being one of the chief purposes for which Parliament exists. But I feel assured that it will be quite possible for Parliament to exercise its proper functions in this respect, without in any way restricting the Government's freedom of action, in that which we must all agree, is today our paramount duty, viz.: to see that Canada puts forth every possible effort for the prosecution of the war to a triumphant conclusion.

> *Yours very sincerely,*
> *(Sgd.)* WILFRID LAURIER

The Right Honourable,
Sir Robert Laird Borden, P.C., G.C.M.G.,
Prime Minister's Office,
Ottawa.

> *Ottawa, Ont.,*
> *November 13, 1915.*

Dear Sir Wilfrid Laurier,
 Your letter of the13th instant reaches me on the eve of my departure for Halifax to attend the funeral of Sir Charles Tupper.

 I observe with regret your conclusion that the time has not arrived when a settled agreement should be reached on the subject discussed at our interviews and in our correspondence. The acceptance of my proposals involves, as I have said—

1. *The extension of the term of the present Parliament for one year.*
2. *The avoidance of a general election during the war.*
3. *An arrangement that by-elections shall not be contested*

—each party holding the seats which it previously held.

4. *The suspension of party warfare while the Empire is engaged in a struggle which threatens its existence.*

I desire to repeat and emphasize the considerations which were expressed in my letter of the 9th instant.

Respecting your reference to the British Parliament I would observe that Parliament of Canada has not the power to prolong its term. That purpose can only be carried into effect by legislation of the British Parliament based upon resolutions passed by the Canadian Senate and House of Commons. This would involve considerable delay and for this reason a decision must be reached at a correspondingly earlier date. We have no assurance that the British Parliament may not prorogue before the conclusion of our next session.

With the possibility of an impending general election the approaching session of the present Parliament would inevitably develop warm party controversy. The responsibilities imposed upon the Government by this war are of an extremely arduous nature and demand the most earnest and unremitting attention from day to day. You cannot fail to realize that in the discharge of these responsibilities which must include every possible provision and safeguard for the gallant men who have gone and who are yet to go to the front, it would be both unfortunate and deplorable that the energies of any Government should be distracted by the possible imminence of a general election and all that it would involve.

The supreme purpose is the attainment of an honourable and lasting peace through the victory of the allied nations. What may afterwards happen in respect of the fortunes of any political party is in comparison of little moment.

For these reasons I must repeat my regret at the conclusion which you announce.

Yours faithfully,
(Sgd.) R. L. BORDEN

The Right Honourable
Sir Wilfrid Laurier, P.C., G.C.M.G.,
Ottawa, Ont.

News of the death of Sir Charles Tupper reached us on October 30; and on November 4 we had word from the Tupper family that they would accept the State funeral which was offered. The funeral took place at Halifax on November 16, and the ceremony was most impressive. I arrived at 9:45 in the morning and was met by a large gathering. I drove at once to the Provincial buildings to take a last look at the features of one of the greatest Canadians. All the arrangements had been worked out well and carefully by Sir Joseph Pope, but upon my return to Ottawa I received a letter of protest from the local Evangelical Alliance as to certain precedence given on that occasion. In my reply I said, "I deeply regret that my attention was not directed to the matter during my brief visit to Halifax, as my colleagues and I would most willingly have yielded our places to the representatives of the churches on whose behalf you have written.". . .

On November 11, I found it necessary to issue a statement asking the public to subscribe to the Red Cross and Patriotic Funds and to leave to the public treasury the provision of further machineguns. Complications ensued regarding Ontario's gift, a large portion of which had already been subscribed. Requests were made by the Ontario Government and in several other instances for the return of monies subscribed for machineguns. These requests were not granted, as the Government realized the confusion which would probably ensue had such a course been followed. Subscriptions already received were used for machineguns but no further subscriptions were accepted for that purpose.

There was difficulty during the year in keeping Hughes down to mere administration of his department. His extraordinary temperament has already been alluded to. It gave me great concern from time to time and constituted a severe handicap upon his usefulness during the war period. Like other very able men with whom I have been associated, he was incapable of forming a just estimate of certain favourites who were able to appeal to him, often through the medium of his excessive vanity. Equally, he was incapable of giving just consideration to other men, capable and worthy, whose attitude and outlook did not happen to appeal to him. And it should be noted with regard to both classes he was prepared not only privately but publicly to speak his mind.

During 1915, he travelled extensively. He was extremely fond of military parade and liked to attend reviews in different parts of the country. His activities included a two weeks' western journey covering 7,000 miles during which he delivered twenty-five addresses and reviewed troops in as many centres. Returning from this he later visited all the cities and principal centres of Ontario. But he especially liked to cross the Atlantic for the supposed purpose of investigating and improving conditions in Great Britain and at the Front. Thus, leaving Ottawa on July 1, he proceeded to England, remained nine days at the Front and was back in Ottawa on September 3. He discussed from time to time the proposal that he should take military command in France. The idea was congenial to him, although I doubt whether he would have had a successful career; but he was unwilling to relinquish his powers as Minister of Militia. To remain Minister of Militia and to hold an important military appointment at the Front would have been the ideal situation so far as his outlook was concerned.

Aside from his numerous trips, he had a stormy time during 1915. The Auditor-General complained of expenditures in his department without Orders-in-Council authorizing them; complaints made by Alderson and Sir George Perley were denied by him as inaccurate; he was denounced for his public speeches, for his language to officers and others, for his growing intimacy and connection with Allison and other honorary colonels; and he was much disturbed by the complaints against the Ross Rifle as well as by the constitution of the Shell Committee and the War Purchasing Commission.

Undoubtedly he was a man of great ability. During this period excellent military camps were being established, enlistments were satisfactory, and military aviation in Canada had its beginning.

In November, Mr. Meighen (then Solicitor-General) was offered the quartermastership of General Meighen's new regiment, the Grenadier Guards, and desired to go to the Front; but the Government required him to remain in Canada.

During the remainder of this month, I pondered long and anxiously over the railway difficulties. In my diary for November 26, I find this note:

> Before rising got an idea that Canadian Northern nightmare might be dissipated by merely putting in an estimate to protect underlying securities. Long discussion with White to whom I eventually unfolded it. Then with him and Meighen. . . .

Towards the end of November there was tremendous excitement occasioned by the Order-in-Council commandeering grain. During the summer a very difficult problem had arisen with regard to the wheat supply. A huge prospective Canadian crop, shortage in transport, steady increase in freight rates, and a current lowering in price, together with the possible opening of the Dardanelles to Russian wheat, combined to create this situation. Although every possible assistance was given in the release of ships for transport, the supply did not meet the demand and congestion of freight at all the ports, increasing rates, and the holding through the winter of 100,000,000 bushels of wheat resulted. By Order-in-Council in April of this year the export of wheat to any except British countries and the Allies and to United States under bond had been prohibited. Special permission for export to neutral countries could be obtained after application and arrangements for delivery had been made. On September 20, a Committee of the Cabinet composed of Rogers (Chairman), Sir George Foster, Reid, Burrell, and Meighen, with Sanford Evans as secretary, was appointed to deal with the whole question of marketing the Canadian grain crop. As a result of the findings of this Commission, Mr. Meighen on November 29, issued the following official statement:

> *The phenomenal crop of wheat in the Canadian West has brought upon the Government the duty of assisting to the farthest extent possible in the marketing. The supply of wheat the world over is known to have been abundant, and the importance of taking advantage of every opportunity to provide for the disposing of our grain is on that account the greater. For many months, the Government has been in touch with the British authorities with a view to procuring orders from the United Kingdom and the Allied Governments, in order that the utmost share of the consuming demand in those countries may be turned toward our Canadian surplus. As a consequence of this, the British Government has required the Canadian Government to provide within a short time a very large supply of Nos. 1, 2, and 3 Northern wheat.*
>
> *The problem of meeting these requirements and of doing so at such prices as would induce the repetition of orders in Canada, then confronted the Government. The effect of Government purchases in the open market, such as were made by different countries a year ago, is well known to the public. The market rises abnormally, adding to the profits of grain dealers and speculators who have purchased the grain which the Government require. The advance in price of the large amounts of grain in store becomes the loss of the owner of the stored grain. To secure the desired end this year the Government determined, Saturday November 27th, to commandeer all Nos. 1, 2, and 3 Northern wheat in store at the head of the Lakes and eastward. This involves the purchase of anywhere from 12 to 15 million bushels. The price paid has not yet been*

settled by the Government but will shortly be fixed on a fair basis.

Much controversy and discussion resulted from the announcement; and members of the Government were deluged with telegrams and messages. Differences of opinion arose between Rogers and Meighen. However, on December 1, Meighen reported that he thought it would all work out satisfactorily.

During this month the affairs of the Canadian Shell Committee also occupied much time and thought. Lionel Hitchens, who had been appointed to succeed D. A. Thomas, was engaged in perfecting the arrangements for the manufacture of shells and in organizing the Imperial Munitions Board.

Hitchens consulted me as to the various steps and as to the personnel of the Board but, of course, took full responsibility, and I declined to do more than give suggestions as to certain aspects. . . .

On the thirtieth, I sent for Hughes, White, and Reid, to whom I put forward the proposal that our military forces should be increased to 500,000 men and that I should send forth a New Year's message to that effect. While still in great pain, I drafted my address to the Canadian people. As a result of my labours, I suffered intense spasms of pain from 3 p.m. to 6 a.m., so that I was absolutely helpless. Dr. Laidlaw pronounced lumbago with inflammation of the sciatic nerve, ordered me not to work. However, I told him I must finish my address which I did. A trained nurse arrived that afternoon.

My message to the Canadian people was as follows:

More than a twelvemonth ago our Empire consecrated all its powers and its supreme endeavour in a great purpose which concerns the liberties of the world and the destinies of its nations. Much had to be learned during the past fifteen months, because we had not prepared for this war. The strongest assurance of ultimate victory lies in the fact that we were not crushed in learning that hard lesson. Those who forced this war upon us may be assured by th traditions of our past that the lesson will be thoroughly learned to the end that there shall be enduring peace. The very character and greatness of the ideals for which we are fighting forbid us to pause until their triumph is fully assured. The Canadian Forces at the Front have indeed fought a good fight and they have crowned the name of Canada with undying laurels. To them and to all the Overseas Forces now under arms and awaiting the opportunity to do their part we bid God-speed, in the sure faith that they will never fail in their duty. On this the last day of the old year the authorized Forces of Canada number 250,000 and the number enlisted is rapidly approaching that limit. From tomorrow, the first day of the New Year, our authorized force will be 500,000. This announcement is made in token of Canada's unflinchable resolve to crown the justice of our cause with victory and with an abiding peace.

It was well received and I had many telegrams and messages of congratulation.

In the tension of my illness* I had omitted to give notice to the Governor-General of the Government's policy to increase our military forces to 500,000; and the following correspondence ensued.

> *Government House,*
> *Ottawa,*
> *31 December, 1915.*

My Dear Blount,
   I am asked by His Royal Highness to request you to express to the Prime Minister his great regret to hear that the Prime Minister is no better and his most earnest hope that he may soon shake off the attack to which so many of Ottawa's citizens have been victims.

   As regards the Prime Minister's message to the people of Canada on New Year's date, His Royal Highness the Governor-General congratulates him and the Government of Canada on so splendid a Resolution which will undoubtedly act as a great stimulus throughout the Empire to other Dominions to prosecute the War with the greatest energy.

   His Royal Highness cannot but feel considerable doubt as to the possibility of increasing the Canadian Forces to 500,000 men. His Royal Highness understands that of the 250,000 men at present authorized, some 50,000 are still deficient and he fears that the magnificent total of 500,000 may be beyond the powers of the Dominion of Canada to provide under voluntary enlistment.

   His Royal Highness assumes that Privy Council have considered and approved of this momentous question, although he has not yet received any notice from them to this effect. He is a little surprised that the notice of the Prime Minister should be given out in the Press before a Minute of Privy Council has been submitted to him for approval on the subject.

> *(Sgd.)* E. A. STANTON

---

* [Borden was in the throes of grippe.]

Ottawa,
January 1, 1916.

Dear Colonel Stanton,

I explained to the Prime Minister (who is still confined to his bed) the purport of your letter of 31st December. He begs that you will convey to His Royal Highness his warm thanks and every good wish for the New Year upon which we have entered.

The Prime Minister also greatly appreciates the congratulations of His Royal Highness on the Message to the People of Canada, which appears in the press today.

As to the possibility of enlisting five hundred thousand men in Canada, the Prime Minister is not inclined to share the doubts which His Royal Highness entertains. Whether or not these doubts are well founded the Prime Minister is thoroughly convinced that more will be accomplished by the proposed effort than could otherwise be achieved.

The Prime Minister learns with regret that His Royal Highness has felt some surprise because an Order-in-Council was not passed before announcing the policy alluded to. For nearly a century it has not been the practice of this country to formulate policies through the medium of Orders-in-Council. That course may be taken as a matter of convenience, but it is by no means necessary or even usual. Frequently an Order-in-Council is requisite to carry out a policy but it is seldom used for the purpose of announcing it. The policy announced by the Prime Minister is merely a development of that which he laid down in his message to the British Government on the first of August, 1914.

(Sgd.) A. E. BLOUNT,
Private Secretary.

A further letter from Colonel Stanton on the following day regretted the misunderstanding and stated that His Royal Highness now fully understood.

25: The Session *1915*

Parliament met on February 4, 1915; the Opening being the usual brilliant affair. In the Speech from the Throne references were made to the loyalty of the Canadian people; to the First Canadian Expeditionary Force of 30,000 which was soon to take its place in the field; to the further large additional forces being organized; and to measures and necessary financial provisions to be introduced for the effective conduct of the war.

The Address in reply was moved by W. G. Weichel (North Waterloo) and H. Achim (Labelle) both of whom made excellent speeches. Sir Wilfrid followed and after a graceful tribute to the devotion of Their Excellencies to Canada and the Empire, he complimented the mover and seconder of the Address commenting on the fact that:

The one thing remarkable in the debate is that the motion for an Address, devoted altogether to the proposition that the War must be continued, should come from one of His Majesty's subjects of German origin. If there be anything significant anything which justifies the very eloquent periods of my hon. friend from North Waterloo, it is the very fact that he, a British subject of German origin, should speak as he speaks and occupy the place which he does. There could be no better justification, if justification were needed, for British institutions.

He referred to the provision of large sums necessary for war purposes and expressed the view that a full statement of expenditure of the money already voted should be supplied by the Government. He referred also to various criticisms of the boots issued to the First Contingent and urged that full investigation should be made.

Following Sir Wilfrid, I agreed that full information should be furnished regarding the expenditure of money voted for war purposes and stated that a committee had been considering the best type of boot and one had been decided upon which would prove very serviceable.

I reviewed the attitude of the Government as to Canada's participation in the War stating that Canada had, in August, 1914, decided to "take her proper place" in the struggle: "Thirty-one thousand men are today in the British Isles or in France; one thousand are at Bermuda; and nearly ten thousand are doing garrison duty in Canada." Nearly fifty thousand men had been enlisted to stand as an armed force for the protection of our country.

I pointed out that Prussian militarism had taught its armies to employ "means and methods, relentless and remorseless, which seem to have been designed to deprive the nations with whom they are contending not only of their material but of their intellectual and moral resources."

Concluding, I said:

The events of the past six months mark a new stage in our nationhood; a new chapter in the book of our destiny has been opened. The strength of our Empire bound by the ties of liberty and autonomous self-government, has been tested and it has held firm and true. In no respect have the expectations of the Prussian autocracy been more utterly disappointed and falsified than in this. From these great Dominions have gone and will still go forth the free manhood of a great Empire to fight for a cause which involves not alone our institutions, our freedom and our destiny, but those of the world. Fighting in such a cause we do not, we dare not, doubt the issue.

In the excited condition of public opinion during a war, rumour is usually accepted as fact and loud outcry gathers headway against the Government, supposed to be derelict in its duty in permitting irregularities. This outcry naturally concentrates itself against the leader of the Government who is supposed to be materially responsible, as he is constitutionally responsible, for maladministration or inefficiency. In most cases this outcry arises in respect of subjects that are of a purely departmental character and with which no human being occupying the position of Prime Minister could possibly keep in touch.

Such an outcry arose with regard to the character of the boots supplied to the First Division. It gathered such volume that on February 16, I moved for the appointment of a Special Committee of the House.

The Committee engaged in a very extensive, thorough and exhaustive inquiry with the result that on April 12, the chairman, Mr. Middlebro, moved for the adoption of the very lengthy majority report. In speaking to his motion he went into the subject very fully. He was followed by the several members of the Committee in support of his motion or in opposition thereto.

It would be idle to attempt any analysis of the findings of the Committee and of the arguments pro and con. The severe weather conditions which prevailed in the Canadian encamp-

ment on Salisbury Plain undoubtedly proved a most trying
test to the boots with which the Canadian soldiers were shod.
These boots were not as heavy as those used in the British and
French armies, but they were somewhat heavier than those
adopted in the army of the United States.

We inherited from the administration of Sir Wilfrid Laurier
not only a type of rifle but a type of boot; and as a result we
were vigorously assailed by supporters of the party which had
established those types. The type of boot which we thus inherited
and which we used had been established by the Laurier Government after the conclusion of the South African War.

We were attacked for using this unsuitable type; and the
minority members of the Committee put forward the extraordinary argument that this type was not intended for war but
for peace.

The Budget and the War Taxes were subjects of lengthy
debate; and on March 10, Sir Wilfrid severely criticized the
Government for extravagance, for omitting to make necessary
retrenchments and reforms, and for the increased tariff duties
which he characterized as "protective in their nature" and as
placing barriers against Great Britain's trade with Canada.
While not hesitating to support the Government in every
possible way in its endeavour to have Canada bear her share in
the War, he maintained the right to criticize war administration.

On February 16, at Sir Wilfrid's request, I made a statement
respecting the resignations of Mr. Pelletier and Mr. Nantel, to
each of whom I paid a well-deserved tribute. Mr. Pelletier had
been succeeded as Postmaster-General by Mr. T. Chase Casgrain and Mr. Nantel had been succeeded as Minister of Inland
Revenue by Mr. Pierre E. Blondin. Naturally, I enlarged upon
the eminent qualifications of both these gentlemen to fulfil the
duties devolving upon them as Ministers.

Sir Wilfrid observed that my explanation was rich in words,
although absolutely lacking in substance as it gave no information except what had already appeared in the public Press. He
took occasion to make mildly adverse comment on Mr. Pelletier's career in public life, expressing surprise that Mr. Pelletier,
unable to serve the country as a Minister of the Crown, had
still sufficient health to undertake the duties of a judge. In this
connection he contrasted the condition of Mr. Doherty,[1] "unable to serve the country as a judge and serving the country as
a Minister of the Crown." He also adverted to Mr. Blondin as

[1] Minister of Justice–a former judge of the Superior Court of Quebec.
[Ed.]

an "arch-Nationalist" and commented on the "irony of fate" that he should have been introduced by Sir George Foster:

When, on the opening of the session, I saw the new Minister walking into this House leaning upon the arm of my hon. friend the Minister of Trade and Commerce, I thought the Minister of Trade and Commerce showed by the way he seemed to be limping that he had a heavy load to carry. . . . When he (Minister of Trade and Commerce) told you, Sir, that the hon. gentleman (Mr. Blondin) had taken the oath and signed the roll, I thought he would add that the hon. gentleman had filled up the holes in the flag and that he would now breathe the atmosphere of liberty.

The reference to Mr. Doherty thoroughly aroused that gentleman who was never in better form than when subjected to unjust criticism. With much vigour he resented and refuted Sir Wilfrid's statement that he had resigned his position as judge by reason of illness. In part he said:

It is certainly a pitiable sight; the leader of a great party compelled to resort to making statements of fact which certainly he cannot know to be true, and which, as I say, the public documents on record in the Department of Justice of this country, demonstrate to be false; and that for the petty purpose of making some jeering remarks.

On the same day Mr. Doherty moved for a special committee to inquire into the operation of the Elections Act and the Contraverted Elections Act and to consider what changes were desirable therein. As a result of this Committee three bills were introduced, two of them unanimously reported by the Committee, and the third reported by the majority.

The first of these Bills was introduced by the Minister of Justice on March 30. It made certain minor amendments and *inter alia* provided that employers should give to their employees an extra hour in addition to the noon hour for the purpose of enabling them to vote. This Bill did not receive extended discussion and was passed without division.

On the same day Mr. Doherty introduced a Bill to amend the Dominion Contraverted Elections Act. The purpose of this measure was to simplify procedure and to lessen the opportunity for technical objections. A good deal of discussion ensued. Many questions were raised and suggestions made. On April 7, both Sir Wilfrid Laurier and I expressed our approval of the measure as it was and the Bill was passed without division.

On April 1, Mr. Doherty proposed the necessary resolution to precede a Bill making provision whereby "every male British subject of twenty-one years of age or upwards serving in the military forces of Canada in the present War might exercise his electoral franchise." This Bill which provided elaborate machinery for the purpose was the subject of lengthy discussion and not a little controversy. Several amendments were moved and negatived on division. Eventually the Bill was passed without division. It proved to be of minor importance as, on an election taking place, it was repealed by the Military Voters' Act of 1917.[2]

Other important matters dealt with during the session included Mr. Cockshutt's motion on March 1:

That in the opinion of this House the circumstances arising out of the present War are such as to justify the Government of Canada in exercising supreme control over the quantity and destiny of our food exports, thereby regulating the prices at which bread, meat and other food products shall be sold for home consumption, while at the same time directing that our surplus food exports should only reach British or friendly countries.

In speaking to this motion Mr. Cockshutt made an elaborate and lengthy review of the grain crops of the world with prices and conditions of supply and demand in these products. After several brief and mostly unfavourable speeches on the subject I stated the Government's policy as follows:

So far as the general question is concerned, the policy which the Government has endeavoured to follow since the outbreak of War is not to interfere with the business activities of the country, except in so far as this is absolutely and imperatively demanded of it by reason of the War or by reason of conditions arising out of the War. . . . I would like to point out that the question of food supply, so far as wheat and wheat products are concerned, is not solely a question of the wheat in this

---

[2] I quote the following extract from my diary for April 13, 1915:

"Last day in House over Votes for Soldiers Bill. At the end Doherty in a condition of physical exhaustion. He talks altogether too much and too often. Hugh Clark said that he thought the Bill would go through, notwithstanding the Minister's explanation. After midnight he (Doherty) became plaintive in his weariness: 'Hell, that is awful', and 'God Almighty, did you ever hear the like?'; and when Laurier rose about a question to me 'H— and D—, didn't he promise to put through the Bill tonight?' "

country, but a question of the wheat available for milling and of the flour in the country. I would like to assure all hon. members that this subject has engaged the attention of the Government . . . and that we do not think conditions in this country at the present time are such as to make any action by the Government necessary so far as that particular feature of the question is concerned.

I then pointed out that prohibition of exports in such a way as to prevent them reaching the enemy was being carried out by co-operation with a British Special Committee appointed for the purpose. As to the regulation of prices, this was attended to largely by the British market; but in any case it did not appear desirable to reduce farmers' prices when the demand was strong and leave them to face the lower rates when the demand was weak.

Mr. Cockshutt's motion was negatived on division.

On June 11, 1914, I had moved an Address to His Majesty praying for the passage of an Act by the Imperial Parliament providing for increasing the number of senators and fixing the representation of the Provinces in the Senate and House of Commons.

The situation created by the Senate's amendments has already been described.

On March 25, 1915, I again moved this resolution and I was followed by Sir Wilfrid who argued that the Senate's action in declaring that the proposed Act should take effect only on the dissolution of the existing Parliament was entirely proper and appropriate. However, the Resolution received the unanimous consent of the House and was transmitted to the Senate for its concurrence.

The subject came up again on April 10 for consideration of the same amendment which had been made by the Senate in 1914. Observing that the majority of the Senate seemed determined to insist upon its postponement, for a very obvious reason, and as it seemed impossible to pass this desirable and necessary legislation without the Senate's unnecessary and obstructive amendment, I felt disposed to accept the Senate's proposal; and therefore I moved that the House should concur. Considerable debate ensued. Later in the discussion I took the opportunity of observing that the House had unanimously concurred in rejecting the Senate's amendment of the previous year for reasons entirely inconsistent with the views now entertained and expressed by Sir Wilfrid Laurier who attempted to justify himself by an ingenuous but fallacious argument. I pointed out that by his assent, for reasons stated, to the rejection of the Senate's amendment in the previous year, he had by his vote committed himself to full agreement and approval of those reasons. The final passage-at-arms was as follows:

SIR ROBERT BORDEN: *"The right hon. gentleman has said that the Senate ought not to degenerate into being a recording clerk of the House of Commons."*

SIR WILFRID LAURIER: *"Hear, hear."*

SIR ROBERT BORDEN: *"There is just one thing worse than that —to have the Senate degenerate into being a recording Clerk of the minority of the House of Commons."*

The motion was eventually agreed to.

By two Orders-in-Council, dated respectively May 10, 1913, and June 27, 1913, Mr. T. R. Ferguson had been appointed:

To investigate and report upon all matters connected with the sale, lease, grant, exchange or disposition by any means whatsoever, since the first day of July, 1896, of (a) Dominion lands; (b) timber and mineral lands and mining rights and privileges, including coal, petroleum and gas lands and rights; (c) water-powers and rights, under the authority or purporting to be under the authority of the Dominion Lands Act, Irrigation Act, or other statutes of the Parliament of Canada; (d) Indian lands and Indian reserves.

Mr. Ferguson's report had been tabled; and on April 14, Mr. Oliver moved adjournment of the House for the purpose of discussing it. Disclosures made in the report involved severe discredit on the administration of Mr. Oliver's Department while he was Minister of the Interior in Sir Wilfrid Laurier's administration and especially condemned irregular alienation of the public domain to political favourites without regard to the statutes and regulations.

Mr. Oliver endeavoured to excuse, or at least to minimize the irregularities which were of a very serious and damaging nature; and he was followed by Dr. Roche (Minister of the Interior). Later, Mr. Meighen and Mr. Bennett (R.B.) in very powerful speeches made devastating attacks upon Mr. Oliver's administration.

The whole subject attracted less attention than it deserved by reason of war conditions and the intense absorption of the people therein.

In the course of the debate, Sir Wilfrid Laurier took occasion to repudiate the suggestion or "insinuation," as he termed it, that he had in any way acted as intermediary in any of the discreditable transactions which were disclosed.

On the following day, April 15, it became my duty, in a lengthy speech, to deal with a report of the Committee of Public Accounts which had conducted a very full investigation into certain expenditures for war purposes.

In the first place, I emphasized my direction to members of the Government on that Committee that there should be the fullest and freest investigation into all matters brought to the Committee's attention. After observing that this course had not been followed under the previous administration, I pointed out that the irregularities exposed had occurred in the first six weeks of the War and under conditions of extreme stress and urgency. In speaking of evidence to the effect that General Jones had declared that "the Government did not desire to purchase directly from manufacturers and producers; but that it desired to employ the services of middlemen," I used the following language:

> *I say that if General Jones ever did make any such observation to Mr. Shaver or anybody else, his conduct must be called into question by this Government, and if he is not able satisfactorily to deny the assertion that he used such language, he is no longer fit to hold a position in the public service. But, in the meantime, I do General Jones the credit of assuming that he never said anything of the kind.*[3]

Dealing one by one with certain unfortunate and discreditable transactions which had been exposed, and emphasizing my desire by legislation, recommendation, audit, and otherwise to prevent any fraud upon the country, I alluded to my letter of November 18, 1914 to General Hughes and to my letter to the Solicitor-General of October 19, 1914. Continuing I said:

> *One can readily understand that persons may desire from time to time to practise fraud or to impose exorbitant prices upon the Government through the very conditions which have arisen. I do not speak of that in a general sense, because I think that there are few people in Canada who would be guilty of anything so dishonest and unpatriotic. But we know that there*

---

[3] The Press distorted this into a statement of my refusal to believe that "that guy, Carleton Jones, every said anything of the kind."

are men who, even in time of war, will seek to make undue profits out of their business relations with the Government, even when all the people of the country are straining every effort and are inspired with the most patriotic desire to assist, and to sacrifice their own interests for that purpose.

I pointed out that such conditions had arisen in many other countries—unfortunately in Great Britain as well.

Then, coming to a certain transaction with regard to the purchase of horses, in which Mr. Foster, M.P. for King's County, Nova Scotia, and to certain other transactions in which the Carlton Drug Company, owned by Mr. Garland, M.P. for Carleton, Ont., were involved, I said:

A member of Parliament, in respect of contracts with the Government, ought to keep himself absolutely above suspicion. Therefore, in respect of the hon. member for Carleton and in respect of the hon. member for King's, N.S., I feel that I owe it as a duty to the Government of which I am the head, to the party of which in Federal affairs I am the leader, and to this House and to this country, to express, as I do here express, my very grave disapproval of their conduct in respect of the matters which have been under investigation by the Public Accounts Committee.

The duty which I thus performed was a painful one; but my declaration had the effect of clearing the air, as it was well received, not only in Parliament but throughout the Country.

Then, after referring to the great success which had attended the work of the Shell Committee and after quoting the report of Colonel Alex. Bertram, the Chairman, I announced my intention of appointing a commission to deal with the whole question of purchases under the appropriation of $100,000,000 which had been passed by Parliament for war purposes. In conclusion, I said:

It remains for the Government of the country to do its duty; that is, to take such means and to employ such safeguards as will result in the wise and economical and efficient expenditure of that sum of $100,000,000 to the end that not one single dollar of it shall be lost or wasted, so that we may be enabled at another session of Parliament to give an account of our steward-ship which shall commend itself not only to the members of this Parliament, but to the people of this country from the Atlantic to the Pacific.

It was recognized, I believe, throughout the country, so far as the Government was concerned, that there was an active and determined endeavour to prevent fraud, irregularities, and undue profits. Naturally, the intense emotion created by war conditions frequently lead to credence in baseless rumours as well as to gross exaggeration.

Parliament was prorogued on April 15.

NOTE ON EDITION
Suggestions for Further Reading, a Note on the Author, and the Index will be found at the end of Volume II.